Employment Claims without a Lawyer

A Handbook for Litigants in Person

Revised 2nd edition

David Curwen, Barrister

Unity Street Chambers, Bristol

BATH PUBLISHING

Also available from Bath Publishing

www.employmentcasesupdate.co.uk

You can read, for free, the full text of all the EAT, Court of Appeal and Supreme Court judgments, together with a short summary of each case at www.employmentcasesupdate.co.uk.

www.employmentclaimstoolkit.co.uk

Finally, if you need to prepare a schedule of loss, visit www.employmentclaimstoolkit.co.uk which will help you to create a mathematically and legally correct document to support your claim. The service is free if you only want to create one schedule.

First published September 2015 (revised January 2017)

Second edition published March 2018

Revised second edition published July 2020

ISBN 978-0-9935836-8-1

Bath Publishing Limited
27 Charmouth Road
Bath
BA1 3LJ

Tel: 01225 577810

email: info@bathpublishing.co.uk

www.bathpublishing.com

Bath Publishing is a company registered in England: 5209173

Registered Office: As above

Contents

1. Introduction

2. Pre-claim matters

3. Unfair dismissal

4. Discrimination

5. Disputes about pay

6. Transfer of undertakings

7. Time limits for bringing a claim

8. Early conciliation

9. Making a claim to the employment tribunal

10. Responding to a tribunal claim

11. What happens next? Summary of procedure after the response has been filed

12. Amending a claim

13. Additional information

14. Preliminary hearings

15. Disclosure of documents

16. Schedule of loss

17. Settlement agreements

18. Witness statements

19. Preparation for the hearing

20. The hearing

21. Remedies

22. Judgments

23. Costs

24. Appeals

Appendix A: Jargon buster

Appendix B: Model letters and precedents

Chapter 1

Introduction

Bringing a case in an employment tribunal can be a frightening prospect even if you are represented by a lawyer, but if you are representing yourself it can appear to be an impossible task; coping with the procedure, preparing witness statements and complying with time limits, particularly if the other side does have legal representation.

A person who appears in an employment tribunal as one of the parties in the claim is called a litigant. This can refer either to the person bringing the claim (the "Claimant") or to the person or company defending the claim (the "Respondent"). A person who represents themselves whether as a Claimant or a Respondent is called a "litigant in person". This book is designed to assist the litigant in person. It is mainly for employees who are considering bringing a claim or who have started a claim but it will also be a useful guide for an employer Respondent who is acting in person or is representing their company. Therefore I will give guidance both on how to bring a claim and also how to defend a claim that has been brought against you. Whether you are bringing a claim or defending a claim it is always helpful to be aware of the procedures and tactics that the other party might be using.

The employment relationship is probably the most important relationship a person will have in their life after their family. When the employment relationship breaks down, if your job is at risk or even where there are problems at work this can have a significant impact on your livelihood and your life. If you have been dismissed and are out of work the financial aspect will probably be the most important motivation for bringing a claim. Another aspect will be the possibility of trying to negotiate a satisfactory reference from your employer, which should make obtaining new employment easier - this will be particularly relevant in those cases where the reason for the dismissal has been misconduct.

Whether you have obtained a new job or not, another important reason for bringing a claim is self-respect, proving that the dismissal has been unfair whether it is a question of proving the allegation of misconduct to be false, showing that you were wrongly selected for redundancy or that the dismissal was motivated by discrimination of some form.

This book is intended to be a guide to tribunal practice. It is not a textbook on employment law although I will give a summary of the law in those different areas of employment law that a tribunal can hear. A litigant in person who wants to research the law will need to obtain a text book or look on the internet. A list of the best text books and internet sites is given in Appendix D. There is also a set of precedents, or model letters, in Appendix B which can be used as guides or templates.

There have been a number of changes in the law in the last few years which have made it more difficult to bring an employment claim; the qualifying period for bringing an unfair dismissal claim has increased from one to two years and there is now a requirement to participate in pre-action conciliation. Faced with these obstacles a person considering bringing a claim might well give up before even starting. I hope that by explaining the procedure in fairly simple and easy to understand language, this will encourage that person to persevere with their claim.

It is important to appreciate right from the outset that bringing a claim in an employment tribunal is not a task to be undertaken lightly. It is a significant commitment both in terms of time and emotional input. Certain steps need to be undertaken by a specific date and failure to comply with tribunal orders or to provide documents or information by that specified date can result in the claim being struck out and possibly an order to pay the Respondent's costs. If the tribunal concludes that the claim has been unreasonably brought or unreasonably conducted it can make a costs order against that party.

In this book I start by considering the pre-claim position where an employee has a complaint or a grievance, how the employee should go about raising this and getting it resolved, and how the employer should deal with a grievance that has been raised. I then consider the most common types of claim that are brought in the employment tribunal; these include unfair dismissal, various types of discrimination claim and breach of the Working Time Regulations. I have deliberately not included claims relating to trade union membership as these are likely to be brought by or with the assistance of union representatives. Nor have I included equal pay claims as these are extremely complex. I would recommend getting a lawyer if you are considering either of these types of claim.

The main part of the book covers Employment Tribunal procedure with provisions about pre-claim conciliation, commencement of a claim and responding to a claim. I will take you through the various procedural steps and pitfalls that you may face leading up to the hearing itself, and describe the law on remedies and costs. Finally I will deal with reconsideration of decisions and appeals.

In this book I have referred to the Claimant as "he". This is not because it is only intended for male Claimants but because I find putting in the alternative each time either "he/she" or "s/he" to be rather clumsy. All government Acts or Statutes use the masculine gender "he" as including the feminine "she" (see section 6 Interpretation Act 1978) so I have adopted the same formula as a matter of convenience.

I have tried to use everyday language but there are many legal words that you will need to know; where these are used I will explain what the word or phrase means. I have tried to limit the references to Statutes (these are Acts of Parliament which set out the law), Regulations or reported cases but where necessary I will refer to these giving the section number or the Regulation and the name and date of the Act or Regulation.

When looking up Acts or Regulations yourself it is important to know the date of the one you want because in some cases a new Act or Regulation will have been passed which has the same name as the old one. Where possible in the text of the book I have summarised the wording of Statutes or Regulations.

Do not be afraid of contacting the employment tribunal if you have a query about the tribunal procedure - they are generally very helpful particularly if you are a litigant in person. You can telephone the employment tribunals public enquiry line on 0300 123 1024 (or 0300 790 6234 in Scotland) but do be aware that they will not give advice about the merits of your particular claim. There is also a huge amount of helpful information on the internet. In particular I can recommend the ACAS Codes of Practice or guides. I have listed these and other helpful websites at Appendix D.

In June 2015 the Law Society published guidelines for lawyers acting against litigants in person. This relates to all court proceedings and not just employment tribunals. It also includes a section for the litigant in person on what to expect from the lawyer acting for the other party in a case and has a list of relevant court decisions involving litigants in person. The document can be found on the Law Society website.

In March 2020 in order to restrict the spread of coronavirus the government took the unprecedented step of shutting down all non-essential businesses and shops. It also imposed restrictions on non-essential travel - a "lockdown". The provisions are set out in The Health Protection (Coronavirus, Restrictions) (England) Regulations 2020, which came into force on 26th March 2020. The schedule to these regulations specified which businesses were required to close down and which shops could remain open.

At the same time the government also announced the setting up of the "furlough" scheme to provide support for those businesses required to shut down and to prevent large scale redundancies. Under this scheme the government would pay 80% of the wages of those workers or employees who were required to stay at home "on furlough". Although initially this scheme was for 3 months it has been extended with some modifications until the end of October 2020.

The lockdown also meant that courts and tribunals could no longer conduct hearings which required the personal attendance of parties, witnesses or lawyers. From 23rd March 2020 all in-person hearings due to be heard before 26th June 2020 were converted into management hearings when directions would be given by the judge for the future progress of the case. It is likely that for the foreseeable future, until a vaccine for the virus has been developed, many employment tribunals hearings will take place either by telephone or by some form of video link where witnesses are required to give evidence. I have included a new section dealing with video hearings at the end of Chapter 20.

The coronavirus has had a huge impact on business, workplaces and those employed there. ACAS has provided an online information document providing advice for employers and employees, which deals with aspects such as safe workplaces, furlough and pay, vulnerable employees, sick pay, holiday and leave, grievance and disciplinary procedures. This document is called Coronavirus (Covid-19): advice for employers and employees.

The President of the Employment Tribunals has provided an online document called FAQ (Frequently Asked Questions) arising from the Covid-19 pandemic. This is dated 30th April 2020 and covers many areas including the position relating to ongoing cases, where there are difficulties preparing for a case, attending telephone or video hearings, the etiquette for video hearings and whether time limits will be extended. There is also a very helpful appendix giving a list of web links.

This is a period of huge uncertainty for businesses and employees. It remains to be seen what impact the coronavirus pandemic will have on the economy and the employment situation. The court and tribunal system has had to adapt quickly to changes caused by the lockdown and to get to grips with the new technology involved in video hearings. Where these changes have had an impact on tribunal procedure I have set out the new position as at June 2020 but it must be borne in mind that the coronavirus situation is altering every week and this will have an effect on tribunal procedure and in particular how quickly tribunals will be able to revert to live hearings on a regular basis.

Chapter 2

Pre-claim matters

In the first part of this chapter I will consider the position with regard to complaints, grievances, disputes that can arise between an employer and an employee and the procedure that should be used to resolve these grievances. I will then go on to consider disciplinary procedures; this will also include the way in which employers should deal with performance related issues and with long term sickness absences.

2.1 Grievances

There is an ACAS Guide to Discipline and Grievances at Work (the "ACAS Guide") which sets out in clear language the way in which grievances should be dealt with in the workplace. It is a guide which is designed for both employers and employees.

There is also an ACAS Code of Practice on Disciplinary and Grievance Procedures (the "ACAS Code of Practice"), the latest edition of which was published in March 2015. It is important for both employees and employers that the steps given in the Code of Practice setting out the way in which grievances should be dealt with are followed. A failure to follow the recommended procedure could result in a reduction or an increase in an employment tribunal award by as much as 25% (section 207A of the Trade Union and Labour Relations (Consolidation) Act 1992) (see Chapter 16).

Both these booklets can be found on the ACAS website at www.acas.org.uk.

2.2 What is a grievance?

A grievance is a concern, a problem or a complaint.

It might be about:

- things you are asked to do at work;

- the terms and conditions of your contract of employment, such as pay, hours of work, place of work etc;

- new working practices or organisational changes;

- the way you are being treated at work, e.g. bullied, victimised, ignored etc;

- being subjected to discrimination.

2.3   Informal procedure

The first step is to try to resolve the problem informally by talking about it with your line manager or someone from Human Resources ("HR" or Personnel Department). If you feel you cannot speak to your line manager about the problem speak to another member of the management team or a person in a position of authority. In smaller firms, which are often run by the owner or by a manager, there might be no other person with whom a grievance can be raised. In these situations it is still important that the grievance is properly dealt with.

If you are the employer it will always be better for you to resolve any concerns or problems at this stage rather than allow them to go unheeded or ignored; while some problems might resolve themselves with time, other problems will become worse and be more difficult to resolve as time passes. Grievances should always be dealt with promptly.

Many companies will have a written grievance procedure which will set out who should be contacted in the case of a grievance and how to go about this. You should check your contract of employment or the company handbook to see if there is a written grievance procedure and make sure you follow it.

ACAS recommends having a written policy to make it clear what the procedures are and how they are to be followed.

2.4   Formal procedure

If the problem is not resolved with an informal discussion the next stage is to make a formal complaint. This will need to be done in writing. You should set out your grievance and give examples of the problems or conduct complained of, ideally including relevant dates and the names of people involved. Keep a copy of this letter for yourself.

Your employer should respond by arranging a meeting to discuss the complaint. ACAS recommends that where possible the meeting should be held within five working days of the grievance being received.

You are entitled to be accompanied by a work colleague or a trade union representative to the meeting (section 10 Employment Relations Act 1999) if your grievance concerns a duty owed to you by your employer. Where the employer refuses a reasonable request to be accompanied you can make a complaint to the employment tribunal. If the complaint is upheld the tribunal can make an award of compensation of up to two weeks pay (section 11 Employment Relations Act 1999).

Paragraphs 35 to 39 of the Code of Practice set out various factors that should be considered when selecting a person to accompany you to a grievance meeting. It suggests an employee be accompanied by a "companion who is suitable willing and available on site". The request to be accompanied must be a reasonable request. What this means is that if you choose someone who works at a very distant location or is going to be absent from work for an extended period, the employer might regard this as an unreasonable request.

Your companion is entitled to address the meeting to sum up and put forward your case.so you should be looking to be accompanied by someone who will help explain your case not someone likely to be disruptive or who might antagonise the employer.

See Appendix B: Model letters and precedents for examples of letters requesting a grievance meeting.

The meeting

The meeting will be an opportunity for you to explain your grievance and to provide any further details you consider might be helpful to your case; this includes providing specific examples of your complaint. If there are a number of different points you want to raise make a note of these before the meeting so that you remember to cover each of them.

You will also need to explain how you would like your grievance to be resolved. It will be an opportunity for your employer to ask you about the problem, about any evidence you have referred to and to put forward any points you might not have taken into account, including any potential difficulties with the resolution you have proposed.

If it is necessary for your employer to investigate any of the matters you have raised, the employer should adjourn (i.e. postpone) the hearing to another day to allow time to investigate these matters.

The outcome

After the meeting your employer should write to you telling you whether they uphold your grievance (i.e. accept it) or not. If they do accept it they should tell you what they propose to do about it; if they do not accept it they should explain why. The letter should also inform you of your right to appeal.

It is good practice for the employer to keep a written record of the grievance meeting and a copy of this record should be given to you so that you have the opportunity to correct any errors. If you do want to correct any mistakes or include anything that you consider was left out, you should make these changes on the copy of the meeting that you were given and ask your employer to agree them.

Appeal

If you do not agree with the decision you can appeal. You will need to write to your employer stating that you are appealing the decision and why you do not agree with it.

Your employer should arrange a further meeting. Usually this will be done with a different manager, although this might not be possible in a very small business. Again you have the right to be accompanied to the meeting.

2.5   Failure to comply with the ACAS Code of Practice

The failure by an *employee* to raise a grievance before bringing a claim in the employment tribunal can have adverse financial consequences for the employee, because the tribunal can reduce an award by up to 25% where it finds that the employee has unreasonably failed to comply with the provisions of the ACAS Code of Practice. Alternatively the tribunal can increase the award by up to 25% where it considers that the *employer* has unreasonably failed to comply with the provisions of the Code of Practice.

2.6   Mediation

The ACAS guide recommends mediation as a possible way of resolving grievances. A mediator is an independent third party who sits down with both sides and tries to help them resolve their dispute. The mediator will not act as judge but will help each side see the other person's point of view and help them try to reach a compromise that goes some way towards satisfying each party, or perhaps suggesting a resolution which neither side had considered.

The ACAS guide sets out different situations that might and might not be suitable for mediation. In particular, where decisions about misconduct have to be taken or where the employee wants an allegation of discrimination investigated, it would probably not be appropriate to have mediation.

2.7   Judicial mediation

The employment tribunals do provide a mediation service which is conducted by an employment judge acting as the mediator. This is called Judicial Mediation and is free of charge. See section 14.15 for more information on how it works.

Summary of Grievance Procedure

(1) Resolve grievances informally - often a quiet word is sufficient.

(2) Use the company grievance procedure (if there is one) where it has not been possible to resolve the matter informally.

(3) Write to the employer setting out the grievance.

(4) Arrange a meeting to discuss the grievance and allow the employee to be accompanied.

(5) Decide on appropriate action, if any, and inform the employee.

(6) Allow the employee to appeal if not satisfied with the outcome.

2.8   Disciplinary procedures

A disciplinary situation can include both an act of misconduct or poor performance. Most employers will have a written disciplinary procedure and some employers will have a separate written procedure dealing with poor performance (often referred to as a "capability procedure").

2.9   Capability

Capability covers those circumstances where an employee is not doing his job properly and where his performance is below the standard expected of him. This could be for any number of reasons, either through lack of skill or experience, because of emotional or domestic problems or simply because he is lazy or cannot be bothered to do the job properly. It will also apply where he is unable to do his job through long-term sickness.

It is important to note that the ACAS Code of Practice includes procedures for poor performance. The contract of employment might contain a procedure dealing with performance issues - the employer can use this as long as it contains the basic principles of fairness, which are set out in the Code of Practice.

If you are the employer you would be well advised to deal with poor performance informally if this is possible. Sometimes a quiet word with the employee concerned will be sufficient to make him aware that his poor performance has been noticed and that an improvement is expected. It is usually preferable that you do this in private - if it is done in front of work colleagues it might cause embarrassment and can lead to accusations of harassment.

There is an ACAS booklet called "How to Manage Performance" which can be found on the ACAS website. This includes a section on dealing with under-performance.

2.10   Formal procedures

If the poor performance continues you, as the employer, might feel the need to implement formal procedures. The first step will be to investigate the problem; you should see whether the employee has been properly trained, you should find out the reason for the incompetence or poor performance and see whether it was the employee's fault or some other cause. This will involve speaking to the employee himself and those responsible for training or supervising him.

First meeting

If it appears that the problem has been caused by insufficient training you should consider whether appropriate training should be organised for the employee.

If the problem appears to lie with the employee then you should invite the employee to a meeting. The letter inviting him should contain sufficient information about the poor performance to enable the employee to respond to the allegation. The letter should also set out possible consequences of a failure to improve and advise the employee of his right to be accompanied to the meeting.

At this meeting the allegation of poor performance will need to be explained to the employee with specific examples being given. The employee should be allowed to ask questions about the allegations or the evidence on which they are based. The employee should have the opportunity to put their case and to call any witnesses they wish to call. If the employee raises matters which require further investigation then the meeting should be adjourned to allow these matters to be investigated.

Warning

If it is found that the allegation of poor performance is justified the employee should be given a warning; this should state that he will need to improve within a specified time period. The time period should be sufficient to give the employee a reasonable period in which he can show that his performance has improved and will often be three months. Where possible the employee should also be told what standard he would be expected to achieve in that period. The letter should also set out the possible consequences in the event of a finding that he has failed to improve his performance.

Second meeting

If the employee fails to achieve the required standard within the given period you should arrange a further meeting. The employee should be invited to attend at a stated time and place. This letter will need to set out the allegations again, and refer to the previous meeting and what was expected of the employee. It will also need to set out why it is considered that he has failed to improve his performance. The employee should be advised of his right to be accompanied to the meeting.

In this meeting the allegation of poor performance should be explained with details being given of what was expected of the employee since the previous meeting and why it was considered that his performance had not improved. You will need to consider what the employee says about this failure, whether he accepts he was at fault and if he does not what explanation he gives. If this explanation is not accepted you should let the employee know why.

The decision

Before deciding to dismiss an employee you should give consideration to whether there are alternatives such as:

* would further training change the situation?

* could the employee be moved to an alternative position?

* should the employee be given a further chance to show that they can improve their performance?

Only if there is no alternative should you be considering dismissal.

A number of factors will affect the consideration of whether dismissal is a reasonable option, including:

* how long the employee had been employed (the longer the period the less reasonable the decision to dismiss becomes);

* the attitude of the employee and whether they have shown efforts to improve but have found some parts of the job beyond their capabilities or whether they have made little effort to improve;

* the size of the organisation and the extent to which other positions are available.

It is advisable that you arrange for someone to take notes of what is said at these meetings. These notes should be typed up after the meeting and a copy given to the employee to make any additions or corrections. Once approved you should arrange for the employee to sign the note to confirm that it is accurate.

The employee should be informed of the decision in writing and reasons should be given for the decision. If the decision is taken to dismiss the employee he should be given the appropriate period of notice as this is not a dismissal for gross misconduct where the employer need not give notice (see Chapter 3). Where the contract of employment has provision for it the employee can be given pay in lieu of notice (i.e. payment instead of working out the period of notice).

Appeal

Whatever sanction the employee is given he should be given the opportunity to appeal and he should be notified of this right in writing. The appeal should be heard without unreasonable delay. It should be heard by someone different from the person who conducted the disciplinary hearing. If the employee raises new matters in his appeal letter these should be investigated before the appeal is heard. Again, employees have a right to be accompanied to the appeal hearing.

The decision on the appeal and the reason for this decision should be given in writing.

Summary of capability procedure

(1) Resolve the issue of poor performance informally - often a quiet word is sufficient.

(2) Use the company capability procedure (if there is one) where it has not been possible to resolve the matter informally.

(3) Write to the employee setting out the allegation and why his performance is considered to be below standard.

(4) Arrange a meeting to discuss the poor performance and allow the employee to be accompanied.

(5) Decide on appropriate action, if any, and inform the employee in what respect his performance is expected to improve and over what period.

(6) Monitor performance over this period and invite the employee to a further meeting if there has been no or insufficient improvement.

(7) Explain to the employee in the meeting why it is considered his performance has not reached the expected standard and listen to the employee's explanation.

(8) Decide on appropriate action, if any, and inform the employee.

(9) Allow the employee to appeal if he is not satisfied with the outcome.

2.11   Sickness absence

Long term sickness can create difficulties for employers, particularly small businesses. Whilst employment tribunals understand the problems long term sickness can create, they also expect employers to be sympathetic and show understanding towards the employees. Appendix 4 of the ACAS Guide gives guidance as to how to deal with absences caused by sickness or injury.

As an employer you will also need to be aware that in some situations there will be an overlap between long term sickness absence and disability discrimination under the Equality Act (see Chapter 4) and you will have to be mindful of the requirement to make adjustments to assist a disabled employee.

Meeting

You should always try to arrange a formal meeting with the employee before coming to a decision whether to dismiss. This will not always be possible - for example, in cases where the employee is off sick with stress, they or their doctor might argue that such a meeting would contribute to the employee's condition and make it worse. Such a meeting will need to be held at a place and a time that is convenient for the employee - this might need to be away from the workplace and possibly even at the employee's home. It is important that the employee is informed if there is any question of his employment being terminated.

Factors to be taken into account

As an employer, when considering whether to dismiss an employee who has been on long term sick leave or on the grounds of capability, the sorts of questions that you should be asking are:

- how long has the employee been off sick?

- how long is it anticipated that the employee will continue to be off sick?

- has medical evidence been obtained to carry out an assessment of the position, either from the employee's doctor or from an occupational health physician?

- what is the nature of the employee's job?

- how important is the employee's position in the organisation?

- can the post be covered by other employees?

If the matter comes before an employment tribunal in a claim for unfair dismissal these are all factors that the tribunal will be considering when assessing how long it would be reasonable for this employer to wait before dismissing the employee. Tribunals expect employers to take a sympathetic and considerate approach towards employees who are on long term sickness absence.

The dismissal of an employee who has been on long term sickness absence should be the last resort and only decided upon when all other possible alternatives have been considered and rejected. If the employee is disabled you will need to consider possible adjustments as an alternative to dismissal.

The decision

The employee should be informed of the decision in writing and reasons should be given for the decision. If the decision is taken to dismiss the employee should be given the appropriate period of notice as this is not a dismissal for gross misconduct where the employer need not give notice.

Whatever the sanction the employee should be given the opportunity to appeal and he should be notified of this right in writing. The appeal should be heard without unreasonable delay. It should be heard by a different person than the person who conducted the hearing. If the employee raises new matters in his appeal letter these should be investigated before the appeal is heard. Again, employees have a right to be accompanied to the appeal hearing.

Summary of procedure for dealing with long term sickness absence

(1) Write to the employee to find out how long they are likely to be absent.

(2) Obtain evidence from a medical practitioner as to how long the employee is likely to be absent.

(3) Invite the employee to a meeting to consider options and allow the employee to be accompanied.

(4) Explain possible options to the employee and ask for his views.

(5) Decide on appropriate action, if any, and inform the employee.

(6) Allow the employee to appeal if he is not satisfied with the outcome.

2.12   Misconduct

Most employers will include their disciplinary procedure either in the contract of employment or in a separate document - it is sometimes included in the company handbook. As long as this procedure contains the basic principles of fairness set out in the ACAS Code of Practice on Disciplinary and Grievance Procedures, an employer can follow his own disciplinary procedures. The ACAS Guide to Discipline and Grievances at Work provides more detailed advice and guidance on disciplinary procedures.

An employer will need to be mindful of the guidelines set out in the ACAS Code because a failure to follow the steps set out in the Code can result in a tribunal increasing an award to an employee who has been unfairly dismissed by up to 25%.

There are three basic stages to the disciplinary process:

- the investigation stage; then

- the disciplinary hearing; and finally

- the decision, and, if the allegation is proved, whether to dismiss or if some alternative sanction is appropriate.

2.13   What constitutes misconduct?

Misconduct is divided into two categories. Less serious misconduct will merit a warning whilst gross misconduct can merit immediate (or "summary") dismissal.

For less serious misconduct there will normally be three stages of warning:

- a verbal warning;

- a written warning; and

- a final written warning.

The disciplinary procedure will normally set out a list of matters that will constitute gross misconduct. These usually include theft or other dishonesty, fighting, bullying, harassment or discrimination, refusing to obey a lawful order, deliberate and serious damage to property, bringing the company into serious disrepute and incapability at work due to alcohol or illegal drugs.

Some disciplinary procedures set out what constitutes ordinary misconduct. This often includes such things as poor attendance or bad time keeping, minor damage to property, failing to observe company procedures and abusive behaviour.

2.14   Warning

The contract of employment will usually provide a period for which the warning (whether it is a verbal, written or final warning) remains on the employee's record - this will normally be six or twelve months and the warning is said to be "live" for this period. If a further instance of misconduct is committed within this period the employer can take the earlier warning into account, but if the further instance of misconduct is committed after this period the earlier warning should not normally be taken into account. Where the employee is already on a final written warning it will only take a fairly minor act of misconduct to justify his dismissal.

The disciplinary procedure will normally set out the various stages that are involved when an employee is accused of misconduct and will set out various examples of acts that would be considered to amount to misconduct or gross misconduct. The significance of gross misconduct is that an employee found guilty of gross misconduct can be dismissed without notice and without any further warning.

2.15   Informal procedure

If you are an employer you should, where possible, try to deal with a disciplinary matter informally. Sometimes a quiet word with the employee concerned will be sufficient to make him aware that the conduct has been noticed and that a change is expected. It will almost always be preferable that this is done in private as if it is done in front of work colleagues it can cause embarrassment and the employee might not feel that he is in a position to put forward an explanation for his conduct.

As an employer you should try to be flexible in dealing with problems that an employee may have. For example if an employee has been getting into work late because of difficulties with public transport it might be possible to change the times when he starts and finishes work to try to accommodate this. If such a change is not possible the employee should be told why this is the case and the need to be on time should be emphasised.

In such circumstances it would be appropriate to warn the employee that if there is no improvement in their conduct this could result in formal disciplinary proceedings. Even though this is not a formal meeting a note should be kept of what has been said.

2.16   Suspension

In some cases of serious misconduct it may be necessary to suspend the employee concerned while the misconduct is being investigated. Such a suspension should be on full pay and should be for as short a period as is necessary.

There are no set circumstances where the suspension of an employee will be appropriate. The ACAS Guide gives some examples: where relationships within the workplace have broken down; in gross misconduct cases; or where there are risks to property. It may also be appropriate to suspend the employee in circumstances where there is a risk of interference with witnesses or with evidence.

If you are an employee who has been informed that you are being suspended but have not been given any reason for this, you should write to your employer asking why you have been suspended. Although the employer does not need to give a reason for the suspension I would suggest that the employer should explain why it considers a suspension to be appropriate in the circumstances. If the employer has no good explanation for the suspension such an action can look unreasonable.

2.17   Formal procedure

If the misconduct continues or is too serious just for an informal chat then formal disciplinary proceedings will need to be undertaken.

It is important that disciplinary matters are dealt with promptly and fairly. This means that the employee must be informed of the allegations against him and must be given an opportunity to answer these allegations before any disciplinary action is taken.

The procedure is referred to as "formal" because if the misconduct is proved and the employer considers a warning is the appropriate penalty, this warning will be recorded on the employee's disciplinary record and remains "live" for the stated period. This will apply whatever type of warning is given.

This formal procedure will apply to all allegations of misconduct even when the allegation is one of gross misconduct. Where an act of gross misconduct is alleged it will be particularly important for the employer to ensure that the correct procedure is followed because such an allegation can lead to the dismissal of the employee.

Investigation

The matter will start with an allegation of misconduct. This will normally be something that has come to the attention of a manager or supervisor either because he has seen something himself or information has been brought to him. He will have to decide whether it merits an investigation. If he decides that there needs to be an investigation this should be carried out by himself, but not if he is a witness to the misconduct, in which case he should appoint someone else to carry out the investigation.

It is important that a full investigation into the misconduct is carried out - failure to carry out a proper investigation and to give the employee an opportunity to know the allegations against him and to put his side of the case will render the dismissal unfair even where the evidence against him is overwhelming.

As an employer your first step will be to investigate the accusation or complaint against the employee concerned to establish the facts of the case. As a general rule the person carrying out this investigation should not be the person who carries out any subsequent disciplinary hearing, although this is not always possible in very small organisations.

Written statements should be taken because these will need to be shown to the employee accused. Normally the name of the witness should be included on the statement - it will only be in unusual circumstances that an anonymous witness statement would be relied on.

Investigation meeting

Once the evidence has been obtained it should be reviewed to see if there is sufficient evidence of misconduct to provide a case that the employee should answer. If there is not sufficient evidence that will be an end of the matter. If there is sufficient evidence the investigating officer should consider whether to conduct a formal interview with the employee. Such an interview is not a requirement under the ACAS Code of Practice but it is an advisable step in most cases as it will be an opportunity to clear up any mistakes or misunderstandings without the need for a formal disciplinary hearing. The employee should be given sufficient information about the allegation to know what he is being accused of - ideally he should be given the witness statements at this stage.

If, during the course of this interview, the employee raises matters that require further investigation, the interview should be adjourned whilst these matters are investigated. The interview should then be resumed with the employee being given the opportunity to comment on any new matters that have been discovered. Once the investigating officer has considered all the evidence and satisfied himself that there is a case to answer he will need to write to the employee informing him that this is the case and invite him to a disciplinary hearing.

What if there are ongoing criminal proceedings?

If the employee has been charged with a criminal offence by the police, for example theft from the employer, the employer will have to decide whether it is appropriate to pursue disciplinary proceedings before the criminal proceedings have concluded. One factor will be whether there is likely to be a long delay before the criminal proceedings are concluded. If there is, it might well be considered reasonable for the employer to proceed with a disciplinary hearing.

If the employee is content for the disciplinary hearing to take place it will probably be reasonable for the employer to continue but if the employee says he has been advised by his lawyer not to say anything in the disciplinary proceedings, as this might prejudice the criminal proceedings, then the employer might have to wait until the criminal proceedings have been finalised before conducting a disciplinary hearing.

2.18   The disciplinary hearing

The employee should then be invited in writing to attend a hearing. Whether or not there has been an interview with the employee, this letter should contain sufficient information for the employee to know the allegation against him with sufficient detail to prepare to answer the case against him. If he has not been provided with the written statements or other evidence beforehand he should be supplied with this information at this point.

The employee will have the right to be accompanied by a colleague or union representative. The place and date of the meeting should be at time and place that is convenient to the employee.

Recording the hearing

It is not unusual at employment tribunal hearings for there to be a dispute as to what has actually been said at the disciplinary hearing. The best way of avoiding such a dispute is to have the hearing recorded, then to have the recording written up (or "transcribed") and both the employer and the employee to sign the transcript confirming that they agree it is an accurate record of the hearing.

If notes of the hearing are taken by a secretary or someone else for the employer, it is important for the employee to obtain a copy of these notes as soon as possible after the meeting and make any corrections or additions. Unless he does this at the time it becomes very difficult many months after the meeting to remember exactly what was said and the tribunal will usually accept what is written as the correct version.

There have been instances recently of employees secretly recording disciplinary hearings or meetings. This is often referred to as a "covert recording". Such recordings have been admitted by the employment tribunals as evidence. This is not a course of action I would recommend unless you have a good reason to believe that the person conducting the hearing might not record truthfully or accurately what has been said. If you do make such a recording and the matter goes to a tribunal hearing you would expect to be questioned as to why you did not ask for permission to record the hearing but felt it necessary to make a secret recording. Secret recording of interviews or meetings can constitute misconduct and potentially gross misconduct if done with the intention of entrapping an employer, trying to gain an unfair advantage or if it is categorised in the contract of employment as an act of gross misconduct - see the case of *Phoenix House Ltd v Stockman* UKEAT/0284/17/00. There is a short ACAS article on covert recordings dated April 2013 which can be found on the ACAS website.

Who should conduct the hearing?

It is always preferable to have the hearing conducted by a person who has not conducted the investigation and is not a witness, although this will not always be possible with very small businesses. There is a danger that, where the person who carries out the investigation and then conducts the hearing, they may be accused of being biased, having prejudged the issue before the hearing, and the tribunal may conclude that the hearing has been procedurally flawed.

At the hearing the employer should explain the complaint or the allegation against the employee. He should go through the evidence that has been obtained. The employee should be given the opportunity to set out their case, to ask questions, put forward evidence and call witnesses. If either the employer or the employee intends to call witnesses they should give the other side advance notice that they intend to do this.

Matters to be taken into consideration

If you are the employer you need to realise that a disciplinary hearing can be both a stressful and an emotional experience for the employee. If the employee considers that he has been wrongly accused of something that he has not done he might well be upset, angry and uncooperative. It is for the employer to ensure as best he can that the disciplinary hearing is conducted fairly, that the employee is encouraged to put his side of the story, that the hearing does not get heated and that matters are dealt with calmly.

If you are the employee it is important to realise that this is your opportunity to put your side of the case. Even if you do not consider you will get a fair hearing you should still put your side of the story. If you do not consider you were guilty of the misconduct alleged you should explain why. If you accept the allegation but consider that there were mitigating circumstances you should put these forward. "Mitigating circumstances" means that you accept the allegation that has been made against you but you consider that there are circumstances or reasons which would lessen the degree of blame. For example, if you have been accused of fighting it would be a mitigating circumstance to show that you had been provoked.

If you are the employee it will not benefit you to refuse to co-operate with the hearing or to be hostile or aggressive in the hearing because, if the matter does end in your dismissal and you bring a tribunal claim, you will want to persuade the tribunal that it was the employer, and not you, who was acting unreasonably.

When the tribunal comes to consider the merits of the case the test they will apply is whether the employer, on the evidence before him, acted reasonably in dismissing the employee. If you had a good case but failed to put forward this case at the disciplinary hearing the tribunal might conclude that on the evidence before him the employer acted reasonably in dismissing you.

The decision

After the meeting the employer will have to decide whether any disciplinary action is justified and if so, what the appropriate action is. If it is a first finding of misconduct against the employee then a written warning will normally be sufficient. If it is serious misconduct then a final written warning may be appropriate. If the finding is gross misconduct or the employee already has a final written warning on his record that has not expired, then the employer will be justified in considering dismissal.

Before reaching the decision to dismiss, the employer will need to take into account not just the misconduct itself but other factors including how long the employee has worked and how the employer has treated similar instances of misconduct by other employees. Employers are expected to act consistently; so, if two employees are involved in a fight and it is not possible to decide who was responsible and they both had the same disciplinary record, then the punishment should be consistent.

If a verbal, written or final written warning is given the employee should be informed in writing of the nature of the misconduct, how long the warning will remain on his file and the possible impact of a further act of misconduct in this period.

Appeal

Whatever the sanction, the employee should be given the opportunity to appeal, and he should be notified of this right in writing. The appeal should be heard without unreasonable delay. It should, where possible, be heard by a different person than the person who conducted the disciplinary hearing. If the employee raises new matters in his appeal letter these should be investigated before the appeal is heard. Again, employees have the right to be accompanied to the appeal hearing.

As with the disciplinary hearing the appeal hearing should be recorded and the record of the hearing agreed between the employer and the employee. The employee should be informed of the outcome of the appeal hearing in writing without any undue delay.

2.19   The Coronavirus Job Retention Scheme

On 23rd March 2020 the government announced that many workplaces would have to close on a temporary basis because of the coronavirus pandemic. Employees were expected to work from home where they could. To prevent the spread of the disease the government introduced social distancing guidelines under which people including employees were expected to keep two metres apart. In order to prevent large scale redundancies the government set up a scheme under which the employees would be put "on furlough", which meant they would remain at home but would continue to be paid 80% of their salary. This is called the Coronavirus Job Retention Scheme. The government would then reimburse the employers this sum. The details of the scheme can be found on the government website. Although originally the scheme was designed to last for three months, on 12th May 2020 the government announced that the scheme would be extended to the end of October 2020.

On 6th May 2020 ACAS published a guidance document entitled Disciplinary and Grievance Procedures during the Coronavirus Pandemic. This confirmed that the ACAS Code of Practice on Disciplinary and Grievance Procedures would still apply. The employer would need to decide if it would be fair and reasonable to start or carry on with a disciplinary or grievance people while employees or workers were still on furlough or working from home and the social distancing and other public health guidelines were in place.

If an employee who is working from home or on furlough wants to raise a grievance the employer must consider whether it can carry out a fair procedure.

If someone is on furlough they can take part in a disciplinary or grievance investigation or hearing if they:

- are under investigation in a disciplinary procedure;

- have raised a grievance;

- are chairing a disciplinary or grievance hearing;

- are taking notes at a hearing or interview;

- are being interviewed as part of an investigation;

- are a witness at a hearing;

- are an employee's companion for a hearing.

This is as long the employee is doing it out of their own choice and the interview or hearing takes place in line with current public health guidance such as social distancing.

The guidance advises that disciplinary and grievance procedures can be stressful. Employees might be facing other stressful circumstances and the guidance suggests that the options are discussed with the employee before making a decision whether to proceed or not. When a decision is made the reason for this decision should be explained to those involved.

Where the workplace is open the employer should consider whether the procedure can be carried out in line with public health guidelines, for example, can interviews and meetings be held in a place that allows for social distancing as well as privacy?

Where people are working from home or on furlough the employer will need to consider if the procedure can be carried out in a fair and reasonable way. They should consider the individual circumstances; whether the case needs to be dealt with urgently or if it could be dealt with more fairly when people return to work. They should consider any reasonable objections to the procedure going ahead at that time.

If the employer intends to go ahead using video meetings, they must consider if this can be done fairly.

- Does everyone have access to the necessary equipment?

- Does anyone have disability or other accessibility issues that might affect their ability to use technology? If so reasonable adjustments should be considered. (See paragraph 4.17 on disability discrimination).

- Can any witness statements or other evidence be seen clearly by everyone involved in the hearing?

- Will it be possible to fairly assess and question evidence given by people interviewed during a video meeting?

- Is it possible to obtain all the necessary evidence needed for the investigation, such as records or files?

- Is possible for the employee to be accompanied?

The right to be accompanied still applies even though it is a video meeting. The hearing must be set up to allow the companion to present the case on behalf of the employee, respond on behalf of the employee to anything said and talk privately with the employee at any point. If the companion is unable to attend the proposed hearing date, the employer can suggest another date as long as it is reasonable and no more than 5 working days after the original date. Where the coronavirus pandemic causes problems for a companion's attendance, a delay of more than 5 days might be reasonable.

Where the grievance or disciplinary meeting is held by video there will normally be no reason to record the meeting. If it is felt there is a good reason to record it, this must be done in line with data protection law.

The employee still has a right of appeal against a disciplinary finding or against a grievance that has been rejected. The employer must follow a fair appeal procedure taking into account the same considerations as with the grievance or disciplinary procedure.

Summary of disciplinary procedure for misconduct

(1) Resolve the issue of misconduct informally - often a quiet word is sufficient.

(2) Use the company disciplinary procedure where it has not been possible to resolve the matter informally.

(3) Investigate the allegation, inviting the employee to an investigation meeting if appropriate.

(4) Write to the employee setting out the allegation and evidence of misconduct.

(5) Arrange a meeting to discuss the allegation, and allow the employee to be accompanied.

(6) Decide on appropriate action, if any, and inform the employee what penalty, if any, is considered appropriate.

(7) Allow the employee to appeal if he is not satisfied with the outcome.

Chapter 3

Unfair dismissal

3.1 What is dismissal?

A dismissal occurs when your employer brings your employment to an end. Unless your employer can show that the dismissal was for a fair reason then it will be an unfair dismissal. Your employer must also show that, in coming to the decision to dismiss you, he acted fairly and reasonably.

The basic law relating to unfair dismissal is set out in sections 94 to 107 of the Employment Rights Act 1996. Section 98 sets out those reasons that can constitute a fair reason for dismissing an employee.

The law as set out in the Employment Rights Act 1996 has been considered by the Employment Appeal Tribunal and the Court of Appeal in many cases and in their judgments they have set out guidelines as to how the law should be interpreted. These judgments can be found on the Employment Appeal Tribunal website at www.gov.uk/employment-appeal-tribunal-decisions. In 2017, Employment Tribunal decisions started to be published on the Gov.UK website - you can access these decisions at www.gov.uk/employment-tribunal-decisions.

For the Court of Appeal the best place to find the judgments are www.bailii.org.

Claims for unfair dismissal can only be brought in the employment tribunal - you cannot bring a claim for unfair dismissal in the County Court.

3.2 Termination of contract of employment

Lawyers often talk about the "termination of a contract of employment". All this means in ordinary language is that the contract has come to an end. The contract can be terminated (or brought to an end) by either you as the employee or by your employer. The effect of the termination of your contract of employment is that you no longer work for that employer.

The phrase "termination of the contract of employment" is a neutral phrase and does not imply blame either on the part of you as employee or your employer. If you choose to leave your employment, perhaps because you are taking up a new job or moving to a different part of the country, you would hand in your resignation. In these circumstances the contract of employment has been terminated by agreement between you and your employer and you could not claim unfair dismissal.

3.3   Resignation

A resignation that has been forced upon you by your employer would constitute a dismissal if your employer says "Unless you resign I will dismiss you" and you resign. This will be treated by the employment tribunal as a dismissal by your employer.

If you are an employee and have been unfairly dismissed you can get compensation. This is an award of money for losing your job and for any money you have lost as a result of being dismissed, such as a loss of earnings.

In some circumstances the employment tribunal can order that an employer who has unfairly dismissed you employs you again - this is called reinstatement. In practice this remedy is rarely used because by the time the case comes to the tribunal the relationship between you and your former employer will usually be so bad that it is unrealistic to expect an employment relationship to work. I will consider this remedy in more detail in Chapter 21.

3.4   Who can make a claim for unfair dismissal?

The following categories of people can make a claim for unfair dismissal:

- an employee, who is not in one of the exempted categories (see 'Excluded employees' below);

- an employee who has been employed for at least two years by the same employer, unless the dismissal is for an automatically unfair reason, in which case no qualifying period is required;

- an employee who is not employed under an illegal contract.

I will consider each of these categories in turn.

An employee

A claim for unfair dismissal can only be brought by someone who is an employee. Therefore, if you are self-employed, you will not be able to bring a claim for unfair dismissal.

The Employment Rights Act 1996 (section 230) defines an employee as someone who is employed under a contract of employment. This might not be considered a very helpful definition but the difficulty is that it has been almost impossible to provide a satisfactory definition of what an employee is.

The employment tribunals and courts have tried to set out various factors or tests that will determine whether the relationship between the two parties is that of an employer and an employee, or between a self-employed person and the client who has agreed to use their services.

In many cases the distinction will be obvious. If you ask a plumber or electrician to come round to your house they will agree to do work for you and you will agree to pay them but it is obvious they are not your employee.

In other cases the distinction will be much more difficult to ascertain. In the case of *Autoclenz v Belcher* [2011] UKSC 41 which went up to the Supreme Court, the Claimant was a car valeter who cleaned cars for the Respondent company. Even though the Claimant had signed a contract stating that he was self-employed the court found that he was in fact an employee. This case is a good illustration of the difficulty of distinguishing between an employee and a self-employed contractor and how the tribunal will apply various tests to the facts of the case.

A detailed consideration of what constitutes an employee is beyond the scope of this book but I set out below some general indications that have been provided by the courts.

- The fact that there is a contract of employment signed or agreed by both parties as a general rule indicates an employment relationship, but not always, and the tribunals are prepared to find the document will be a sham if it does not actually represent the relationship between the parties.

- If the worker is paid holiday pay and sick pay, or if he has to work set hours at a set place of work, these are all factors which indicate a contract of employment while if he pays his own tax and national insurance, or uses his own tools and equipment, these factors suggest he is not an employee.

- One of the more recent tests relied on by the courts is referred to as "mutuality of obligation". This means that if the "employer" is not required to offer work and, if offered, the worker is not required to accept that offer, then it is unlikely that there is a contract of employment.

As a general rule it will be the Claimant who is trying to allege that he is an employee so that he can bring a claim for unfair dismissal, and it is the "employer" or client who is denying that there is such a relationship. This dispute can arise in a variety of different situations, such as agency workers, workers who start on a self-employed basis working for an organisation but over time are gradually integrated into the organisation, or casual or zero-hours workers who do not have fixed work times but are hired when and if they are needed for a particular job.

There are a couple of websites that set out the differences between a worker, an employee and a self-employed person:

www.gov.uk/government/collections/employed-or-self-employed

www.nidirect.gov.uk/index/information-and-services/employment/under-standing-your-work-status/employment-status.htm

Excluded employees

There are various categories of employees who cannot bring a claim for unfair dismissal. These include:

- police officers, unless it is a whistleblowing claim;

- members of the armed forces;

- fishermen who are paid with a share of the profits;

- persons who work abroad.

3.5 The qualifying period

The qualifying period is the length of time you must have been continuously employed for before you can bring a claim. The qualifying period for unfair dismissal changed on 6th April 2012 from one year to two years. This means that if you started working for your employer before this date you would only need one years' continuous service to bring a claim. If you started working for your employer after this date you will need to have worked for two full years to be able to bring a claim for unfair dismissal, unless you can show that the reason for the dismissal falls into that category of dismissals which are automatically unfair where no qualifying period is required.

3.6 Automatically unfair dismissals

If you have been dismissed for a reason such as raising concerns about a health and safety issue or for asserting a legal (or "statutory") right, such as the right to have rest breaks or the right to a minimum wage, then it will not matter that you have been employed for less than two years - you can still claim unfair dismissal.

No qualifying period is required if it can be shown that the reason for the dismissal was for one of the following reasons (all sections refer to the Employment Rights Act (ERA) 1996):

- Relating to health and safety (s100);

- Asserting a statutory right (s104);

- Asserting a right under the Working Time Regulations (s101A);

- Making a protected disclosure (s103A);

- Acting as an employee representative (s103);

- Asserting a right under the National Minimum Wage Act (s104A);

- Dismissal due to employee's political opinions (s108);

- Relating to pregnancy or maternity/paternity leave (s99);

- Discrimination under one of the protected grounds in the Equality Act.

There are various other reasons but these are the most common. For a full list of reasons see www.gov.uk/dismissal/unfair-and-constructive-dismissal.

What this means is that however long you have been employed, if you can satisfy the tribunal that the reason you were dismissed is for any one of the reasons set out above, the tribunal will hold that the dismissal was unfair.

If you have been dismissed before you have been employed for two years there is a temptation to try and see if you can bring the dismissal within one of those categories that qualifies for automatic unfair dismissal. You will need good evidence that this is the case as tribunals are alert to Claimants trying to argue that the dismissal was for an automatically unfair reason just in order to avoid the requirement of two years' employment.

First of all you will need to show that you do potentially fall into one of the above categories, for example that you have raised health and safety concerns or that you have made a protected disclosure. You will then need to show that the reason your employer has given for dismissing you had no real merit, for example if your last appraisal was favourable but your employer dismissed you soon after the appraisal for poor performance. Once you have satisfied the tribunal on these two issues you should have a reasonable prospect of persuading the tribunal that you were dismissed for an automatically unfair reason.

3.7 Protected disclosure ("whistleblowing")

Part IVA of the ERA 1996 sets out the statutory provisions dealing with protected disclosures. Section 43B defines a "qualifying disclosure". This is any disclosure of information which in the reasonable belief of the worker is made in the public interest and tends to show:

- a criminal act has been or is likely to be committed;

- a person has or is likely to fail to comply with a legal obligation;

- a miscarriage of justice has or is likely to occur;

- the health and safety of an individual has been or is likely to be endangered;

- the environment has been or is likely to be damaged; or

- information tending to show any matter within the preceding paragraphs has been or is likely to be deliberately concealed.

The requirement that the disclosure be made in good faith has now gone, although the tribunal can reduce the amount of compensation awarded by up to 25% if the disclosure is not made in good faith. What good faith means is that the disclosure should be made for the benefit of the public and not for a personal motive, for example where a disclosure is made to get a particular person into trouble because the worker dislikes that person.

The requirement that the disclosure be "in the public interest" means that it must affect others, e.g. the general public. A complaint by an employee about a breach of their contract by the employer will not normally be a protected disclosure because it is not in the public interest.

Sections 43C, D, E and F set out the categories of persons to whom a qualifying disclosure must be made - these include the employer.

Under section 47B a worker has the right not to be subjected to a detriment on the ground that he has made a protected disclosure. A "detriment" means being subjected to unfair treatment by the employer, for example by being denied overtime or other benefits, or being singled out for unpleasant tasks. It does not include dismissal, which is dealt with separately under section 103A of the ERA 1996. Section 103A states that an employee who is dismissed for making a protected disclosure will be regarded as unfairly dismissed.

It is worth noting that if you can prove that you have been subjected to a detriment for making a protected disclosure under section 43B, you are entitled to damages for injury to feelings. If you are *dismissed* for making a protected disclosure you are entitled to a basic award and a compensatory award but not to injury to feelings. For further information about damages see Chapter 21 on Remedies.

3.8 A worker

This is another category that is used in employment law. A "worker" includes employees but also covers people who work under a contract to perform personally some work or service but can not be classed as an employee because they do not have a contract of employment. The definition of a worker is set out in section 230(3)(b) of the Employment Rights Act - referring to this subsection they are sometimes called "limb (b) workers". Examples of limb (b) workers might include an agency worker, a short term casual worker, a freelance worker or a zero hours worker. A person who is a limb (b) worker but not an employee cannot bring a claim for unfair dismissal but does have certain employment rights including the right to a minimum wage and to holiday pay. Limb (b) workers can also bring a discrimination claim and since April 2020 they are also entitled to itemised pay slips.

3.9   Zero-hours contracts

This term is used to describe a number of different types of agreement under which work is performed by an individual, the general principle being that the employer does not guarantee any set hours of work in any period. The employer will offer work and the worker can either accept or turn down this offer of work. As long as the agreement is to carry out the work personally the worker is likely to be classified as a limb (b) worker with the rights as set out above. One disadvantage of being a zero hours worker is that, because there are no guaranteed minimum hours, an employer need not dismiss the worker but just decide not to offer them any more work.

A zero hours worker is protected from suffering a detriment or being dismissed for working for another employer - section 27A Employment Rights Act 1996. In the case of *Obi v Rice Shack Ltd* UKEAT/0240/17/DM an employee on a zero hours contract was entitled to be paid her average weekly earnings for the period whilst she was suspended pending disciplinary proceedings.

The government published Guidance on Zero Hours Contracts in October 2015 and ACAS have a short guide to Zero Hours Contracts.

3.10   Illegal contracts

Another important exclusion to the right to bring a claim for unfair dismissal is where you are employed under an illegal contract in circumstances where you knew and participated in that illegal contract. One situation when this occurs is where you are entirely or partly paid in cash and the intention on the part of your employer is to avoid having to pay tax on this money.

If your employer has paid your salary either fully or partly in cash as a way of reducing the amount of tax that should have been paid, then there is a real possibility that a tribunal will conclude that this constitutes a fraud on the revenue. As such it will be an illegal contract and your claim for unfair dismissal will be dismissed. This will be the case even where your employer has suggested that the payments be in cash and even if your employer does not raise this issue in their ET3. I have had cases where this issue did not come to light until evidence was being heard in the tribunal and once the judge became aware of the position the claim was dismissed.

If your employer has paid you fully or partly in cash and it appears that the purpose might have been to avoid paying tax I would suggest you should get legal advice as to whether a tribunal is likely to conclude that this is an illegal contract. Otherwise you might spend a lot of time bringing the claim to the tribunal only to get it dismissed at the hearing.

3.11   Dismissal

I will now go on to consider different ways in which an employee can be dismissed from his job. The most common way is when the contract is terminated or brought to an end by the employer dismissing the employee. There will also be a dismissal when a fixed term contract comes to an end and is not renewed. In addition there are cases when the employee resigns in circumstances where the employer has been in breach of contract and this entitles the employee to regard the contract as having come to end - this is called "constructive dismissal".

3.12   Fixed term contract

The contract of employment might be for a fixed term where it has been agreed that the employee will work for a specific period, for example 6 months or one year, and at the end of that period the contract will come to an end. The employer and employee can agree to extend the contract by a further set period. Although the employer does not actually sack the employee, the termination of the contract amounts in law to a dismissal (section 95(1)(b) ERA 1996).

The same will apply where the contract is for the performance of a specific task. Once that task has been completed the contract of employment comes to an end. Again, this will in law amount to a dismissal of the employee.

Where the employer unreasonably fails to renew the contract of employment this can amount to an unfair dismissal.

3.13   Constructive dismissal

Constructive dismissal applies where it is employee who actually terminates the contract (section 95(1)(c) Employment Rights Act 1996), when his employer has been guilty of a serious breach of contract. Usually this will be by the employee writing a letter to the employer setting out his complaint, what the employee has tried to do about it, that nothing has been done by the employer to improve the situation, that the employee can put up with it no longer and is therefore tendering his resignation (see Appendix B: Model letters and precedents for two examples of resignation letters).

Unless the employee has raised his complaint by way of a formal grievance there is a risk that any damages he might be awarded at the end of a tribunal hearing will be reduced by up to 25% for failing to comply with the ACAS Code of Practice (see Chapter 16).

If you are the employee in such circumstances you will have to satisfy the tribunal that your employer has committed a breach of the employment contract. This must be a serious breach of contract (sometimes referred to as a "fundamental breach") and not just a minor breach. You will need to show that you resigned because of the breach and not for some other reason, for example that you had an offer of a better job elsewhere. You will also need to show that you have resigned within a reasonable period from the time you became aware of the breach of contract and have not delayed too long.

There are a large number of reported cases where the Employment Appeal Tribunal and the Court of Appeal have considered the circumstances which entitle an employee to resign and claim constructive dismissal. See Appendix C: Table of cases for a list of cases.

Examples of constructive dismissal

You should be aware that each case will depend on the facts of that case. Just because a tribunal found that there was a breach of contract in a reported case does not necessarily mean it will do so in your case, but it is a good starting point if you can show that there are similar facts or circumstances.

I will give some examples of the sort of behaviour that has been found to constitute a fundamental breach of contract which has entitled the employee to resign and claim constructive dismissal:

- As a general rule any attempt to reduce your pay or other contractual entitlements by your employer;

- If your employer significantly changes your job responsibilities or demotes you;

- A refusal by an employer to investigate grievances or complaints;

- Where an employer has been abusive towards an employee or has criticised an employee in front of their subordinates in a humiliating and degrading manner.

Breach of contract

The first requirement is that the employer's conduct must constitute a breach of contract. What the law says is that where an employer has committed a serious breach of contract, the employee is regarding himself as no longer bound by the terms of the contract and is, in effect, treating the contract as ended. The legal phrase is that the employer has "repudiated the contract".

It is important to be aware that merely because the employer does something which the employee does not like, but which the employer is entitled to do under the contract, this will not be a repudiation of the contract. For example, if the employer believes that the employee is guilty of some misconduct and starts an investigation or a disciplinary hearing this will not normally entitle the employee to resign. The position would be different if the employee can show that the employer has acted in bad faith i.e. that the employer does not actually believe that there was any real evidence that the employee was guilty of misconduct but was using this as a reason to harass or get rid of him. It is often difficult to prove bad faith which is unlikely to be admitted by the employer.

The breach of contract must be a serious breach and not a minor or trivial breach of contract. The difficulty for an employee is to know when a breach of contract is sufficiently serious to merit resigning - if he gets it wrong and the employment tribunal does not consider that the breach was sufficiently serious to amount to a fundamental breach of contract, the employee will lose his claim for unfair dismissal.

The "last straw doctrine"

The only time that a minor matter can constitute grounds for an employee resigning and claiming constructive dismissal is when the employer has been guilty of a course of conduct which has the effect of undermining the contract of employment. The employee puts up with this conduct until the time comes when some matter, and it might be a relatively minor incident, results in him saying that he has had enough and then resigns. This is called the "last straw doctrine".

I have set out the names of a number of cases where this doctrine has been considered in Appendix C. It is important to note that an innocent act by the employer, which he is entitled to do under the contract, cannot constitute the last straw.

Breach of an implied term

The contract of employment will contain a number of actual or "express" terms, including the amount of pay, the number of hours to be worked, the place of work etc. In addition the law considers that there are certain "implied" terms which are not specified in the contract of employment. For example, it will be regarded as an implied term that the employer will not require the employee to work in a workplace which is unsafe or provide the employee with tools or working equipment which are unsafe to use.

In addition there is an implied term that neither an employer nor an employee will act in such a way as to undermine the relationship of trust and confidence that exists between an employer and an employee. In general terms this is behaviour which is harsh, oppressive, unlawful or likely to cause either physical injury or mental harm. In an extreme case this will apply where the employer is involved in illegal activities. This occurred in the case of *BCCI v Malik* [1998] AC 20 where the bank was involved in fraudulent transactions, and this entitled the employees to treat the contract of employment as repudiated.

It is difficult to identify what actions by an employer will amount to a breach of trust and confidence but again there are a number of reported cases where the Employment Appeal Tribunal and the Court of Appeal have considered the law on this point - see Appendix C: Table of cases.

Delay

If the employee continues to go into work after the breach of contract, without resigning, there is a danger that the tribunal will consider that he has "waived" or accepted the breach of contract and he will no longer be entitled to claim breach of contract. Where the employee is off sick and does not go into work he will not be treated as having waived the breach unless he does some other act indicating that he regards himself as still bound by the contract.

Can a constructive dismissal be a fair dismissal?

The answer is "yes". The fact that the employer has been guilty of a breach of contract and the employee resigns does not always mean that the employee will succeed in a claim that the dismissal was unfair. There will be circumstances where an employment tribunal will find that it was a fair dismissal, for example when an employer is forced, because of financial problems, to reduce the wages or the hours of employees and the employer proposes changing the terms of the contract accordingly. Whilst the reduction in pay or hours would constitute a fundamental breach of contract, the tribunal might consider that the dismissal of any employee who has resigned as a fair dismissal if it regarded the decision to reduce pay as reasonable and justified by the circumstances, and there has been full consultation with the affected employees.

I have listed some cases where the tribunal has held the constructive dismissal to be fair in Appendix C.

3.14   Unfair dismissal

The Employment Rights Act 1996 at section 98(2) sets out five circumstances in which the dismissal of an employee can potentially be a fair dismissal. These are:

- if the dismissal is for a reason relating to the capability or qualifications of the employee;

- if the dismissal is for a reason relating to the conduct of the employee;

- if the dismissal is the redundancy of the employee;

- if the employee continued to work in the position he held, it would contravene some duty of the employer;

- if the dismissal is for some other substantial reason.

When deciding if a dismissal is fair or unfair the tribunal will consider whether, in the circumstances, the employer acted reasonably in treating the reason for dismissal as a sufficient reason to dismiss the employee. These circumstances include taking into account the size and administrative resources of the employer (section 98(4) ERA). What this means is that, for example, a larger company will be expected to make greater efforts to find an alternative position for a potentially redundant employee than a small company with only a few employees.

Burden of proof

In a case of constructive dismissal, where the *employee* has resigned, it is for the *employee* to prove that his employer was guilty of a breach of contract which entitled him to resign. In other words, the "burden" of proving breach of contract is on the employee. In cases where the *employer* has dismissed the employee, it is for the *employer* to prove that the reason for the dismissal comes within one of the five categories of potentially fair reasons for dismissal (above). This means that when cases of constructive dismissal are heard by the tribunal the employee will go first and give his evidence first. In cases where the employer has dismissed the employee it will be for the employer to go first. I will consider this in more detail in Chapter 20.

3.15   Capability

The first category of potentially fair reasons for dismissals is capability. This covers circumstances where an employee is incompetent, meaning that he is unable to do his job properly either through lack of skill or experience or simply that he is lazy or cannot be bothered to do it properly. It will also apply where he is unable to do his job through long term sickness.

It is important to note that the ACAS Code of Practice includes procedures for poor performance. The contract of employment might contain a procedure dealing with performance issues and the employer can use this as long as it contains the basic principles of fairness, which are set out in the Code of Practice.

I have considered the appropriate procedures and the factors that need to be taken into consideration in Chapter 2 dealing with pre-claim matters.

Summary of procedure for dealing with poor performance

(1) Resolve the issue of poor performance informally - often a quiet word is sufficient.

(2) Use the company capability procedure (if there is one) where it has not been possible to resolve the matter informally.

(3) Write to the employee setting out the allegation and why his performance is considered to be below standard.

(4) Arrange a meeting to discuss the poor performance and allow the employee to be accompanied.

(5) Decide on appropriate action, if any, and inform the employee in what respect his performance is expected to improve and over what period.

(6) Monitor performance over this period and invite the employee to a further meeting if there has been no or insufficient improvement.

(7) Explain to the employee in the meeting why it is considered his performance has not reached the expected standard and listen to the employee's explanation.

(8) Decide on appropriate action, if any, and inform the employee.

(9) Allow the employee to appeal if he is not satisfied with the outcome.

Sickness

Long term sickness comes within the definition of capability and as such can constitute a fair reason for dismissal. In some situations, particularly where the condition has lasted, or is likely to last, more than a year and has a substantial adverse effect on the employee's ability to carry out day-to-day activities, there is likely to be an overlap with disability discrimination under the Equality Act - see Chapter 4. The employer will have to consider what reasonable adjustments could be made to assist the employee before considering whether a dismissal is appropriate.

I have considered the appropriate procedures and the factors that need to be taken into consideration in Chapter 2 dealing with pre-claim matters.

Summary of procedure for dealing with long term sickness absence

(1) Write to the employee to find out how long they are likely to be absent.

(2) Obtain evidence from a medical practitioner as to how long the employee is

likely to be absent.

(3) Invite the employee to a meeting to consider options and allow the employee to be accompanied.

(4) Explain possible options to the employee and ask for his views.

(5) Decide on appropriate action, if any, and inform the employee.

(6) Allow the employee to appeal if he is not satisfied with the outcome.

3.16   Misconduct

The second category of potentially fair dismissals is misconduct. As with poor performance the contract of employment will often contain disciplinary procedures, and as long as these contain the basic principles of fairness set out in the ACAS Code of Practice, an employer can follow his own disciplinary procedures. An employer will need to be mindful of the guidelines set out in the ACAS Code because a failure to follow the steps set out in the Code can result in a tribunal increasing an award to an employee who has been unfairly dismissed by up to 25%.

The disciplinary procedure consists of three stages:

• the investigation stage;

• the disciplinary hearing, and then;

• if the allegation is proved, there is the decision as to the appropriate penalty, whether this is dismissal or some other alternative sanction.

It is particularly important in cases of misconduct to ensure that the allegation is thoroughly investigated, and that the employee is provided with all relevant evidence and given an opportunity to respond to the allegations.

Once the investigation has been concluded and the employer considers that there is sufficient evidence of misconduct the employee should be invited to a disciplinary hearing. This letter should contain sufficient information for the employee to know the allegation against him with sufficient detail to prepare to answer the case against him and it should notify the employee of his right to be accompanied by a colleague or union representative (see Appendix B: Model letters and precedents).

Ideally the meetings should be tape recorded and then transcribed. It is not unusual in employment tribunal cases for there to be a dispute about what was said in the investigation meeting or disciplinary hearing.

If notes of the hearing are taken by a secretary or someone else for the employer, it is important for the employee to obtain a copy of these notes as soon as possible after the meeting and make any corrections or additions. Unless he does this at the time it becomes very difficult many months after the meeting to remember exactly what was said and the tribunal will usually accept what is written as the correct of version of what has been said.

In order to consider whether a dismissal for misconduct is fair a tribunal will follow the guidelines set out in the case of *British Home Stores v Burchill* [1976] IRLR 379. The employer will need to show that:

- he believed that the employee had been guilty of the misconduct alleged;

- he had reasonable grounds on which to sustain that belief; and

- he carried out as much investigation into the matter as was reasonable in all the circumstances.

It is important to note that the employer does not need to prove that the employee was guilty of the misconduct alleged - only that he had a reasonable belief that the employee was guilty. A tribunal will then consider whether dismissal was within the band of reasonable responses that was open to the employer. The test that the employment tribunal will apply is not whether they would have dismissed this employee but whether dismissal came within that band of sanctions that was open to a reasonable employer. In other words, if no reasonable employer would have dismissed this employee the dismissal is likely to be found to be unfair.

I have considered what constitutes misconduct, the appropriate procedures and the factors that need to be taken into consideration in Chapter 2 dealing with pre-claim matters.

Summary of disciplinary procedure for misconduct

(1) Resolve the issue of misconduct informally - often a quiet word is sufficient.

(2) Use the company disciplinary procedure where it has not been possible to resolve the matter informally.

(3) Investigate the allegation, inviting the employee to an investigation meeting if appropriate.

(4) Write to the employee setting out the allegation and evidence of misconduct.

(5) Arrange a meeting to discuss the allegation and allow the employee to be accompanied.

(6) Decide on appropriate action, if any, and inform the employee what penalty is considered appropriate.

(7) Allow the employee to appeal if he is not satisfied with the outcome.

3.17   Redundancy

Redundancy can constitute a fair reason for dismissing an employee. In my experience this is probably the most common reason for an employee being dismissed.

ACAS has published an online guidance for employees called "Your rights during redundancy" and for employers called "Manage staff redundancies" both of which can be found on the ACAS website - www.acas.org.uk.

It can be difficult to prove that you have been unfairly dismissed where the reason for the dismissal is given as redundancy. It will be particularly difficult if there appears to be a redundancy situation (which I will go on to consider later in this section), that your employer held consultation meetings with you and you are not aware of any suitable alternate vacancies within the company.

If you have been made redundant it can sometimes be quite hard to accept that out of all the people in your department or section it is you who have been selected for redundancy. You might feel that you are much more hard-working or experienced than another employee in your department who was not made redundant. It can be difficult to accept on a personal level that you are an employee, or one of a number employees, who do not appear to be valued by your employer and in these circumstances you might look for some other reason to explain why you have been picked on. I have represented many employees who consider that they have been unfairly selected for redundancy for some personal reason, perhaps because they did not get on well with their line manager, rather than because of their work record. The difficulty is proving to an employment tribunal that this was the case.

The problem that employment tribunal judges have is that they are faced with an employer who says "I had to make some employees redundant and I fairly selected the Claimant" and on the other hand there is the Claimant who says "It should not have been me". In these circumstances the Claimant will need to have good evidence that his employer acted unfairly. I will go on to consider these circumstances.

What is a redundancy situation?

It is important to understand what a redundancy situation is. The legal definition is set out at section 139 Employment Rights Act 1996 and there are three circumstances which are covered:

- where the employer has stopped, or intends to stop, the business in which the employee was employed;

- where the employer has stopped, or intends to stop, carrying on business *in the place* where the employee was employed;

- where the requirements of the business for employees to carry out work of a particular kind, or for them to carry out that work in the place they were employed, have ceased or diminished i.e. there is less work available.

Ceasing business

The first of these categories does not generally cause much difficulty. If an employer shuts down his business there will clearly be a redundancy situation in respect of those employees working in the business. The situation will be different if the business is transferred (see Chapter 6 on Transfer of Undertakings).

Ceasing business in current place

Where an employer moves his business to a different location, whether or not an employee is redundant will depend on the terms of his contract. If the contract specifies that he works at a particular location, he will be redundant if the employer moves to a completely different location, although, if the new location is only a short distance from the old location, this move might not be sufficient to result in a redundancy situation. If the contract is silent on this point and the employee works at different locations, only one of which is moving, then it is unlikely that this will constitute a redundancy situation.

Less work available

The last category is where there is less work available for the employees to do or the employer requires fewer employees, for example if the employer introduces machinery to do some of the tasks that had previously been done by hand. Either of these circumstances will create a redundancy situation whereby some of the employees are redundant. The fact that the work being done by the employee still needs to be done does not prevent there being a redundancy situation. This will be the case where the workload has declined and the employer only needs one employee for work that was previously done by two employees. But if a new employee is brought in from outside to do the work that an existing employee was doing, even if the new employee is on a lower pay level, then there is a good argument for saying that the job was not redundant.

As a general rule it is not open to an employee to claim that his dismissal was unfair because the employer acted unreasonably in choosing to make workers redundant. The employment tribunals take the view that it is not for them to investigate the commercial and economic reasons for the closure of a business or the need to reduce the workforce. But it is open to the employee to challenge whether his job was in fact redundant and suggest that there might be other motives for dismissing him.

Bumping

There can be occasions when an employee is dismissed in circumstances where a more senior employer, who would otherwise have been made redundant, has been transferred to their position. This is called "bumping" - the junior employee is "bumped" out of the job by the transfer. In these circumstances the junior employee is redundant. This can be a fair dismissal as long as the proper procedure has been followed.

Redundancy procedure

An employer is expected to comply with certain procedures when considering making employees redundant. In this book I will concentrate on the position when the redundancy involves fewer than 20 employees. Where there are more than 20 employees being made redundant stricter consultation procedures will apply (see sections 188-192 of the Trade Union and Labour Relations (Consolidation) Act 1992).

In the case of *Williams v Compair Maxam* [1982] IRLR 83 the Court of Appeal set out various standards to be applied by employers when carrying out a redundancy procedure:

- employers should give as much warning as possible of impending redundancies. which will give unions and employees an opportunity to consider possible alternatives to redundancy;

- the employer should consult the appropriate union as to the best means by which the redundancies can be achieved fairly and with as little hardship to the employees as possible;

- the employer will try to agree the criteria in selecting employees;

- whether or not the criteria are agreed the employer will try to establish objective rather than subjective criteria;

- the employer must ensure that the selection is made fairly in accordance with these criteria;

- the employer will consider whether the employee could be offered alternative employment.

I will consider each of these steps in turn.

Notice of redundancy

An employer should inform any employee who is likely to be made redundant as soon as possible. The purpose of this is to give as much time as possible for the employee to consider and propose potential alternatives to employment or to look for another job.

Alternatives to redundancy

The sort of alternatives that might be appropriate to redundancy dismissals would include reducing overtime, considering job sharing, transferring employees to other departments or premises or inviting voluntary redundancies.

Consultation as to method

Where there is a union or worker's representative in the workplace the employer should consult with them about the best way in which to carry out the redundancies. Where there is no union the employer will, in my experience, normally just announce the method of the redundancy procedure to be followed.

Even though the procedure might not have been agreed with the employees concerned it will be rare to successfully argue that such a procedure was unfair unless it was quite clear that it was not a procedure that any reasonable employer would have adopted.

Consultation

Consultation is fundamental to a fair redundancy procedure. Where the employer has failed to have a consultation meeting with the employee before making him redundant an employment tribunal is almost always going to find that the redundancy procedure was unfair.

The consultation with the employee must be a genuine consultation. This means that the decision to make the employee redundant must not have been taken before the meeting otherwise the consultation would have been pointless. What most employers tend to say is that they were considering redundancy as a possible option subject to anything the employee might say but they had taken no definite decision.

If you are the employer it is important that you explain to the employee why the need to make redundancies has arisen, explain any attempts to look for alternatives to redundancies, the method of selection that is being used and why that employee has been chosen for redundancy.

If you are the employee I would suggest finding out as much about the redundancy, the reasons for it and the selection procedure as you can before the meeting. You will then be in a position to plan what you are going to say in the meeting and to make sure that you cover all the important points you want to make to your employer.

This meeting will be your opportunity to put forward any alternatives to redundancy that you can suggest, to explain why you do not consider that your role is redundant or why it is that you should not be made redundant. If you consider that there is someone else in the department or section who should be made redundant rather than you explain why this is so. If you consider that there are flaws in the selection procedure or the way the marking for the selection has been carried out you should say so.

Selection procedure

If it is a question of selecting one or a number of employees to be made redundant the employer will need to set out the basis on which employees are to be selected for redundancy. It might be that the employer will have a formal policy or agreement as to the selection method it will use, in which case the employer would have to have a good reason to justify using a different selection method.

There are different selection methods that employers use but whichever method it chooses this should be on a fair and objective basis which is applicable to all the relevant employees. An objective basis means one which is impartial and lacks bias. It is the opposite of a subjective basis. For example, if a line manager chooses to make employees redundant on the basis of those employees he disliked, this would be a subjective basis.

It is unfair to make a selection for redundancy on discriminatory grounds; that is on the basis of an employee's age, race, disability, sex (this would include maternity related reasons), sexual orientation or religion. It is also unfair to dismiss an employee for redundancy for participation in trade union activities, for carrying out duties as a worker's representative, for being a health and safety representative, for asserting a statutory right or making a protected disclosure.

The selection pool

All those employees holding the same or similar positions would be included in the pool of employees from which those to be made redundant would be selected. It is a common complaint by employees that they should not have been included in the selection pool or alternatively that one or more other employees who were not included in the pool should have been. The tribunal will not usually regard the selection as unfair unless it is clear that the employer has acted unreasonably in including or not including a particular employee in the pool.

A common method of selecting for redundancies is by means of a grid or chart with various different categories such as skills, experience, work performance, punctuality, attendance or disciplinary record. Each employee would then be marked from 1 to 5 or 1 to 10, with the highest marks given for the best employees. The marks would be added up and the employee or employees with the lowest marks would be made redundant. An employer must be careful not to apply discriminatory criteria, for example a disabled employee might have a poor attendance record due to their disability. In these circumstances an employer would need to make reasonable adjustments to prevent that employee being discriminated against.

Once the scores for the various employees have been obtained there would need to be a further meeting with those employees likely to be made redundant on the basis of their low scores. They should be given the opportunity to discuss the scores and, if they disagree with them, an opportunity to explain why. An employee is entitled to be provided with his own scores and it has been suggested that it would be good employment practice to provide the employee with the scores of the other employees who have been subjected to the same procedure. The names of these employees can be blanked out (or "redacted") from the score sheets.

Alternative employment

An employer should make reasonable efforts to find an alternative position for an employee who is at risk of being made redundant. An employer would be well advised to make arrangements to ensure that those employees at risk of redundancy are provided with copies of any internal job vacancies that are being advertised.

Where the employer makes an offer of suitable alternative employment and the employee unreasonably refuses that offer, he will not be entitled to a redundancy payment and, even if he is able to show that he was unfairly dismissed for redundancy, he will be unlikely to recover any ongoing loss of earnings.

In order to constitute suitable alternative employment the terms and conditions of the new job must be substantially the same as the old job. If the new job would result in a loss of benefits or result in personal difficulties for the employee, such as having to move house, a tribunal might well regard the employee's refusal to accept the new position as a reasonable decision.

Where an employee has been dismissed for redundancy and is required to work out his notice period that employee is entitled to a reasonable amount of time off work to look for alternative employment.

An employee selected for redundancy and dismissed must be allowed to appeal against his dismissal.

"*Polkey* reduction"

In cases of unfair dismissal, where an employment tribunal finds that the dismissal procedure followed by the employer has been unfair, the tribunal will go on to consider what would have occurred if a fair procedure had been followed. Where there is a chance that the employee would have been dismissed in any event the amount of the compensatory award (see Chapter 21) would be reduced by the percentage chance that the employee would have been dismissed in any event. This is referred to as a *Polkey* reduction from the case of *Polkey v AE Dayton Services Ltd* [1988] AC 344. For example, if the tribunal took the view that if a correct procedure had been carried out there was a 50% chance that the employee would have been dismissed in any event, then his compensation will accordingly be reduced by 50%.

3.18   Contravention of a duty

Under section 98(2)(d) of the ERA a dismissal can be fair if the reason for the dismissal is that the employee could not continue to work in the position which he held without contravention, on the part either of the employer or the employee, of a duty or restriction imposed by an enactment.

An example of such a dismissal is where it would be against the law for the employee to do the job for which he is employed, for instance where a van driver loses his driving licence. In these circumstances the employer would need to show that there were no alternate positions that the employee could do which did not require a driving licence.

3.19   Some other substantial reason (SOSR)

I have considered in this book the various reasons for dismissal that can constitute a fair dismissal under section 98(2) of the Employment Rights Act 1996. The final category is a catch-all category which includes reasons that do not come within the other four specified categories. This is where the dismissal is for some other substantial reason.

It is not possible to set out all the potential reasons that could fall into this category but the reported cases on this point give some indication of the sort of dismissals that tribunals will accept as being for some other substantial reason.

For example where an employer is faced with reduced income and, rather than make any employees redundant, it proposes to reduce the salary of all its employees, if, after proper consultation with the employees, this is generally accepted by all but one or two employees, then the dismissal of those one or two employees might be accepted as constituting a fair dismissal for some other substantial reason.

Similarly where an employer has a good business reason for asking an employee to accept a variation to his contract of employment, and the employee unreasonably refuses to accept the variation, a tribunal might accept that a dismissal in these circumstances was fair for some other substantial reason. The position is more difficult where the employee has a valid reason for refusing the variation.

Where there has been a serious breakdown in the relationship between employees to such an extent that it is causing a significant disruption to the business, then the dismissal of one of the parties responsible for this breakdown can come within this category of some other substantial reason (see *Perkin v St George's Healthcare NHS Trust* [2005] EWCA Civ 1174). The employer will need to have followed a fair procedure, informed the employee of the problem and given them adequate opportunity to change their behaviour.

3.20   Written reasons for dismissal

Under section 92 of the Employment Rights Act 1996 an employee who is dismissed is entitled to written reasons for the dismissal. The employee must ask for this written statement, unless the employee is dismissed when pregnant or during her period of maternity leave in which case she does not need to ask, and the employer should provide this statement within 14 days.

If the employer does not provide this written statement the employee can apply to the employment tribunal if he is bringing a claim for unfair dismissal. If the tribunal finds that the employer failed to provide such a statement it shall make an award of two weeks pay to the employee.

Chapter 4

Discrimination

4.1   Introduction

Bringing a claim for discrimination in the employment tribunal can appear to be a frightening task. There are various technical words and terms, such as indirect discrimination, comparators, protected characteristics, a proportionate means of achieving a legitimate aim and reasonable adjustments, which may not mean much to a person unfamiliar with employment law.

There will often be the problem of persuading a tribunal that the reason you have been badly treated by your employer, for example you have not been promoted, you have been given the most unpleasant jobs or you have been dismissed, is because of your colour, your sex or because you have a disability.

In this chapter I will try to explain in clear terms who can bring a discrimination claim against their employer, the different types of discrimination and provide some tips about bringing discrimination claims. It will be necessary to refer to the technical words and terms because these are terms that are used in the Equality Act 2010 but I will try to explain what they mean.

Before 2010 there were a number of different Acts dealing with different discrimination. Amongst them there was the Race Relations Act, the Sex Discrimination Act and the Disability Discrimination Act. In 2010 all these individual Acts were abolished and discrimination law was incorporated into the Equality Act 2010. In general the Equality Act did not make any significant changes to discrimination law except for the law relating to disability discrimination, where it clarified what amounts to disability discrimination (I will deal with this later in the chapter). As a result many of the reported cases under the old discrimination acts are still good law under the Equality Act.

4.2   Who can bring a claim?

In order to bring a claim you will need to show that you come within one of the categories set out in the Equality Act 2010. These are referred to as "protected characteristics". Some of these categories apply to all employees - race, sex, sexual orientation and age. For the other categories you will need to show that you come within that category e.g. that you have a disability or that you are married.

It is often thought that you can only bring a claim for race discrimination if you are a member of a racial minority but in fact anyone can bring a claim for race discrimination if they can show that the reason they were treated badly, when compared to other employees, was because of their race or colour. Equally a man can bring a claim for sex discrimination if he can show that the reason he has been treated badly is because he is a man and not a woman. The difficulty lies in proving that the motive for the treatment was discrimination and not some other reason. For example, if you are a woman and have been treated badly by your manager who is also a woman, you are likely to find it more difficult to persuade a tribunal that your manager was motivated by sex discrimination than if your manager was a man.

4.3   The layout of the Equality Act 2010

If you are bringing a discrimination claim or defending a discrimination claim which has been brought against you, it is helpful to have an idea about the layout of the Equality Act as all discrimination claims brought since 2010 will come under this Act.

Part 2 of the Equality Act sets out the two key concepts. In Chapter 1 these are the nine "protected characteristics" and in Chapter 2 they are the different forms of "prohibited conduct".

Part 5 of the Act relates to discrimination at work. In this part Chapter 1 deals with employment and who is protected under the provisions of the Act. Chapter 3 deals with Equality of Terms and includes sex equality, pregnancy and maternity equality.

Part 8 extends prohibited conduct to cover employment relationships that have ended and the liability of employers for acts of discrimination by their employees or agents.

Part 9 deals with enforcement. Chapter 2 deals with bringing discrimination claims in the civil courts and Chapter 3 deals with bringing discrimination claims in the employment tribunals. This chapter includes provisions as to time limits for bringing claims and the remedies available. Chapter 4 deals with equal pay claims. Chapter 5 has various miscellaneous provisions but of particular importance are the provisions dealing with burden of proof and obtaining information.

Part 11 of the Act deals with advancement of equality. Chapter 2 deals with positive action in terms of recruitment and promotion.

Part 13 deals with reasonable adjustments in respect of disability discrimination.

There are also 28 Schedules to the Equality Act. The most important are:

- Schedule 1 - this sets out the definition of disability;

- Schedule 8 - this deals with reasonable adjustments;

- Schedule 9 - this sets out various exceptions to the provisions of the Act including occupational exceptions and exceptions relating to age.

4.4   Protected characteristics

Since 2010 all discrimination claims brought in the Employment Tribunal come under the Equality Act 2010. This Act makes it unlawful for an employer to discriminate against an employee or a worker on the basis of that person's:

- race;

- sex;

- disability;

- age;

- religion or belief;

- gender reassignment;

- marriage or civil partnership;

- pregnancy or maternity;

- sexual orientation.

These are all described as "protected characteristics" (see sections 4 to 12 of the Equality Act 2010).

What this means is if you have one of these characteristics and are treated unfairly or discriminated against by your employer because of this characteristic, you can bring a claim in the Employment Tribunal.

4.5   Prohibited conduct

There are various types of conduct that constitute discrimination and these types of conduct are described as "prohibited conduct" in the Equality Act. They include:

- direct discrimination (section 13);

- indirect discrimination (section 19);

- harassment (section 26);

- victimisation (section 27);

- the duty to make adjustments for disabled persons (section 20).

4.6   Direct discrimination

A person discriminates against an employee if he treats that employee less favourably than he treats other employees because that employee has one of the protected characteristics (see section 13 Equality Act 2010).

This will include the situation where an employee is discriminated against not because *they* have one of the protected characteristics but because they have an *association* with a person who does have that characteristic (for example an employee who is subjected to unfair treatment because they have a disabled child who requires extra care).

Less favourable treatment means that you must be able to point to another employee, called a "comparator", who has not received such treatment (except if the allegation is one of pregnancy-related or maternity discrimination where no comparator is needed).

Where the allegation is one of direct discrimination it does not matter what the motive of the employer is. The question is:

> *"What was it that the employer did?"*

not:

> *"Why did he do it?"*

The treatment must be less favourable treatment. The fact that an employer might treat his female employees differently from his male employers does not in itself mean that he is acting in a discriminatory way. For example, a rule that male employees should not grow their hair below collar length has been held not to be discriminatory.

The fact that an employer treats an employee unreasonably does not in itself constitute discrimination unless it can be shown that the reason for this treatment is based on a protected characteristic.

4.7   Indirect discrimination

A person indirectly discriminates against another if he applies a provision, criterion or practice (often abbreviated to "PCP") which is discriminatory and which has the effect of putting an employee, or a person applying for employment, who has a protected characteristic at a particular disadvantage when compared to a person who has not got that protected characteristic (section 19 Equality Act 2010).

In simple terms indirect discrimination is when an employer has some rule or policy which applies to everyone, but it has a worse effect on some people than others and has the effect of putting those people at a particular disadvantage. One example of this is an employer who refuses to allow any employees to work part time, since this rule puts women, particularly women with young children, at a disadvantage as they are less likely to be able to work full time than men.

Defence

It is a defence to a claim for indirect discrimination for the employer to show that the policy or rule is a "proportionate means of achieving a legitimate aim" (section 19(2)(d)). This defence does not apply to a claim for direct discrimination except if the protected characteristic is age (section 13(2)).

A "legitimate aim" means a good reason or purpose for the discrimination. A "proportionate means" makes it clear that there must be a fair balance between the discrimination and the reason or purpose for it. For example, a factory making food products might have a rule that prohibits employees having beards for health and hygiene reasons. This would discriminate against a Sikh who did not shave for religious reasons. In these circumstances a tribunal might well consider that the provision or rule was a proportionate means of achieving a legitimate aim. But if the employee was able to show that there was another cheap and easy way to prevent facial hair being a hygiene risk then the tribunal might consider that the rule was not proportionate.

To take another example, it would be a defence for an employer, who insisted that a particular job be done full time rather than part-time, to show that because of the nature of the particular work required it would not be possible to do the job on a part-time basis or for two people to do it on a job share basis. To succeed in this defence the employer must show that there is a real need for the rule or policy and it must be appropriate and reasonably necessary.

This defence is one of the main differences between direct and indirect discrimination - an act of direct discrimination, unless it is age discrimination, can never be justified but if an employer can show that his policy or rule is justified this will be a defence to a claim of indirect discrimination.

4.8   Comparators

If you want to show that you have been subjected to discrimination you will first need to compare your treatment with the treatment of another employee who does not have your protected characteristic (called a "comparator"). You will need to satisfy the tribunal that you were treated less favourably than that employee and that the reason for the less favourable treatment was because of the protected characteristic. You need to remember that the comparator must be someone who is in a similar situation to you *but does not have your protected characteristic.* What the Equality Act 2010 says, in section 23, is that there must be no material differences between the circumstances of the victim and their comparator, apart from the protected characteristic.

For example if you are a woman and have been made redundant, whereas various male employees doing a similar job were not made redundant, you would want to choose as your comparator a male employee who has been employed for a similar or shorter length of time than you have. You would not want to choose an employee who has been employed for much longer, as the employer is likely to say that it was your shorter length of service that was the reason for you being made redundant.

Hypothetical comparator

Whilst it is preferable for the comparator to be a real person, you can use a hypothetical comparator if you are unable to find another employee who is in the same or a similar position. For example a female employee who has been dismissed for lying might not be able to point to a male employee who had not been dismissed for lying but might be able to point to a male employee who had committed an act of dishonesty but had not been dismissed. This male employee was in a different situation but the circumstances might be sufficient to allow a tribunal to construct a hypothetical comparator.

4.9   Harassment

Harassment is prohibited conduct under section 26 of the Equality Act. Harassment is described as unwanted conduct, related to a protected characteristic, which is designed to or has the effect of violating that person's dignity, creating an intimidating, hostile, degrading, humiliating or offensive environment. It also includes unwanted conduct of a sexual nature and less favourable treatment of a person because they have refused to submit to conduct of a sexual nature.

In everyday language harassment means much the same as bullying. When the bullying behaviour is linked to the employee's protected characteristic the employee can bring a claim for harassment under the Equality Act.

The examples given by ACAS in their Guide to Bullying and Harassment at Work include:

- spreading malicious rumours;

- copying memos that are critical about someone to others who do not need to know;

- ridiculing or demeaning someone;

- overbearing supervision;

- unwelcome sexual advances, which can include touching or displaying offensive materials;

- making threats or comments about job security without foundation;

- undermining an employee by constant unfair criticism.

It is not unusual to include a claim for harassment in addition to a claim for race or sex discrimination and less frequently in claims of disability discrimination. In some cases it will be clear that behaviour amounts to harassment - in other cases it will not be so obvious. What an employer might regard as justified encouragement might be seen by the employee as unwarranted coercion or criticism.

Where your employer is able to show that the same standards are applied to all the staff and you are claiming that you were being singled out it will be more difficult for you to succeed than if you can show that the treatment has only been applied to you.

4.10   Victimisation

Victimisation is prohibited conduct under section 27 of the Equality Act 2010. Victimisation occurs where an employee is treated less favourably because they have made a complaint, or helped someone else make a complaint, in connection with the Equality Act 2010 about the way they have been treated in the workplace.

There are various protected acts including:

- bringing proceedings under the Equality Act;

- giving evidence or information in connection with proceedings under the Act;

- doing anything else in connection with the Act; and

- making an allegation that another person has contravened the Act.

The Claimant needs to prove that the person who has been responsible for the victimisation did so because the Claimant had done one of the protected acts. This protection does not apply if the allegation is made in bad faith (see section 27(3)).

A person may be victimised even though the employment relationship has ended. For example it will apply if you have left your job but your former employer gives you a bad reference because you had done one of the protected acts. This also applies to discrimination generally and harassment (section 108 Equality Act 2010).

Discrimination and victimisation applies not just to existing employees but also to persons applying for employment and applies in relation to the terms on which the employment is offered or by not offering employment (section 39 Equality Act 2010). Discrimination can apply to job advertisements as well as questions asked in job interviews.

4.11   Discrimination in employment

Section 39 of the Equality Act 2010 sets out the different ways in which discrimination can occur in employment relationships. The Act specifically prohibits discrimination:

- in the terms of employment;

- in the way the employer gives to or withholds from employees access for promotion, transfer, training or receiving any other benefit, facility or service;

- by dismissing the employee; or

- by subjecting him to any other detriment.

One of the defences open to employers when applying a requirement that the applicant or employee must have a particular protected characteristic, is that, having regard to the nature or context of the work, that protected characteristic is an occupational requirement. An example of this could be a job which involves searching female prisoners and is only open to female applicants. The application of the requirement must be a proportionate means of achieving a legitimate aim.

4.12   Contract of service

The Equality Act applies to people who are employed under a contract of service, an apprenticeship or a contract to do work personally. This does not normally include people working as volunteers - nor does it apply to self-employed people.

4.13   Vicarious liability

Where an employee, in the course of his employment, discriminates against another employee or against a job applicant this will be treated as an act of discrimination by the employer, even if the act is done without the employer's knowledge or approval (section 109). The legal term for this is "vicarious liability", where the employer is vicariously liable for the discrimination carried out by one of his employees in the course of his employment.

The employer will have a defence if he can show that he took all reasonable steps to prevent the person from carrying out the act complained of. The sort of thing that a tribunal would want to see is that the employer had provided equality training and that it had a proper system for acknowledging and dealing with complaints of discrimination. If the tribunal considers that the employer could and should have done more to prevent the discrimination it will probably find that the employer has not made out its defence.

4.14   Joint liability

An employee can bring a claim against both the individual who has been responsible for the discrimination and against their employer. If both are found guilty of discrimination then the tribunal can order that they are both "jointly or severally liable" to pay the compensation. What this means is that the Claimant can recover all his damages awarded to him from either one of two Respondents, so that even if the individual Respondent has no money to pay an award of damages the Claimant can recover the whole amount of the award from the Respondent employer.

4.15   Burden of proof

One of the difficulties that can be faced by a Claimant alleging discrimination is proving that the motivation for the treatment he was subjected to was because of his protected characteristic. This is dealt with in section 136 of the Equality Act which has the effect of reversing the burden of proof in circumstances where the Claimant is able to put forward facts from which discrimination can be inferred unless the employer is able to put forward some explanation showing that the reason for the conduct was not because of the Claimant's protected characteristic. For example, where a male employee has been promoted rather than a more qualified female employee a tribunal can infer that she has been discriminated against unless the employer can show a good reason for promoting the male employee which did not relate to his sex. In this example the burden of proof would initially be on the female employee to prove that she been discriminated against. Once the female employee provides evidence from which a tribunal can infer discrimination (in this case it would be that she, as the more qualified employee, should have been promoted) the burden of proof shifts to the employer to prove that there was some reason, other than her sex, that she was not promoted.

4.16   Age discrimination

Age is a protected characteristic under section 5 of the Equality Act 2010. A person discriminates against another if, because of a person's age, he treats that other person less favourably than he treats others.

It is a defence to show that the treatment was a proportionate means of achieving a legitimate aim. For example it has been held that the requirement for a person applying to work as a fire-fighter to be under the age of 30 was justifiable because of the physically demanding nature of the job. But it was discrimination to dismiss an employee for redundancy in order to avoid him becoming entitled to an early retirement pension.

It is likely to be indirect discrimination when a disguised age barrier is imposed as a requirement for a job. For example, if only people with 'O' levels can apply this would prevent anyone younger than 47 applying, as GCSE's were introduced in 1984 in place of 'O' levels.

Where an employer imposes a retirement age he will have to justify it by showing that it was a proportionate means of achieving a legitimate aim, in effect that it was a justified business need.

4.17 Disability discrimination

Disability is a protected characteristic under section 4 of the Equality Act 2010. If a person treats another person less favourably because they are disabled, this is prohibited conduct under section 13 and would constitute direct discrimination.

Under section 15 of the Equality Act 2010 a person discriminates if he treats a disabled person unfavourably because of something arising in consequence of that person's disability and he cannot show that the treatment was a proportionate means of achieving a legitimate aim. There is a defence available if the person can show that he did not know and could not reasonably have been expected to know that the person discriminated against had the disability.

A person has a disability if he has a physical or mental impairment which has a substantial and long term adverse effect on his ability to carry out normal day-to-day activities (section 6 Equality Act 2010).

The Office for Disability Issues has provided a Guidance Document on matters to be taken into account when determining questions relating to the definition of disability. If you are bringing a claim for disability discrimination this is an important document that you should read because it sets out clear and helpful guidance and explanations of all the main aspects of disability discrimination. This includes the definition of disability, the meaning of the phrase "substantial adverse effect" including the cumulative effects of an impairment and progressive conditions. It also provides guidance on the meaning of "long-term effects" and "normal day-to-day activities" with reference to specialised activities and the effect of treatment or correction measures.

Impairment

Schedule 1 of the Equality Act 2010 provides further details as to what constitutes a disability. An impairment means a condition or illness which can be a physical illness or a mental illness. In order for the condition to have a long term effect it must have lasted at least 12 months or be likely to last 12 months. Some conditions which become progressively worse are treated as being a disability including cancer, HIV and MS. Some conditions are excluded from being a disability including addictions to drink or drugs.

In order to assess whether an impairment has a substantial adverse effect the tribunal should concentrate on what the Claimant cannot do or what he can only do with difficulty. This does not mean whether or not that person is able to carry out his job, nor does it mean whether the person can do a particular sport or not, but whether he is able or not to carry out the sort of daily tasks that everyone will do.

In the Appendix to the Guidance document there is a list of examples of impairments which would be reasonable to regard as having a substantial adverse effect on normal day-today activities, for example a total inability to walk, or an ability to walk only a short distance without difficulty. There is also a list of examples which it would not be reasonable to regard as having a substantial adverse effect on normal day-to-day activities, for example experiencing some tiredness or minor discomfort as a result of walking unaided for a distance of about one mile.

Comparator

If you can show that you have been treated unfavourably because of your disability you do not need a comparator because the Equality Act does not say that you have to have been treated less favourably than a person without the disability. However, in practice you will often be able to point to other non-disabled employees who have not been treated in the same way that you have, to show that you have been discriminated against.

For example, if everyone in the business has had their hours reduced, you can argue that you have been treated unfavourably but you will be unlikely to persuade a tribunal that it was because of your disability, whereas if you are disabled and you are the only employee to have had your hours reduced you are more likely to persuade a tribunal that this treatment was on account of your disability.

The employer will have a defence if he can show that the treatment was for a justified business need. For example, if you suffer from blackouts an employer might be justified in not appointing you for a job working at height where this condition would put you at risk of serious injury.

Job applicants

There is specific provision in section 60 which says that an employer must not ask about the health of a job applicant before offering him a job. The Equality Act makes it clear that it is not asking the question that is wrong - it is the conduct based on the information. Thus if the applicant is suffering from a particular condition and is asked in the job interview about his health, he refers to this condition and then is not offered a job, it will be for the employer to show that the applicant's health was not the reason he was turned down. This provision does not prevent the employer asking whether the job applicant can comply with a requirement to undergo an assessment, or whether he will be able to carry out a function that is intrinsic to the job.

Duty to make adjustments

Under the Equality Act (section 20) an employer has a duty to make adjustments in relation to disabled employees. The duty consists of three requirements:

- Where a provision, criterion or practice (often referred to as a "PCP") puts a disabled person at a substantial disadvantage in comparison to a person who is not disabled the employer must take such steps as are reasonable to have to take to avoid the disadvantage.

  What is a "PCP"? It is anything in the way that an employer organises or arranges how work is carried out. For example, a requirement that employees turn up for work at 9.00am is a provision or practice that might put a disabled person at a disadvantage if they need to attend regular hospital appointments at that time. A reasonable adjustment might be to allow the employee to work flexible times so that they do not have to be at work at 9.00am. Similarly a requirement that employees have to be able to lift heavy items might be a provision or criterion that puts a disabled person with a serious back condition at a disadvantage. Here, a reasonable adjustment might be to change the employee's duties so they do not have to lift heavy items.

- The second requirement is where a physical feature of the workplace puts a disabled person at a substantial disadvantage in comparison to a person who is not disabled. The employer must take such steps as are reasonable to have to take to avoid the disadvantage. This refers to some physical feature in the design or construction, either inside or outside a building, such as steps leading up to an office, and the adjustment might be the provision of a ramp to allow access for wheelchair users.

- The third requirement is to take reasonable steps to provide an auxiliary aid or service without which the disabled person would be put at a substantial disadvantage, including making sure that information is provided in an accessible format.

If the employer fails to comply with a duty to make reasonable adjustments this will constitute discrimination.

4.18 Gender reassignment

If a person is proposing to undergo, is undergoing or had undergone a process for the purpose of changing their sex then that person will have a protected characteristic. If that person is absent from work because they are undergoing treatment for gender reassignment they will be discriminated against if they are treated less favourably than a person who is absent because of sickness or illness (section 16 Equality Act 2010).

4.19 Marriage or civil partnerships

Being married or in a civil partnership is a protected characteristic. A person discriminates against another person if he treats that other person less favourably because he is married or in a civil partnership (section 13 Equality Act 2010).

4.20 Pregnancy and maternity

Pregnancy and maternity are protected characteristics. A person discriminates against a woman if, because of pregnancy or maternity, he treats her less well than he would treat others. A person discriminates against a woman if he treats her unfavourably because of her pregnancy or because of an illness suffered by her because of her pregnancy (section 18 Equality Act 2010).

The period of the pregnancy is referred to as the "protected period". It begins when she becomes pregnant and ends at the end of her maternity leave period if she has the right to maternity leave or if not, two weeks after the end of the pregnancy. The discrimination against pregnancy does not require a comparator. For example, if a woman is dismissed because of pregnancy-related sickness this would be discriminatory even if a man would be dismissed for the same period of sickness absence.

A refusal to employ a pregnant woman would constitute discrimination.

4.21 Race discrimination

The protected characteristic of race includes colour, nationality, ethnic or national origins. A person discriminates against another if he treats that person less favourably than he treats others. Section 13 of the Equality Act 2010 prohibits direct discrimination. The motive for the discrimination is not relevant.

It constitutes indirect discrimination if a person applies a provision, criterion or practice ("PCP") which puts that person at a disadvantage because of his race and he cannot show that it is a proportionate means of achieving a legitimate aim (section 19 of the Equality Act 2010 prohibits indirect discrimination). Thus a rule that an employee cannot have long hair might be indirect discrimination against a Sikh but if the rule can be justified on health and safety grounds it might be permitted.

4.22   Religion or belief

Any religion is a protected characteristic, and some philosophical belief can be a protected characteristic but it must be a belief rather than just an opinion. The discrimination must be on the grounds of holding the belief. A registrar who refused to marry same sex couples because it was contrary to her belief and was dismissed was not discriminated against because the dismissal was not on the grounds of her belief but because she refused to comply with her contractual obligations to conduct marriages (section 13 of the Equality Act 2010 prohibits direct discrimination and section 19 of the Act prohibits indirect discrimination).

4.23   Sex discrimination

A person discriminates against another if he treats that person less favourably than he would treat others because of their sex (section 13 of the Equality Act 2010 prohibits direct discrimination). The motive for the discrimination is irrelevant.

An employer discriminates against a person if, because of that person's sex, he applies a provision, criterion or practice which is discriminatory or puts him at a disadvantage and cannot show that it is a proportionate means of achieving a legitimate aim (section 19 of the Act prohibits indirect discrimination).

Justification can be a defence to indirect discrimination while it is not a defence to direct discrimination. It can be indirect discrimination for an employer to refuse to allow a woman to work on a part time basis because more woman look after children than men and this can indirectly discriminate against women. The employer will have a defence if he can show that the requirement for full time work is justified.

The employer will also have a defence if it can be shown that it is an occupational requirement that it is crucial to the job that it is done by a person of a specific sex.

4.24   Sexual orientation

A person discriminates against another if he treats that person less favourably than he would treat others because of their sexual orientation (section 13 of the Equality Act 2010 prohibits direct discrimination). An employer discriminates against a person if, because of that person's sexual orientation, he applies a provision, criterion or practice which is discriminatory or puts him at a disadvantage and cannot show that it is a proportionate means of achieving a legitimate aim (section 19 of the Act prohibits indirect discrimination). Sexual orientation means whether a person is attracted to persons of the same sex, persons of the opposite sex or persons of either sex.

Chapter 5

Disputes about pay

5.1   Introduction

There might be any one of a number of different issues relating to your pay that cause you to think about bringing a claim in the employment tribunal. It could be that your employer has failed to provide you with written details about your pay or an itemised pay slip. It could be that your employer has failed to pay you the basic wage you are due or failed to give you the sick pay, holiday pay or notice pay that you are entitled to under your contract of employment. It could be that your employer has been making deductions from your pay, has failed to pay you commission you are owed or has paid you less than the minimum wage. In any of these circumstances you can bring a claim in the employment tribunal.

The duty of your employer to pay you for the work you have carried out is fundamental to the contractual relationship between you and your employer and any failure by your employer to pay you the money to which you are entitled is obviously going to be a matter of concern. Such concerns should be raised by way of a complaint to your line manager and if not resolved you should submit a written grievance (see Chapter 2). A refusal to pay you the money to which you are contractually entitled can constitute a breach of contract by your employer which entitles you to resign (see Chapter 3).

I have set out below the various circumstances where a complaint by you as an employee with regard to your pay can entitle you to bring a claim in the employment tribunal.

5.2   Statement of particulars of employment

The rate of pay and the frequency of pay (i.e. weekly, monthly etc) should be included in the contract of employment (Employment Rights Act (ERA) 1996 section 1(4)(a) and (b)). The other required particulars include hours of work, holiday entitlement, provision for sick pay, length of notice, job title and place of work. For a full list of required particulars see ERA section 1(4)(a) to (k).

Under section 8 ERA an employee has a right to an itemised pay statement, which gives the gross amount of pay, any deductions and the net amount. As from April 2020 all limb (b) workers are also entitled to an itemised pay slip.

If your employer fails to provide you with a written contract of employment or the contract of employment does not include all the required terms (including the rate and frequency of pay) within one month of the employment commencing, or he fails to provide you with an itemised pay statement, you can bring a claim under section 11 ERA 1996 for the employment tribunal to determine what particulars ought to have been included.

Damages for failing to provide particulars of employment

Under section 38 of the 2002 Employment Act, where an employer has failed to provide a statement of particulars of employment, the tribunal must make an award of at least two weeks pay, and can make an award up to four weeks pay if appropriate in the circumstances. But the tribunal can only make this award if you have brought a claim of a type listed under Schedule 5 of the Employment Act 2002, which includes unfair dismissal, wrongful dismissal and discrimination, and you have succeeded on that claim.

In effect what this means is that if you just bring a claim under section 11 ERA 1996 for failure by your employer to provide you with a statement of particulars of employment, the tribunal cannot award you damages. But if you have another principal claim, such as unfair dismissal or discrimination, and include in your claim form (the ET1) a complaint that your employer has failed to provide you with a statement of employment, so long as you succeed on the main claim the tribunal must award you at least two weeks pay (one week's pay is currently capped at £538 - see Chapter 16), if they also accept that your employer failed to provide you with a statement of particulars of employment.

5.3   The rate of pay

The rate of pay will normally be agreed between the employer and the employee before the contract commences and they are generally free to agree the amount of the pay. The two exceptions to this are under the Equal Pay Act 2010 which indirectly prohibits unequal rates of pay between men and women and under the National Minimum Wage Act 1998 which requires the employer to pay no less than the minimum wage.

5.4   Deductions from wages

Part II of the ERA 1996 sets out provisions dealing with the protection of wages. The basic principle in section 13 is that an employer is not entitled to deduct any sums from his employee's wages unless the deduction is authorised by law, or the employee or worker has consented in writing to the deduction.

Certain deductions are excluded from this principle and these are set out in section 14 ERA. They include a deduction made for the purpose of reimbursing the employer for an overpayment of wages or expenses and a deduction made following disciplinary proceedings.

The definition of wages in section 27 ERA includes any bonus, commission, holiday pay or any other pay due under the contract. If your employer has made deductions from your wages which you consider to be unlawful then you can bring a complaint in the employment tribunal, but the complaint must be made within three months of the deduction being made.

5.5   Sick pay

Most employees will have a right under their contract of employment to be paid whilst off sick and the provision for sick pay should be included in the required particulars of employment. The contract of employment should state the amount of sick pay and the period for which it will be paid.

The contract will normally require that a sick note (this is now referred to as a "fit note") be provided by the employee. If the employee is absent for seven calendar days or less they will inform their employee that they are not well enough to work. This is called self-certifying their sick leave. They should still be paid their contractual sick pay. If they are absent for more than seven days they must get a fit note from their doctor. A common provision is that the employee be paid full pay for a period, possibly three months, and then go on to half pay for a further period of three months, at which time the entitlement to sick pay under the contract will come to an end.

An employer does not have to agree to pay contractual sick pay but even if the contract of employment does not provide for any sick pay to be paid, the employer must pay Statutory Sick Pay (SSP). This is currently £95.85 a week and is payable for up to 28 weeks. The employee cannot claim for the first three days of absence but after that three day period the employer must pay SSP at the required rate.

If there is a dispute about an employee's entitlement to SSP the remedy lies with an application to HM Revenue and Customs and not to an employment tribunal.

5.6   Minimum/living wage

With certain exceptions most workers are entitled to be paid at a rate not less than the national minimum/living wage (section 1 National Minimum Wage Act 1998). It applies to employees who work under a contract of employment and any other contract whereby an individual undertakes to work personally for another - therefore it would include agency workers and people working under a zero-hours contract.

There are various categories of workers to which the National Minimum Wage Act does not apply. These include employees who are below the compulsory school age, voluntary workers working for a charity, au pairs or family members in a family business.

On 1st April 2016 the Government introduced the new National Living Wage. From 1st April 2020 any employee/worker over the age of 25 is entitled to a national living wage of £8.72 per hour. Employees/workers between the ages of 21 and 24 are entitled to a national minimum wage of £8.20 per hour, 18 to 20 year olds to £6.45 per hour, 16 to 17 year olds to £4.55 per hour and apprentices aged under 19 or in the first year of their apprenticeship to £3.90 per hour.

Benefits in kind such as a company car, a company phone, private health care insurance etc are not included when calculating the rate of pay. If an employee is paid below the national minimum wage, he is entitled to the difference. The employee can bring a claim for breach of contract rather than a deduction of wages claim. This claim can be brought in the employment tribunal or in the County Court.

There is an online government document called "Calculating the Minimum Wage" which provides advice about the National Minimum Wage Act with examples to explain:

- what counts and does not count as pay and working hours under the Act;

- eligibility for minimum wage;

- how to calculate the minimum wage;

- how the minimum wage will be enforced.

5.7   Working time

Under the Working Time Regulations ("WTR") 1998 employees or workers have various rights, the most important of which are:

- entitlement to a minimum 20 minute rest break during any working day longer than 6 hours, (for young workers the entitlement is 30 minutes every 4 ½ hours) (regulation 12);

- the average working time for an adult worker (averaged over a four month reference period) must not exceed 48 hours unless they agree in writing to work more than 48 hours (regulation 4);

- every full time employee is entitled to 5.6 weeks paid annual leave which consists of four weeks leave under regulation 13 and 8 bank holidays;

- on termination of employment an employee must be paid in lieu of untaken leave pro rata for the year (regulation 14).

There are various other regulations relating to rest periods, night workers and young workers.

Some, but not all, of the provisions provide a right to complain to an employment tribunal under regulation 30. These include the right to have rest breaks, rest periods, annual leave and the right to have pay in lieu of untaken leave on termination. Otherwise enforcement of the Working Time Regulations will be by the Health and Safety Executive.

5.8   Detriment

There is also the right not to be subjected to a detriment or to be dismissed for asserting a statutory right under the WTR in section 45A of the ERA 1996. This would constitute automatically unfair dismissal and you would not need the two year qualifying period (section 101A ERA). An example might be if an employee is dismissed for refusing to work more than 48 hours a week when they had not signed a document agreeing to this.

There are various sectors of employment which are excluded from some of the provisions of the WTR. These include seafarers, and civil aviation and road transport workers (regulation 18).

It is important to note that there is no statutory entitlement to paid holidays on bank holidays and if the employee is given paid leave on a bank holiday this counts towards his statutory entitlement.

Also, the right to annual leave continues to accrue even where the employee is off work with sickness which means that even if you are off sick for a year you will still accrue your annual holiday entitlement in this period.

5.9   Holiday pay

The basic right to holiday pay is given by regulation 16 of the WTR. The rate of pay for a week's holiday is the same as a normal week's rate of pay. The calculations in respect of rate of pay are set out in sections 221 to 224 of the ERA 1996. Holiday pay is calculated by reference to your normal working hours or by taking an average of your weekly pay over the last 12 weeks. When calculating the amount of holiday pay commission should be included - so should both guaranteed overtime and overtime which, although not guaranteed, is regularly worked. There is an ACAS guide on "Calculating Holiday Pay" which can be found on the ACAS website.

An employee who has not been paid for a period of annual leave can bring a claim under the WTR based on the obligation to pay under regulation 16, or he can bring a claim for unlawful deduction of wages. The remedy is an award for the unpaid pay. The time limit for bringing a claim in the employment tribunal is three months beginning with the date on which it is alleged that the right should have been permitted or the payment made. The award of compensation is discretionary and will depend on the employment tribunal considering whether it is just and equitable having regard to the employer's default and the employee's loss.

5.10   Effect of the Coronavirus Job Retention Scheme

Under the CJRS (see Paragraph 2.19) the government provides a grant to employers to cover 80% of the pay of those employees who have been furloughed up to a maximum figure of £2,500 a month. The scheme only applies to employees or workers paid under PAYE who were on the payroll on 19th March 2020. Where an employer proposes to lay off employees under the scheme and reduce their pay whilst they are on furlough to 80% of their normal pay it is necessary to get the employee's agreement to this as it constitutes a variation of the terms of the contract of employment. If the employee does not agree they are likely to be made redundant. ACAS has provided information about the scheme which can be found at their website - Coronavirus (COVID-19): advice for employers and employees.

Statutory Sick Pay

As from 13th March 2020 employees and workers must receive statutory sick pay from the first day of isolation if it is because of coronavirus symptoms, if someone in their household has coronavirus symptoms or if they have been told by their doctor to self-isolate. If the illness is not related to coronavirus the normal rules will apply (see Paragraph 5.5 above) and they will be entitled to sick pay on their fourth day off work.

Holiday pay

Workers and employees continue to accrue their entitlement to holiday whilst on furlough. If a worker or employee does take their holiday whilst on furlough they are entitled to their full contractual pay for this holiday period and not just 80% of their pay. Employers can require their employees to take their holiday whilst on furlough - see the government guidance document: Holiday entitlement and pay during coronavirus (COVID-19).

Notice pay

If an employee gives notice or is given notice by their employer whilst on furlough they will be entitled to notice pay. The amount of notice pay will depend on the terms of the contract of employment and how long they have been employed (see Paragraph 21.3). The notice pay will normally be 100% of their normal salary but in some circumstances it might only be 80%. This will be the case where the employee is contractually entitled to at least one week's more notice than their statutory entitlement - section 87(4) ERA 1996.

Chapter 6

Transfer of undertakings

6.1   What is a transfer of undertakings?

In simple terms a "transfer of undertakings" applies when one business is taken over or transferred to another business. If you are employed by the company being transferred there are three significant legal effects of this transfer:

- if you are dismissed because of the transfer, it is an unfair dismissal unless your employer can show that the dismissal was for a business reason;

- you are entitled to be employed by the new employer (the "transferee") on the same terms as you were employed by your old employer (the "transferor");

- any action you had against your old employer is transferred to your new employer.

This is the law on transfer of undertakings reduced to its very simplest form - in fact the legal cases arising from this area of law are amongst the most complicated in the whole of employment law. Each of the three effects described above have been considered by the tribunals and courts on many occasions and are subject to exceptions arising in different circumstances.

6.2   TUPE

The provisions regarding such transfers are set out in the Transfer of Undertakings (Protection of Employment) Regulations 2006 ("TUPE").

When a business shuts down the normal position is that the employees of that business will be made redundant. The position is different where the business is taken over or transfers to another business and the new business can acquire responsibilities towards the employees of the old business under the provisions of TUPE. A transfer to which they apply is called a "TUPE transfer", the old business is called the "transferor" and the new business is the "transferee". For the sake of simplicity I will use the phrase "old business" and "new business" in this section.

The TUPE regulations were brought into force as a result of a European Directive on Acquired Rights. The regulations have given rise to considerable amount of litigation and there are a large number of reported cases including decisions from the European Court of Justice providing interpretations of the regulations. It is a complex area of law and in this section I will do no more than give a brief outline of the general principles.

6.3   Who does the transfer apply to?

The TUPE regulations apply where a business or part of a business is transferred. They will relate to any employee of that business. An employee is defined as any individual who works for another - this is a wider definition than is used in the Employment Rights Act 1996 and may include an agency-supplied worker.

For the TUPE regulations to apply the business transferred must be a distinct economic entity which retains its identity after the transfer. For example, if a garage business sold its equipment to another business this would probably not be sufficient to constitute the transfer of a distinct economic entity. The position would probably be different if the new garage took over the premises and the equipment of the old garage and continued to run a motor repair business from these premises - in these circumstances it is likely that the TUPE regulations would apply.

6.4   Change of service provision

A TUPE transfer will also occur where there has been "service provision change". This will apply where, for example, a service such as catering or cleaning which had been done by employees of the old company (in many cases this is a local authority) is transferred to an external service provider such as a catering or cleaning company. It is also a transfer when an outside contractor had provided this service which is then brought back "in-house".

6.5   Effect of the transfer

The effect of the transfer is to provide that the contracts of employment of employees of the old company are transferred to the new company and any contract of employment with the old company will be treated as a contract of employment with the new company. Therefore the employee's length of service with the old company will be transferred over to the new company. Similarly, if an employee had been discriminated against when working for the old company he would be able to bring a claim for damages against the new company.

6.6   Dismissal

If an employee is dismissed because of the transfer, whether this is before the transfer by the old company or after the transfer by the new company, this dismissal will be automatically unfair. In these circumstances the employee would have a claim against the new employer.

The employer has a defence to such a claim if he can show that the dismissal was for an economical, technical or organisational reason ("ETO"). This reason must be something that relates to the way that the company's business is conducted and not, for example, a way of getting a better price for the company that is being sold.

An employee can refuse to work for the new company but, except in special circumstances, this will be treated as a resignation and not a dismissal. The employee would not be able to claim for unfair dismissal or for a redundancy payment. The special circumstances would apply where the terms of employment with the new employment are substantially worse than with the old employer and the employee can treat himself as having been constructively dismissed by the new employer.

6.7 Consultation

Under Regulation 13 there is a duty on an employer to inform and consult with representatives of any employees who may be affected by the transfer. The representatives shall be informed of the fact that the transfer is to take place, the proposed date of the transfer and the reasons for it, the implications of the transfer for those employees and measures which he envisages will be taken in relation to the affected employees. If the employees fail to elect a representative within a reasonable time the required information shall be given to the affected employees.

Under regulation 13A where the employer has fewer than 10 employees and there are no appropriate representatives the employer may comply with his duty to inform and consult if he does so with each of the affected employees.

Where an employer has failed in his duty to inform and consult, a complaint to the employment tribunal may be made by any of the affected employees. The tribunal can order that the employer pay compensation of up to 13 weeks pay for the affected employee.

Chapter 7

Time limits for bringing a claim

Introduction

If you are considering making a claim in the employment tribunal it is most important to be aware that there are strict time limits for bringing the claim and if you do not submit your claim in time you will not be allowed to bring it at all, unless there is a very good reason for the delay.

As a general rule a claim of unfair dismissal must be lodged with the employment tribunal within three months of the date of dismissal (section 111(2) Employment Rights Act 1996 (ERA)). If the claim is for discrimination it must be brought within three months of the act of discrimination complained of (section 123 Equality Act 2010).

There are some exceptions to this:

- An application for interim relief must be brought within seven days of the dismissal (an application for interim relief under section 128 of the ERA 1996 is where the employee claims they were automatically unfairly dismissed for whistleblowing, union membership or acting as an employee representative and applies to the tribunal for an order that their employment should continue pending a full hearing).

- A claim for a redundancy payment must be brought within six months of the relevant date (section 164(1) ERA).

- Claims for equal pay must be made within six months of the last day of employment (section 129(3) Equality Act 2010).

- Claims based on dismissal connected with industrial action must be brought within six months (section 239(2) Trade Union & Labour Relations (Consolidation) Act 1992).

7.1   Continuing act in discrimination cases

Under section 123(3)(a) of the Equality Act 2010, conduct extending over a period is to be treated as done at the end of the period. This is an important principle in discrimination claims and what it means is that if your employer has discriminated against you over an extended period then, if the tribunal accept that this treatment was part of a continuing act and the last act was within three months of bringing your claim, you will still be able to complain of acts of discrimination that had taken place many months or even years earlier.

It has been held that a series of discriminatory acts over a period of time can amount to evidence of a discriminatory practice or state of affairs on the part of an employer, which would constitute a continuing act. In these circumstances the employee would need to prove that the acts are linked to each other and are not isolated incidents.

7.2   Effect of submitting a claim for early conciliation

Where your claim has been submitted to ACAS for early conciliation (see Chapter 8) the three month time limit clock stops running until ACAS sends out the early conciliation certificate, and then the time limit clocks starts running again (see Chapter 8 section 8.10).

7.3   Effective date of termination

With claims for unfair dismissal the claim must be brought within three months of the effective date of termination (section 111(2) ERA). The effective date of termination is the actual date on which the employment comes to an end. The definition of effective date of termination is given in section 97 of the ERA.

If the termination is "with notice" it is the date on which the notice expires. This will apply whether you have to work your notice period or if you are not required to work during your notice period (referred to as "garden leave"). If you are informed that you are being dismissed on 15th June and told that you will need to work your notice period of four weeks, the effective date of termination will be 13th July and any claim for unfair dismissal will need to be brought before midnight on 12th October, i.e. within three calendar months of 13th July.

Where the dismissal is with notice section 111(3) of the ERA states that you can bring your claim within the notice period even though the employment has not technically ended.

If your contract of employment does not specify the amount of notice you are entitled to then the statutory minimum periods of notice, as set out in section 86 ERA, will apply. If you have been employed for less than two years you are entitled to at least one week's notice. You are then entitled to one week's notice for each full year of employment up to a maximum of 12 years.

If the termination is "without notice", this is called a summary dismissal and usually occurs in cases of misconduct. The effective date of termination in this case is the date on which you are dismissed. If you are informed that you are summarily dismissed on 15th June you will need to bring your claim before midnight on 14th September i.e. within three calendar months of 15th June.

If your employer dismisses you without notice but gives you a payment in lieu of notice the effective date of termination will be the date of dismissal.

In the case of a fixed term contract the effective date of termination is the date on which the termination takes effect.

7.4   Extending the effective date of dismissal

Under section 97(2) of the ERA the effective date of termination is extended by the appropriate statutory notice period for the purposes of bringing an unfair dismissal claim but not for computing the time in which the claim must be brought. This means that if you are dismissed less than one week before your two year qualifying period for bringing an unfair dismissal claim then, taking into account the one week statutory minimum notice period, you will be treated as having been employed for more than two years and therefore can bring a claim for unfair dismissal.

For example if your employment started on 15th November 2017 and you are dismissed on 13th November 2019 with one week's notice, the effective date of termination is 20th November 2019 and you will have the two years qualifying period, which allows you to bring a claim for unfair dismissal. The three month period for bringing a claim will begin on 20th November and therefore you will need to submit your claim before midnight on 19th February 2018.

7.5   Effect of an appeal

It is important to be aware that the three month time period for bringing a claim will start running from the date you are dismissed even if you have submitted an appeal to your employer against the dismissal. In these circumstances you must not wait until the appeal is heard before submitting your tribunal claim, because if the appeal procedure drags on you might find yourself out of time for bringing the claim. If your appeal is successful and you are reinstated then you can discontinue your tribunal claim. In some cases the employer's procedure provides for the dismissal procedure to be suspended whilst the appeal process is being carried out but this is an unusual provision.

Even if your employer has not sent you your P45 form this does not alter the effective date of termination and the time for bringing the tribunal claim will still be running.

7.6   Presentation of claim

A claim is presented when it is received by the employment tribunal and not when it is sent. In the case of *Beasley v National Grid* [2008] EWCA Civ 742 the Claimant sent his claim form by email at 11.57pm on the last day of the three month period but it was not received by the tribunal until 1 minute and 28 seconds after midnight.

It was held to be out of time by the tribunal and this decision was upheld by the Court of Appeal. In this case the Claimant had tried sending the email earlier that evening but had typed in the wrong email address and the email had been returned undelivered.

This case illustrates the disastrous consequences of leaving it until the last minute to submit your claim even when you are submitting it by email.

7.7   Sundays and Bank Holidays

If you are presenting your claim by email the fact that the last day of the three month period is a Sunday or a Bank Holiday will make no difference so long as the claim is received before midnight on the last day on the employment tribunal's computer system.

The position is different if you are sending in your claim by post. Because the claim is only presented when it is received by the tribunal office it will not be delivered by the post office on a Sunday and it therefore will not be presented until the next working day. You will need to make sure your claim is received before the Sunday - this can be a Saturday because the claim form should be delivered to the tribunal office by the post office on a Saturday even though the office itself is closed. If the last day of the three month period is a Sunday and your claim is delivered on the Monday it will be out of time and you will have to ask the tribunal to extend time (see section 7.8 below). This is the effect of the decision in the case of *Consignia v Sealy* [2002] EWCA 878.

The decision in *Consignia v Sealy* concerned a case where the expiry date fell on a Sunday, although the position appears to be different if the expiry date falls on a Bank Holiday. In the case of *Ford v Stakis Hotels* [1988] IRLR 46, the expiry date fell on Bank Holiday Monday and the claim form was presented the following day. The Employment Appeal Tribunal held that because there was no proper means of delivering the claim form on the Bank Holiday the time limit was extended by one day and so it was not presented out of time.

If you are sending your claim by post do not leave it until the last day. Letters sent by first class post are expected to arrive on the second working day after posting and letters sent by second class post are expected to arrive on the fourth working day after posting. If the expiry date is a Sunday you need to post your claim by first class post no later than Thursday to be sure that your claim is in time.

7.8   Extending the time limits

If the claim is for unfair dismissal and it is presented out of time (that it is after the three month time limit has expired) the tribunal can allow it in late if you can persuade them that it was not reasonably practicable to present it within the three month time limit (section 111(2) ERA). This applies to most claims brought under the ERA.

If the claim is for discrimination under the Equality Act 2010 and it is presented out of time the tribunal can allow it in late if you can persuade the tribunal that it is just and equitable to extend the time limits (section 123(1)(b) Equality Act).

The "reasonably practicable" test

The test for extending time is harder to pass in unfair dismissal cases than in discrimination cases. In deciding whether to allow a claim for unfair dismissal out of time the tribunal will look at the circumstances that led to the claim being submitted late and it will also consider whether the delay between the expiry of the time limit and the date when the claim was in fact presented was reasonable. What this means is that even if you can show that it was not reasonably practicable to present the claim within the three month period you will still need to show the tribunal that you presented it within a reasonable time after the three month period.

"Reasonably practicable" means the same as reasonably feasible or reasonably possible. The tribunal will look at all the circumstances which have resulted in the claim not being presented in time. The tribunal will consider whether it was physically possible to submit the claim, so if you were too ill to be able to present the claim the tribunal is likely to extend time.

The tribunal will also consider whether there was some mental impediment to bringing the claim in time, for example if you did not know of some fact that would have entitled you to bring a claim. If you have been made redundant but only find out some months after your dismissal that your employer has been advertising your job as a vacancy, the tribunal might accept that it was not reasonably practicable for you to bring a claim until you became aware of the advertisement.

Ignorance of your legal rights, or of the three month time limit, is not normally accepted by the tribunals as a good excuse for failing to bring your claim in time. The tribunal is likely to take the view that most people considering bringing a claim will find out what the time periods are for bringing a claim. The position could well be different if your employer has misled you about your rights to bring a claim, for example if your employer has told you that you cannot bring a claim in the employment tribunal until the internal appeal against your dismissal has been concluded - in these circumstances a tribunal might extend the time limit for bringing a claim.

If you have had a professional representative or advisor acting for you (this can include a trade union official) and they have advised you incorrectly about your rights or they have failed to present the claim in time, this will not normally be a good reason for the tribunal to allow an extension of time. The position appears to be different if the person at fault is not a professional advisor but you will have to persuade the tribunal that it was reasonable for you to rely on the advice of this person and not make an independent enquiry into the position.

The "just and equitable" test

In discrimination cases the tribunal can extend time if it appears to the tribunal that it is "just and equitable" to do so. This phrase gives the tribunal a wider discretion to extend time than the phrase "reasonably practicable" for unfair dismissal claims. There are various factors that a tribunal would be expected to consider and these include:

- the length and reasons for the delay;

- whether any evidence has been lost or deteriorated as a result of the delay;

- whether the Respondent had provided evidence when asked;

- whether the Claimant acted promptly when the Claimant had all the facts;

- steps taken by the Claimant to obtain advice.

When considering the "just and equitable" test, the tribunal can take into account incorrect advice given by the advisor, whether this was a professional advisor or not.

If the claim is out of the time the tribunal will usually list the case for a preliminary hearing (see Chapter 14) to consider whether it should be struck out. The Claimant will be required to provide a statement setting out why the claim was out of time.

If you are making a statement in support of your application to extend time you should include as much detail as possible as to why you failed to submit your claim in time. You will also need to show that once you had all the relevant facts or knowledge you acted promptly in bringing the claim.

7.9   Coronavirus and time limits

The President of the Employment Tribunals has provided an online document of FAQ (Frequently Asked Questions) arising from the Covid-19 pandemic. Question 18 reads:

> *Given the problems caused by the pandemic will the employment tribunal extend the time limits within which a claim should be brought ?*

In the answer it is recognised that the pandemic may well have an impact on how and when individuals are able to take legal advice but it goes on to state that the strict time limits will continue to apply. If a claim is presented late the question of time limits will be considered at a preliminary hearing. It is at this hearing you will have to explain why it was not reasonably practicable to bring the claim in time if it is an unfair dismissal claim or to argue that it would be just and equitable to extend the time limit if it is a discrimination claim.

Chapter 8

Early conciliation

8.1 Introduction

If you want to bring a claim in the employment tribunal, your claim will be rejected by the tribunal unless your claim form, the ET1, includes the reference number provided by ACAS on the Early Conciliation certificate. This certificate is the document that ACAS sends out to confirm that conciliation has been tried and was unsuccessful in settling the dispute.

The employment tribunal has strict time limits for bringing a claim, which are normally three months from the date of the matter complained of, whether it is your dismissal or the date on which you were discriminated against (see Chapter 7 on Time limits).

When you submit your Early Conciliation form this has the effect of stopping the time limit clock from running. So, if you only have a month left out of the three month time limit to bring your claim when you submit your Early Conciliation form, you will still have a month left when you are provided with the early conciliation certificate. Even if you have less than a month left out of the three month time limit you will still have one month to submit your claim after the Early Conciliation certificate is sent out (see section 8.9 below).

The law relating to early conciliation is set out in The Employment Tribunals (Early Conciliation: Exemptions and Rules of Procedure) Regulations 2014.

8.2 Relevant proceedings

The Early Conciliation Regulations apply to all relevant proceedings. These are those proceedings set out in section 18 of the Employment Tribunal Act 1996. In summary they apply to:

- Unfair dismissal cases;

- Workplace discrimination including those cases involving detriment;

- Redundancy payment cases;

- Deductions from wages and holiday pay cases;

- Contractual claims including unpaid notice;

- Right to have time off or flexible working;

- Equal pay.

They do not apply to employers' contract claims.

8.3   Exemptions

There are various cases which are exempt from the requirement for early conciliation, but in practice these exemptions will be fairly rare. What it means is that an
employee or worker can bring a claim without complying with the requirement for
early conciliation.

The exemptions are set out Regulation 3:

- **Where another person has complied with the requirement in relation to
  the same dispute and the prospective Claimant wishes to institute proceedings on the same claim form**

  If two or more employees or workers are intending to bring a claim in respect
  of the same dispute and one of the employees has already complied with the
  early conciliation requirements, any other employee or employees intending
  to use the same claim form need not comply with the requirement for early
  conciliation. In practice this would mean that the first employee would have
  been provided with an Early Conciliation Certificate and the reference number
  given on this form would be entered on the ET1 that is being used by all the
  other employees.

- **A person institutes relevant proceedings on the same form as proceedings which are not relevant proceedings**

  If you are bringing a claim that is not a relevant proceeding on the same ET1
  as you are bringing relevant proceedings you need not comply with the requirements for early conciliation.

- **Where the prospective Claimant can show that the prospective Respondent has contacted ACAS in relation to a dispute and ACAS has not
  received an EC form from the Claimant in relation to that dispute**

  If the prospective Respondent has already contacted ACAS about the dispute
  there is no need for the prospective Claimant to do so. In this case if no settlement is reached both parties will be sent an EC certificate.

- **The proceedings are under part X of the Employment Rights Act (ERA)
  1996 and accompanied by an application under section 128 ERA 1996**

or section 161 Trade Union and Labour Relations (Consolidation) Act (TULR(C)A) 1992

Where the claim includes an application for interim relief either under section 128 of the Employment Rights Act 1996 or section 161 TULR(C)A there is no requirement for the underlying unfair dismissal claim to be submitted for early conciliation. These claims need to be brought within 7 days of the effective date of termination (s128(2) ERA and s161(2) TULR(C)A).

- **The proceedings are against the security service, the intelligence service of GCHQ**

8.4 Contacting ACAS

In order to satisfy the requirement for early conciliation you must either present a completed Early Conciliation form (EC form) to ACAS in accordance with rule 2 of the Regulations or you must telephone ACAS in accordance with rule 3 of the Regulations. The EC form can be found at www.acas.org.uk/earlyconciliation.

ACAS have made it clear that they would prefer to be contacted by email and that contact by post or telephone would not be encouraged. If you are unable to access the ACAS website you can telephone early conciliation support on 0300 123 1100 to discuss your options.

If you are an employer and consider that early conciliation might be helpful in resolving a dispute with an employee you can contact ACAS early conciliation support on 0300 123 1122 to discuss your options.

8.5 The Early Conciliation form

The normal way to commence the procedure for early conciliation will be to complete an Early Conciliation form (EC form). This requires your full name and address including an email address and a main contact number.

The form also requires the name and address of the employer/Respondent you are intending to bring the claim against and the telephone number for ACAS to contact your employer. If there is more than one prospective Respondent you need only provide the name of one of them on the EC form.

The form requires the date your employment started and, where applicable, the date it finished; what job you did for your employer; and the date on which the event that you intend to make a claim about took place.

Finally there is a box where you can give the name of someone else to be contacted or if you have some accessibility needs.

It is important to note that ACAS may reject a form that does not contain the required information. Alternatively they may contact you to obtain the missing information. If ACAS rejects the form it must return it to you.

When you are contacted by the ACAS Early Conciliation Support Officer they will ask you if you are represented and whether contact should be made directly with your representative.

8.6   Submission of the form

The EC form must be either submitted using the online form on the ACAS website or sent by post to the ACAS address set out on the EC form;

> EC Notification
>
> ACAS (Phoenix)
>
> PO Box 10279
>
> Nottingham
>
> NG2 9PE

8.7   Contact

ACAS will try to make contact with you either by email or telephone within 48 hours of receiving your form. This contact will be by an Early Conciliation Support Officer ("ECSO") who will confirm the basic information about the claim and set out the next stage of the process. You will be asked if you consent to ACAS contacting the prospective Respondent. If ACAS is unable to contact either you or the Respondent it will conclude that a settlement is not possible and issue an Early Conciliation Certificate (EC Certificate).

8.8   Period for Early Conciliation

The next contact will be by a conciliation officer. The conciliation officer will have one month starting from the date of receipt by ACAS of the EC form or the prospective Claimant's telephone call to promote a settlement. This period may be extended by a maximum of 14 days if both parties consent and the officer considers that there is a reasonable prospect of achieving a settlement before the expiry of the extended period. This extension may occur only once.

If at any point during the period for early conciliation or the extension period the officer concludes that a settlement of a dispute or part of it is not possible ACAS must issue an EC certificate. If the period for early conciliation or the extension period expires without a settlement having been reached ACAS must issue an EC certificate.

8.9   The Early Conciliation certificate

This must contain the following details:

- the name and address of both the prospective Claimant and Respondent;

- the date of receipt by ACAS of the EC form or the date the Claimant telephoned;

- the unique reference number given by ACAS to the EC certificate;

- the date of issue of the certificate, which will be the date that the certificate is sent by ACAS; and

- a statement indicating the method by which it is sent.

ACAS must send a copy of the EC certificate to the Claimant and, if it has had contact with the Respondent, to that Respondent. If an email address has been provided by either party ACAS must send the certificate by email and in any other case must send it by post. An EC certificate will be deemed to have been received:

- if sent by email, on the day it is sent; or

- if sent by post, on the day on which it would be delivered in the ordinary course of the post.

It is the reference number given by ACAS on the certificate that you will need to put on your ET 1 form (see Chapter 9).

8.10   Time limits

When you submit your Early Conciliation form this has the effect of stopping the time limit clock from running. When ACAS sends out the EC certificate this has the effect of starting the time clock running again but, under the provisions set out in s207B of the ERA, you will get at least a month in which to submit your claim form, even if you only contacted ACAS a few days before the expiry of the original three month time limit.

I will use some examples to explain how this works. In these examples Day A is the day you present your Early Conciliation form and Day B is the date you are treated as having received your Early Conciliation certificate. Day B will be the day the certificate was sent if it is sent by email but if the certificate was sent by post you will be treated as having received it on the second day after it was posted. For example, if it was posted on Tuesday you will be treated as having received on Thursday.

Example 1

You were dismissed on 31st May. The three month time limit would expire at midnight on 30th August. You submit your Early Conciliation form on 20th August (this is Day A). The conciliation period lasts one calendar month starting on 21st August. No settlement is reached and ACAS sends out the certificate by email on 20th September (this is Day B). The new time limit is one month after Day B, so you need to submit your claim before midnight on 19th October. Even though you originally only had ten days left before the expiry of the original time limit, under the new provisions you will have a month left after receiving the certificate.

Example 2

You were dismissed on 31st May. The three month time limit would expire at midnight on 30th August. You submit your Early Conciliation form on 1st July (this is Day A). The conciliation period starts on 2nd July. Your employer makes it clear he is not willing to negotiate and ACAS sends out the Early Conciliation certificate on 14th July (this is Day B). The conciliation period has taken 13 days. These 13 days are added to the original expiry date of 30th August and the new expiry date will be 12th September, which means that you will need to submit your claim before midnight on 12th September. The effect of this is that you do not lose the time spent during the conciliation period - this is added on to the original time limit expiry date, although unlike example 1 above you have not been given any extra days.

In summary the early conciliation procedure is:

- Before a claim can be lodged in the employment tribunal you must send ACAS an Early Conciliation form. This form contains contact details for both you and the prospective Respondent. ACAS will send an acknowledgement of receipt. Receipt of the form will stop the time limit clock for bringing a tribunal claim.

- ACAS will contact you and, if you wish, the prospective Respondent to try to see if a settlement is possible. If not an Early Conciliation certificate will be sent to the parties.

- If you and the Respondent are willing to try to reach a settlement a Conciliation Officer will contact both of you and try to negotiate a settlement. A period of one month is allowed to reach a settlement which can be extended by two weeks if the parties agree. If agreement is reached a settlement agreement in the form of a COT3 document will be drawn up.

- If it is not possible to reach an agreement or time runs out without an agreement being reached an Early Conciliation certificate will be sent to you and the Respondent. Once the Early Conciliation certificate is sent out by ACAS the time limit clock starts running again.

Chapter 9

Making a claim to the employment tribunal

9.1 How to make a claim

In order to make a claim in an employment tribunal you must present details of your claim in writing. The claim has to be made on an approved form which is called the ET1. There are three different ways of obtaining this form:

- the form can either be obtained as a paper version from an employment tribunal;

- by printing off the form which can be found at www.employmenttribunals. service.gov.uk;

- it is available on the internet and can be completed and submitted online. The online version can be found at www.employmenttribunals.service.gov.uk.

9.2 Submitting your application

There are three different ways to submit your application:

Paper version sent through the post
If it is a paper version you can send it to:

> Employment Tribunal Central Office (England and Wales)
>
> PO Box 10218
>
> Leicester
>
> LE1 8EG

Or if you live in Scotland the appropriate address is:

> Employment Tribunal Central Office Scotland
>
> PO Box 27105
>
> Glasgow
>
> G2 9JR

If it is a paper version and you do not want to send it by post or it is more convenient, you can take your completed claim form to one of the individual tribunal offices listed in the schedule to the Practice Direction on presentation of claims. You can find this list at www.gov.uk/employment-tribunal-offices-and-venues.

It is important to note that this list only contains the main tribunals - not every tribunal office can receive an application. For example there is only one office in London and the only one in the South West is in Bristol.

Online version
If you have completed the online version of the form you will need to submit it online. Submitting the form online is the quickest way of making your application.

9.3   Completing the ET1

You need to go through the form very carefully and complete all the necessary boxes because a failure to include information can mean that the form will not be accepted by the tribunal. It is important that you put down the correct name and address of your employer so that they can be contacted by the tribunal. It is important to write the correct postcode of the address where you worked because your claim will eventually be dealt with by the tribunal office which is closest to that postcode. There is a public enquiry line 0845 795 9775 to ring if you do not know the postcode of your employer's business address.

If your claim is accepted you will be sent a letter confirming this.

Your claim will NOT be accepted if:

- it is not on the approved form; or

- you have not completed all those boxes that require information. The form contains a number of boxes to be filled in and some of these boxes HAVE to be filled in (they are marked with an asterisk *). Some boxes need to be filled in if you have the information but the form will not be rejected if they are not. When considering the different sections on the form I will indicate which boxes have to be filled in.

9.4   The ET1 form

Section 1

The first section of the form requires you to fill in your personal details (name, address and contact details). You HAVE to fill in boxes 1.2 (your first name), box 1.3 (your surname) and box 1.5 (your address including the postcode) or your claim will be rejected.

Section 2

Section 2 deals with the Respondent's details. The person you are making a claim against is called the "Respondent" and there can be more than one. The Respondent will normally be your employer which will be either the company, the firm or the person who employed you but in a discrimination case, for example, you might wish to include a particular individual who works for your employer who you consider to have been guilty of discrimination against you (see advice in section 2.5 below).

You can also bring a claim against that person alone without making a claim against your employer in which case you would need to complete the box at section 4 "Cases where the Respondent is not your employer". You will need to state the type of claim in this box and then go to section 8.

The claim has to be connected to your employment. In most cases you will bring the claim against both the other employee and your employer, who will normally be liable for any acts of discrimination committed by the other employee (see Chapter 4 section 4.13). You cannot make a claim against someone, either a person or an organisation, who is not your employer or part of your employer's organisation. For example if you consider that someone such as a customer has discriminated against you, you cannot bring a claim against the customer but you can bring a claim against your employer if your employer knows about this behaviour and has allowed or permitted it to happen and does nothing to protect you.

You HAVE to fill in box 2.1 (the name of your employer or the person or organisation you are bringing a claim against).

You HAVE to fill in box 2.2 (the address of your employer or the person or organisation you are bringing the claim against). This information should be set out in your contract of employment or your wage slips.

The box at 2.3 requires you to give your ACAS Early Conciliation certificate number (see Chapter 8 on Early Conciliation). If you fall into one of the exempt categories you will need to tick the appropriate box. If you do not fill in the EC certificate number your claim form will be rejected. It is important to make sure that you fill in the *correct* ACAS EC certificate number as the claim form will be rejected if the wrong number is entered.

Fill in box 2.4 if you worked at a different address from the address given in box 2.2 above.

More than one Respondent

There are some cases where you might be considering bringing a claim against more than one person or organisation. There are a number of boxes at 2.5 which allow you to provide the name and address of additional Respondents. For example in cases where your employment has been transferred from one organisation to another or your dismissal is connected to such a transfer you can bring a claim against both the employer you worked for before the transfer and the new employer.

In a discrimination case you might wish to bring a claim against an individual employee who you consider has been responsible for acts of discrimination against you as well as your employer. In this case you would put the name of the individual and, unless you know their address, you would put the address of their workplace.

Although you can name specific people in your employer's organisation that you consider to have been guilty of acts of discrimination against you there are a number of disadvantages in doing this and only a few advantages.

Disadvantages

One major disadvantage is that this person becomes a separate party in the proceedings and that person might get their own representative. Any correspondence you have with the tribunal will have to be sent to both parties. Where there is more than one Respondent tribunal proceedings tend to take longer than where there is just one - this is particularly the case where the Respondents are separately represented. Each Respondent or their representative will be entitled to cross-examine you and will be entitled to call their own evidence, bring their own witnesses to any hearing and make submissions at the end of the hearing (see Chapter 20).

Any settlement negotiations will normally have to include that individual because, even if you reach an agreement with your employer, there will still be the proceedings against that individual which will continue unless they are withdrawn or otherwise disposed of. You will run the risk of paying that person's legal costs if the tribunal considers that you have acted unreasonably in bringing that person into the proceedings. Another matter to take into consideration is that some individuals might not have the financial means to pay an award if you succeed in obtaining an award of damages against them.

Advantages

One advantage of bringing a claim against an individual employee you consider has been guilty of discrimination against you is that if your employer succeeds in the defence under section 109(4) of the Equality Act 2010 that they have taken all reasonable measures to prevent that individual committing acts of discrimination, then your claim against your employer would fail and you would only succeed in getting an award of damages against the employee.

Section 3

Section 3 relates to multiple claims. This will apply if there are other employees who are bringing claims against the same employer and the claims arise from the same or similar circumstances. This might apply where a number of employees have been dismissed at the same time for a connected reason or if a number of employees are bringing the same claim against an employer for equal pay or breach of the Working Time Regulations.

Section 4

Section 4 applies in those cases where the Respondent you have named in section 2 has not actually employed you. This will be an unusual situation but might arise where you have applied for a job but have been turned down on grounds that you consider give rise to a claim for discrimination.

Section 5

Section 5 requires you to set out the details of your employment. It states that the information should be given if possible, which means that if there are any details which you do not know, a failure to include them on the form does not mean your application will be rejected.

The first question is: "When did your employment start?". If you can only remember a year, or a month and a year, this will be sufficient - your employer should have the exact details and will be able to enter this on their response form, the ET3.

You are then asked if your employment is continuing and if not when it ended, or, if you have been given notice, when that period of notice will end. You are also asked to provide your job title.

Section 6

Section 6.1 requires details about the basic number of hours that you work or worked on average - do not include overtime even if this was worked regularly.

Section 6.2 has two boxes. In the first you should put your earnings before tax and any other deductions (this is your gross pay) but don't include overtime payments. In the second box you will need to put the amount of your normal take home pay, including overtime, commission and bonuses. This will be your earnings after deductions including tax and national insurance (this is your net pay). You can provide either a weekly or monthly figure, which you will be able to get from your latest pay slip.

Section 6.3 asks whether, if your employment has ended, you worked (or were paid for) a period of notice and, if so, the amount of notice you worked or were paid for.

Under box 6.4 you will need to indicate if you were in your employer's pension scheme.

Under the box at 6.5 you should also include any other benefits you receive from your employer. This will include such benefits as a company car, mobile phone or medical insurance. If you have an idea of how much the benefit is worth you can include that figure.

Section 7

Section 7 relates to the position where your job with the Respondent has ended and you will need to indicate whether or not you have a new job.

If you are setting up your own business or working on a self-employed basis you will need to tick the box saying you have a new job and indicate how much you expect to be making from this business in the box at 7.3. It will be better to underestimate this figure rather than overestimate it - in most businesses there will be a number of expenses and costs that will have to be paid out and these will be deducted from your gross earnings to calculate your actual net earnings. This figure in box 7.3 will be used to calculate the amount of your compensatory award, which is the difference between the amount you were paid in the job with the Respondent and the amount you are now being paid. You will only get a compensatory award if the amount you are now paid is less than the amount you were paid.

Section 8

Section 8 requires you to indicate the type or types of claim you are making. You must tick at least one of the boxes.

Tick the first box if you are claiming unfair dismissal, whether the dismissal was by your employer or you resigned and are claiming that you were constructively dismissed by your employer.

Tick the second box if you are making a claim for discrimination - you will then need to tick another box to indicate the type of discrimination you are claiming. You are not restricted to ticking just one box - you might be claiming both unfair dismissal and discrimination, or you might be claiming both sex and race discrimination. Make sure that, if you are claiming for a pregnancy or maternity discrimination, you also tick the box for sex discrimination. It is important that you tick the boxes indicating all the possible types of claim you might wish to bring in the tribunal.

There is a box for claiming a redundancy payment and boxes for different types of pay you might be owed - again you are not restricted to ticking just one box. You need to explain why you consider that you are owed this payment. If you know the exact figure you are owed put this figure down and explain how you have calculated it.

At section 8.2 there is a full page for you to provide details of your claim. If you do not complete this page, the claim will be rejected. If necessary you can continue on the blank sheet at the end of the form (see section 9.5 below for more information on how to complete this page).

Section 9

Section 9 asks what remedy you want. For unfair dismissal you can ask for your old job back (called "reinstatement") or another job with the same employer (called "re-engagement"). I will consider this remedy in more detail in the section dealing with remedies but at this stage it is worth pointing out that it is rare for a tribunal to order either reinstatement or re-engagement because, by the time the tribunal hearing has taken place, the relationship between the employer and the employee will probably have broken down to such an extent that it would not be realistic for the employee to return.

The main award is that of compensation but in discrimination cases the tribunal can also make a recommendation. Again I will consider this remedy in more detail in the section on remedies but essentially it is a recommendation to change some aspect of the employment that has resulted in discrimination. This can be either a positive step to do something or an order that something which the tribunal regards as discriminatory not be done.

Under section 9.2 you are asked to give as much detail about the compensation you are seeking (see Chapter 16 on Schedule of loss). The figures you put in this section are not binding on you and you will be allowed to alter this figure at a later date. The purpose is to give the Respondent some idea of the amount you are claiming.

Section 10

Section 10 applies only to cases where you are claiming that you have been dismissed for making a protected disclosure. Tick that box at 10.1 if you wish your claim to be forwarded to the relevant regulator.

Section 11

Section 11 deals with details of your representative if you have one. If you fill in this section the tribunal office will send all correspondence to your representative's address.

Section 12

Section 12 deals with disability. You need to explain what your disability is and whether it means you are likely to need assistance from the tribunal staff. For example they can produce documents in Braille or in large print; they can put them on a disc; or they can make adjustments in the tribunal hearing room.

Section 13

Section 13 provides further space to include additional Respondents.

Section 14

Section 14 asks you to confirm that you have checked that the information you have put down is accurate.

Section 15

Section 15 provides a page to include any additional information. If your claim is out of time and you want to explain why, you can do so here.

9.5   Providing details of your claim

This is your opportunity to set out in your own words why you are bringing the claim and what it is that your employer has done wrong. I find that the best way to do this is to set out a history of the complaint using the main dates when something significant happened. I have provided some examples at Appendix B.

It is important that you stick to a factual account of what has occurred. However strongly you feel about the way in which you have been treated you will not help your case by including abusive terms or criticisms that you cannot prove. If you are able to remember the date on which an event occurred or something was said, put down that date as this will make the narrative more convincing. If you are not sure of the exact date use the phrase "on or about" 17th June for example. Do not write that a certain event occurred on a certain date if you are not sure about it because your employer might be able to show that the event could not have happened on that date and this will undermine your account. For example, if you state that your line manager made some discriminatory remark to you at lunchtime on 15th January 2014 and your employer is able to show that the manager was in fact on holiday on 15th January then you might have difficulty persuading the tribunal that the remark was ever made.

It is preferable to limit the facts to those things that you have seen and heard. Where necessary you can include things that you have been told but this is regarded by tribunals and courts as second hand or "hearsay" evidence.

As an example, if you tell the tribunal that your manager used a discriminatory term directly towards you and he denies it, the tribunal will have to decide which of you is telling the truth and they will do this by asking you about the circumstances in which the words were spoken. But if all you can say is that "Jane told me the manager said this" and he denies it or said she misheard him than the tribunal is likely to accept his evidence.

You will need to put down all the facts that support your claim. If you are claiming unfair dismissal and you had been dismissed for misconduct, you will need to set out the factual circumstances leading up to your dismissal explaining the misconduct you were accused of.

You will need to explain why you say you did not do the thing you were accused of and why your employer should not have believed that you were guilty. If you consider that your employer had some other motive for wanting to dismiss you, you should set that down and explain what evidence you have for believing he had that motive.

If you were dismissed for redundancy you will need to explain why you consider that you were not redundant, and whether there were other jobs available that you could have done.

If you consider that the selection procedure was unfair you will need to explain why it was unfair. For example, if you are alleging that the marking of the selection matrix was wrong you will not only need to explain why but also that if it had been marked correctly why you would not have been made redundant. If there was someone else you say should have been included in the selection pool you will need to explain why and also why that person would probably have been selected for redundancy before you.

If you are alleging discrimination you should try to set out all the examples of discriminatory conduct that you rely on. You should set out the incidents in chronological order; that is starting with the earliest incident and listing them in date order until the most recent one. It does not matter that the earliest incident might have occurred a number of years earlier because a tribunal might accept that it is part of a series of events. Try and give as much detail as you can about the date on which the incident occurred, where it occurred and who it was that said the thing or did the thing complained of.

If you are alleging disability discrimination you will need to explain your disability and how it limits your ability to carry out everyday tasks.

Chapter 10

Responding to a tribunal claim

10.1   Receipt of the ET1

Under the new provisions relating to early conciliation (see Chapter 8) the employer will have been contacted by an ACAS Conciliation Officer about the Claimant's intention to bring a claim and should be able to indicate the type of claim that the Claimant is intending to bring. If you are dealing with the response on your own behalf as the employer of the Claimant or if you are dealing with the matter on behalf of the Respondent company you will know if conciliation has failed and the receipt of the Claimant's ET1 will come as no surprise to you.

The tribunal will send you a copy of the ET1 with an accompanying letter. This letter will give the case number that has been allocated to the case. You will need to use this case number for reference purposes in any letters or emails you send to the tribunal. It will give the names of the Claimant and the Respondent (or Respondents if there are more than one). It will state that the tribunal has accepted one or more claims made against the named Respondent(s). It will provide the date by which the response must be received at that office.

10.2   How to respond

The most important thing you must be aware of is that you only have 28 days to submit your response. The 28 days runs from the date when a copy of the claim form was sent by the tribunal and not the date it was received by you.

In responding to the claim as set out on the ET1 it is obligatory to use the prescribed form ET3 and to comply with the requirements on the form. The ET3 response form can be found on the website www.employmenttribunals.service. gov.uk. You can print off this form and send it to the tribunal or you can submit your response online. If you are sending it by post you must ensure that it is sent in time so that the tribunal will receive it no later than 28 days after they sent out the ET3 form. It is worth checking with the tribunal office to ensure that they have received your ET3.

If you respond online your form will be automatically sent to the tribunal office dealing with the case. You should print out a copy of your ET3 for your own benefit. Whenever you communicate with the tribunal office you will need to provide the case number.

10.3   Default judgments

A tribunal can make a "default judgment" which is where judgment is entered for one party, normally the Claimant, in circumstances where the Respondent has failed to submit an ET3 or the form submitted has not been completed correctly. This means judgment for the Claimant on all the claims they have made. If the tribunal judge has sufficient information he can determine the remedy (normally the amount of money the Respondent will have to pay the Claimant) or he can list the case for a remedies hearing at which the amount of compensation that the Respondent will have to pay the Claimant will be decided. Because the Respondent has failed to enter a response to the claim he would not be permitted to address the tribunal as to the amount of compensation (see section 10.7: Reconsideration of rejection of the response, below).

10.4   The ET3 form

Section 2

In section 2 of the ET3 you will need to set out the Respondent's details. These include the name of the company, firm, partnership or individual who employed the Claimant. It is not unusual for a Claimant to have incorrectly identified the name of the company employing him - you will need to put down the correct name even if this is different from the name the Claimant has put down.

If it is denied that the Claimant was employed you will still need to enter the Respondent's name and details in this section but you will need to specify in section 4 that the dates of employment are incorrect and explain that the Claimant was not an employee but was working for you on a self-employed basis. You do not need to go into any further details in this section but you will need to set out in section 6 those facts which you rely on to support your argument that the Claimant was self-employed.

Section 3

Section 3 relates to the details given by the Claimant about the early conciliation with ACAS. If you disagree with the details the Claimant has put down on his form you will to explain why you disagree. For example, if the Claimant has given the wrong conciliation certificate number you will need to enter the correct number. If the Claimant has stated that his claim is exempt from early conciliation and you disagree with this you will need to explain why you disagree.

Section 4

Under section 4 you will need to confirm the details given by the Claimant with regard to their employment with you. If you disagree with the dates the Claimant's employment started and finished you will need to explain why you disagree. If you disagree with the job title or job description that the Claimant has put on his ET1 you will need to put down what you consider to be the correct job title.

Section 5

Section 5 deals with the Claimant's earnings and benefits. Again it is important to correct any facts or figures you consider that the Claimant has incorrectly entered on his ET1. Even if you are alleging that the Claimant is self-employed you should put down the correct hours of work or the pay details if you disagree with the figures that the Claimant has entered.

Under section 5.2 the information about pay includes overtime, commission and bonuses etc. This is based on normal or average pay before and after tax. If you disagree with the figure that the Claimant has entered for his pay, there is no opportunity in this section to explain why you disagree - all you can do is enter what you consider to be the correct figure.

Section 5.3 deals with notice pay. An employee is entitled to notice pay based either on the provisions in the contract of employment or the number of years he has been employed. If the Claimant has been dismissed summarily for gross misconduct he will not be entitled to any notice pay. If the Claimant is claiming for unfair dismissal in such circumstances he will normally claim his notice pay. You will need to explain that the Claimant was dismissed summarily for gross misconduct and therefore he was not entitled to any notice pay.

Section 5.4 relates to the company benefits that the Claimant has referred to in his ET1. This is relevant to the amount of the compensatory damages that the tribunal would be looking to award if the Claimant was successful in his claim. For example, if he had health insurance that was worth £25 a month then any compensatory award would include the value of this benefit. If you are disputing that he was entitled to these benefits or disputing that these benefits would have continued if the Claimant had not been dismissed, you will need to explain this in section 5.4.

Section 6

Section 6 is your opportunity to set out the facts that you want to rely on in defending the claim. There is a continuation sheet at the end of the form if you need further space (see section 10.5 Providing details of the response, below).

Section 7

Section 7 of the form makes provision for you to bring a counterclaim against the Claimant. This will only apply in those cases where the Claimant has included a breach of contract in his ET1. The most common breach of contract claims made by an employee are for failure to pay notice pay (this is sometimes referred to as a "wrongful dismissal" claim as distinct from an unfair dismissal claim), or a failure to pay holiday pay, commission, bonus or some other sum due under the contract. It is important to note that if the Claimant is only claiming statutory notice pay or holiday pay under the Working Time Regulations and claiming them as a breach of the terms of the contract of employment, these would not be classed as "contract claims".

The counterclaim must be a claim that arises out of, or is outstanding on, the termination of the employment, so the Claimant's employment must have come to an end. You have six weeks from the date of receipt of the breach of contract claim to bring a counterclaim.

The most common counterclaims are for the failure to return tools or property belonging to the Respondent, an overpayment of salary or holiday pay, the repayment of a loan made to the Claimant by the Respondent, or re-payment of money taken by the Claimant.

The maximum award a tribunal can make on a counterclaim is £25,000.

Section 8

Section 8 applies where you have a representative acting for you and you will need to put down his details.

Section 9

Section 9 applies if you have a disability, which would mean that you require assistance as the claim progresses or when hearing the claim.

10.5   Providing details of the response

If the claim is for unfair dismissal this is your opportunity to tell your version of the events leading up to the Claimant's dismissal and why the dismissal was fair.

If it is a discrimination case you need to admit if it is accepted that discrimination took place, or deny that the Claimant was subjected to discrimination. Then you will set out your version of the events.

If you are contending that the claim has been brought out of time or, in a discrimination case, some of the allegations are out of time, you will need to set out the basis for this contention here. You will still need to set out your version of events because it might be that the tribunal will allow the claim to be brought even though it is out of time.

If you are claiming that the Claimant was self-employed you will need to set out the basis for this contention here. You will still need to set out your version of events because it might be that the tribunal does not accept you contention that the Claimant was self-employed, in which case you will still need to show that the dismissal was fair.

There are no set rules for setting out your response but it is important that, where the Claimant has included facts that you disagree with, you state this and set out what you consider to be the true facts. The normal formula is to state:

> *"It is not accepted that Mr Smith said to the Claimant that ... What Mr Smith in fact said was..."*

If it is denied that the conversation took place at all then this is all that needs to be said:

> *"It is denied that Mr Smith said to the Claimant that... "*

Where you are setting out your version of events it is always best to set out the history in chronological order starting with the earliest incidents and leading up to the most recent ones. It is helpful to use numbered paragraphs and make the paragraphs fairly short with no more than two or three sentences to each paragraph, since this will make the document much easier to read. If the Claimant has used numbered paragraphs you can refer to these paragraphs when responding to the point made as follows:

> *"As stated in paragraph 4 of the claim it is accepted that Mr Smith told the Claimant ... but it is denied that he also told the Claimant that..."*

It is worth putting in a paragraph at the end of your response making it clear that you are denying all the claims brought by the Claimant or, if there are some of the claims that you accept, stating that you accept this claim, e.g. a claim for holiday pay, but denying all the others.

If there are matters that you consider would be relevant to the amount of compensation claimed or to which the Claimant might be entitled, these points can also be included in this part of the response. These might include for example an admission that following his dismissal the Claimant was not notified of his right to appeal but that this failure did not make the dismissal unfair, and in any event it would not have made any difference to the decision to dismiss the Claimant. In a redundancy case it might refer to the fact that the Claimant was offered an alternative position which he unreasonably turned down.

10.6   Extension of time

If it becomes clear that you need more time than the 28 days allowed in order to submit the ET 3 you can apply for an extension, but it is important that this is done before the 28 days has expired. Otherwise you will be treated as having failed to file a response and a judgment can be entered against you by the tribunal.

You must explain why you are unable to comply with the time limit. For example, an important witness is abroad on holiday or off sick and cannot be contacted and you need to obtain information from them in order to respond to the claim. The more details you can provide including any relevant dates will make it more likely that the tribunal will agree to the extension of time.

If you are applying for an extension of time and have a representative you must send to the Claimant (or if there is more than one, all the Claimants) details of the application and why it is being made. You must also notify them that any objections to the application must be sent to the tribunal within 7 days of receiving the application and that copies of the objection must be sent to the tribunal, to yourself and to any other parties to the claim. If you do not have a representative the tribunal will send a copy of your application to all the other parties and notify them of the requirements if they wish to lodge an objection.

If you become aware that you might have difficulty complying with the 28 day time period you should make your application as soon as possible because, if the application is refused, you will still need to submit your ET3 within the 28 days providing as much information as you can about your response to the claim. The tribunal will inform you in writing if your application is refused.

The tribunals recognise that the coronavirus pandemic might well have an impact on respondents taking legal advice about claims, contacting individuals to understand whether the account set out in the ET1 should be challenged or where business premises have been temporarily closed. The 28 day time limit for submitting a response will still apply but the tribunal has the power to extend this time limit. This will apply even where the time limit has passed. Where a respondent is unable to take instructions about an account given in the ET1 one option might be to complete a "holding" ET3 response and explain that full details will be provided at a later date.

10.7   Reconsideration of rejection

You can apply for a reconsideration (a "review") of the decision not to extend time or not to accept a response on the grounds that it is in the interests of justice. Where the ET3 has been presented out of time this reconsideration may be used if you have not appreciated that the ET3 would arrive late because of some problem with the transmission or where you have been prevented for some reason from lodging the response. The tribunal will allow the reconsideration where it is just and equitable to do so.

If you are asking the tribunal to reconsider the decision it is important that you provide the tribunal with all the relevant documentation, a full explanation of what went wrong and explain the merits of the defence. This reconsideration procedure will also apply in circumstances where the Respondent has not received a copy of the claim form.

Regulations 17 and 18 of the Employment Tribunal (Constitution and Rules of Procedure) Regulations 2013 schedule 1 set out the regulations relating to rejection of the response because the correct form was not used, where there was a failure to supply the required information or where the form was presented late.

Regulation 19 deals with reconsideration of rejection. You have to notify the tribunal in writing within 14 days of the date of the notice of rejection and explain why the decision was wrong. You also need to state if you require a hearing, otherwise the judge will determine the application without one.

Regulation 20 deals with applications for extension of time for presenting the response. You must send a copy of the application to the Claimant as well as the tribunal. You must state the reason for the extension and send a draft copy of the response. You also need to state if you require a hearing otherwise the judge will determine the application without one.

10.8   Amending the response

A response can only be amended or changed with permission from the tribunal. This can be done at any stage of the proceedings but as a general rule the sooner this is done the less likely it is to cause prejudice to the Claimant and therefore the more likely it is to be allowed.

An application will need to be made to a Tribunal Judge to allow the ET3 to be amended. Normally this will be granted unless the Claimant is able to show that the change would cause prejudice to his case and result in injustice.

If it becomes clear when preparing for the hearing that the ET 3 will need to be changed then the application should be made before the hearing starts. Where the amendment is substantial and would result in the Claimant having to call new evidence the tribunal might adjourn the hearing to another day, in which case you would be expected to pay the Claimant's costs that have been wasted by the hearing not going ahead that day. Alternatively the tribunal might refuse to allow the amendment.

Where the amendment involves withdrawing an admission that you have made, the tribunal will consider why you wish to withdraw the admission and whether this is because new evidence has come to light. The tribunal will also consider the conduct of the parties particularly whether the Claimant has done anything which led to the admission being made or withdrawn. The tribunal will also consider whether withdrawing the admission would cause prejudice to the Claimant and whether refusing to allow the admission to be withdrawn would cause prejudice to the Respondent.

Chapter 11

What happens next? Summary of procedure after the response has been filed

You have lodged your claim and received a copy of the Respondent's ET3 setting out the Respondent's defence to the claim. It should be clear from this document what matters are in dispute and what matters, if any, are agreed.

In this chapter I will set out a summary of the different steps and actions that need to be taken before the hearing of the case and the sorts of problems that might arise. In the following chapters I will consider these different steps in more detail.

11.1   Procedural rules

The rules setting out the procedure to be followed in the tribunal can be found in Schedule 1 of the Employment Tribunals (Constitution and Rules of Procedure) Regulations 2013. Section 2 of this Schedule sets out the overriding objective, which is that cases should be dealt with fairly and justly and so far as is practicable:

- ensure that the parties are on an equal footing;

- deal with cases in a way which is proportionate to the complexity and importance of the issues;

- avoid unnecessary formality and seek flexibility;

- avoid delay; and

- save expense.

11.2   Presidential guidance

There is provision for the President of the Employment Tribunals to publish guidance documents. One in particular is very useful - general case management - and it can be found at www.judiciary.gov.uk/wp-content/uploads/2013/08/presidential-guidance-general-case-management-20180122.pdf

This guidance was updated in January 2018 and it provides helpful guidance in everyday non-technical language about:

- disclosure of documents and preparing bundles for the hearing;

- witness statements;

- amendments to the claim and response;

- disability;

- remedy;

- costs;

- timetabling;

- concluding cases without a hearing; and

- judicial meditation.

Another document produced by the President is called an *Agenda for Case Management at Preliminary Hearing*. This provides a useful checklist of the issues and steps to take in the action before the hearing and can be found by typing in 'Employment Tribunal Presidential Guidance General Case Management' into Google.

11.3   Summary of procedure

To some extent the procedure followed will depend on the Respondent's ET3 and what matters have been put in dispute. For example if the Respondent has denied that you were an employee or has alleged that your claim has been brought out of time then the tribunal might consider that this issue should be dealt with at a preliminary hearing (see Chapter 14).

Further information

If the Respondent says that you have not provided sufficient information to enable it to deal with an allegation, the tribunal might require you to provide further details of that allegation. This procedure is considered in more detail in Chapter 13.

Amending the claim

If the Respondent says that you have made some mistake either about the correct name of the Respondent or some mistake of fact in your details of the claim as set out in section 8.2 of the ET1 you might want to apply to amend the ET1 to correct the mistake (see Chapter 12).

Striking out

It might be the case that the tribunal judge, having looked at both the ET1 and the ET3, decides that either the claim or the response is so weak that the matter should be listed for hearing to consider whether the claim or response should be struck out;

or in the case of the claim whether a deposit order should be made (see Chapter 14).

If you are the Claimant and, having read the ET3, consider that it does not put forward any real defence to your claim you can apply to have the response struck out. This will not be appropriate if you are merely disputing the facts put forward by the Respondent because the tribunal will not normally decide factual disputes at a preliminary stage - it would need to hear evidence from both sides. But if for example the Respondent accepts that it dismissed you for gross misconduct without conducting any disciplinary hearing and gives no explanation for this failure you might well consider applying to have the response struck out.

It is far more common for the Respondent to make an application to have the claim struck out or that a deposit order be made against the Claimant on the basis that the claim has no real prospects of success (see Chapter 14).

Preliminary hearing

A preliminary hearing is a hearing which is conducted by an Employment Judge after the ET3 has been filed by the Respondent but before the final hearing. At this hearing the Employment Judge will conduct a preliminary consideration of the claim and can make directions for various steps to be taken before the final hearing. If the claim includes a claim for discrimination or protected disclosure the Employment Judge considering the papers will normally set the case down for a preliminary hearing to clarify the issues and make appropriate directions. If this is the case the tribunal will send each party a copy of a questionnaire called *Agenda for Case Management at Preliminary Hearing*. This is a way of summarising the issues between the parties for the benefit of the Judge conducting the preliminary hearing. You will need to fill out this form and send a copy to the other side and to the tribunal before the hearing.

If there is an application to strike out a claim or a response, or for a deposit to be paid, the case will be listed for a preliminary hearing. This might be either dealt with on the telephone or heard at an employment tribunal. The procedure for such a hearing is considered in detail in Chapter 14.

Judicial assessment

This is a procedure introduced to try to encourage the parties to resolve their dispute by agreement. At the preliminary hearing the Employment Judge will provide an assessment of the strengths and weaknesses of each side's case, as well as the risk involved. This will only occur where both parties agree to it. If you go to the Employment Cases Update website there is a helpful note on Judicial Assessments with a link to the Presidential Guidance. The procedure for judicial assessments is considered in more detail in Chapter 14 on Preliminary hearings.

Judicial mediation

Judicial mediation is a process where both parties attend the employment tribunal, without their witnesses, and an Employment Judge will act as a mediator and try to encourage the parties to settle their dispute. The procedure for judicial mediation is considered in more detail in Chapter 14 on Preliminary hearings.

Further information about the response

It might be the case that, having read through the ET3, you consider that you want further details of the response, in which case you should set out a list of questions to ask the Respondent. This is not an opportunity to dispute facts or allegations in the ET3 but to ask for more detail about matters that they have included. For example, if they mention a particular letter without referring to the date you can ask them for the date of the letter and who sent it.

Directions

When the tribunal judge has read the ET1 and the ET3 and does not consider that any further clarification of the claim or the response is required or that the case needs to be set down for a preliminary hearing, he will make directions for the steps to be taken before the hearing.

"Directions" are orders that a tribunal judge gives for the procedural steps that each side must take to ensure that all the appropriate evidence is available for the hearing. The usual directions will include:

- disclosure of relevant documents by a specified date;

- Claimant to provide the Respondent with a schedule of damages claimed;

- witness statements to be exchanged (in straightforward cases this will often be a week before the hearing);

- preparation of a bundle of relevant documents;

- hearing date with a time estimate i.e. one day or two days.

Disclosure

This means showing the other party all those documents that you have which you consider to be relevant to the case to be heard by the tribunal. This includes any documents which help your case but also those documents which do not help your case. You must not conceal these just because you consider that they are damaging to your case.

In most cases it is the Respondent employer who will have most of the relevant documents but it is equally important for the Claimant employee to disclose any relevant documents that he has. If you turn up on the day of the tribunal hearing with a document that you want the judge to see but have failed to disclose this document to the other side this is likely to cause problems. You might find that the judge will refuse to allow it in as evidence or the other side might say that they need a postponement of the hearing to deal with the points raised in this document. You might also have to pay any costs wasted as a result of this postponement (see Chapter 15 for a more detailed consideration of disclosure).

If you have received the other side's list of documents and believe that there are documents missing from this list you can contact the other side and ask for these documents to be produced. If they say they do not have the documents, or say they do not exist or refuse to disclose the documents and you have good reason to believe that they do have them and they are important to your case, then you can apply to the tribunal for an order that the documents be disclosed.

Before the hearing all the relevant documents will be gathered together into a bundle of documents, which each party and the tribunal judge will have at the hearing.

Schedule of loss

In most cases the Claimant will be asked to produce a schedule of loss. This is a document setting out what damages he is claiming and how the figures are calculated. In a complicated case involving different types of claim the Respondent might be asked to produce a counter-schedule setting out which of the Claimant's figures are accepted and which are disputed and the basis on which they are disputed (see Chapter 16 for a more detailed consideration of schedules of loss).

Witness statement

Each side will be required to draw up a statement for every witness they wish to call at the tribunal hearing. These witness statements are exchanged with the other side, normally a week before the hearing, but sometimes earlier than that. If you have not sent the other party a copy of the statements for witnesses you want to call then it is unlikely that the tribunal judge will allow that witness to give evidence, or the hearing might have to be postponed with you paying any wasted costs (see Chapter 18 for a more detailed consideration of witness statements).

The hearing

The case will be listed to be heard on a specified day at the stated employment tribunal. People unfamiliar with employment tribunals are often surprised at how much longer the hearing takes than they expect. A very short case might be listed for half a day but even with two witnesses, one for the Claimant and one for the

Respondent, a case might well take one day. If there are more than about four witnesses or the evidence from the Claimant or the Respondent is particularly involved the case might well be listed for more than one day. You will need to make sure that any witnesses you wish to call are available for the day listed for the hearing

See Chapter 20 for a more detailed consideration of the hearing.

Chapter 12

Amending a claim

12.1   What is an amendment?

An "amendment" is the technical legal term for making a change or an alteration in a document, including making an addition or removing part of the document. It can also include adding or removing a party to the claim - I will consider this at the end of the chapter.

Once you have sent your ET1 to the tribunal you cannot change what you have put in this document without the permission of the tribunal. Tribunals have a general power (or "discretion") to allow a Claimant to make changes or amendments to their ET1 but whether they will allow this depends on a number of factors, most importantly how significant the change is. The tribunal will also consider whether the change will cause prejudice or difficulty to the other side and take into account when the request to make the change is made.

12.2   Guidance document on amendments

If you go to the Presidential Guidance on General Case Management you will find Guidance Note 1 on *Amendment of the Claim and Response including adding and removing parties*. This is a helpful guide to making amendments to the claim or response in the employment tribunal and also deals with adding or removing a party to the claim.

This guidance states that the tribunal can allow amendments but generally will only do so after careful consideration and taking into account the views of the other party in the case.

12.3   Time limit

There is no time limit to making an amendment and it can even be made during the course of the hearing but the later the date is, particularly if it is after the hearing has begun, the less likely it is the tribunal will allow the change to be made.

Where you are trying to introduce a new claim which is not connected to the original claim in your ET1 you will have to satisfy the tribunal that you have complied with the rule relating to time limits for bringing a claim (see Chapter 7).

12.4   Types of amendment

The application to amend may cover a variety of different matters; it might include small changes such as correcting a typing error, or adding a word or words that have been missed out. It might include some changes to the facts that have been included, which make no difference to the allegations you have made against the Respondent. Where the changes are minor it is unlikely that the Respondent will object to them and it is likely that the tribunal will allow the change to be made.

If you do make a change to a fact in your ET1 you must be aware that you can be asked about this by the Respondent or their representative at the hearing when you are cross-examined by them. It might be suggested that because you have changed this fact you are not sure about it and therefore the tribunal should not trust your memory of the incident. It is for this reason that it is so important to make sure that the facts you include in your ET1 are accurate and that you do not need to change them at a later date.

12.5   Substantial changes

If the change you are asking for is substantial but the Respondent does not object the tribunal will normally allow the change. It will be in those circumstances where the Respondent *does* object to the change, or where the change has the effect of bringing in a new claim, that the tribunal will normally arrange a hearing so that you have the opportunity to explain why you need to make the change and the Respondent has the opportunity to explain why they are objecting to the change being made.

When deciding whether to allow the change or not the tribunal will take account of all the circumstances. The tribunal will have to balance the problems that you would be caused if the change was not allowed against the problems that the Respondent would have if the change was allowed.

12.6   Categories of amendment

If it is not a minor change your amendment is likely to fall into one of two categories, which will affect the way the application to make an amendment is treated by the tribunal. It is important to appreciate which category your amendment will be likely to fall into because if it is the second category, which is introducing a new claim not connected to the original claim, you will have to satisfy the tribunal that you have complied with the rule relating to time limits for bringing a claim (see Chapter 7). If you are outside the time limit you will have to get the tribunal's permission to make the change even if the Respondent agrees to it.

First category

This is where you are not seeking to alter the basis on which you are making an existing claim, and such a change would not be affected by the rule relating to time limits. An example of this type of change is where you have claimed unfair dismissal but are seeking to change the way, or add an additional way, you say the dismissal was unfair. You might want to add a claim that the dismissal was also unfair because the Respondent failed to advise you that you could appeal the decision to dismiss you.

If the Respondent objects to the change being made you will have to satisfy the tribunal that in all the circumstances it is fair to allow the change. The three main points you will need to deal with are:

- why you did not include the claim in your original ET1;

- why you would be prejudiced if the tribunal did not allow the claim; and

- why the Respondent would not be put to a disadvantage if the change was allowed.

Re-labelling

This first category also includes amendments where you seeking to add or substitute a new cause of action or claim but one which is linked to or arises out of the same facts as you have already included in your existing claim. This would be regarded as putting a new label on a claim that has already been included. For example, if you claimed unfair dismissal but then apply to include a claim for a redundancy payment, this would normally be regarded as a different type of claim but based on the same facts that you had already included in your ET1. Again if the Respondent objects to the amendment you will have to deal with the three main points set out above.

It can be more difficult to add or change a claim for unfair dismissal to one for discrimination arising out of the same facts or alternatively adding or changing a discrimination claim to one of unfair dismissal. If the facts are essentially the same and there has been reference to the protected characteristic (see Chapter 4) in the ET1 but the box claiming discrimination in the ET1 form has not been ticked, the tribunal might allow an amendment, but you will have to show that the Respondent has not been prejudiced by such a change. The longer you have delayed in making your application to amend the ET1 the more difficult it will be to persuade the tribunal that such an amendment is fair.

Second category (new claim based on new facts)

The second category is when you are seeking to add or amend a new head of claim which is not based on the facts set out in the ET1 and is unconnected with the existing claim. In this case you will have to satisfy the rules relating to time limits for bringing a claim. For example, if the new claim is based on an act of discrimination which occurred more than three months earlier you will have to satisfy the tribunal that it is just and equitable to allow you to bring in a new claim outside the three month time limit. If your amendment has the effect of bringing in a new claim for unfair dismissal you will have to persuade the tribunal that it was not reasonably practicable to present this claim within the three month time limit.

The courts have held that a claim for indirect discrimination is a different type of unlawful act from a claim for direct discrimination (see Chapter 4) and you would therefore have to satisfy the rules relating to time limits. The same applies to adding a claim for victimisation to an existing claim for discrimination.

In addition you will have to satisfy the tribunal that it is fair and equitable to allow the change. As with the other category of amendment you will need to explain why you did not include the claim in your original ET1, why you would be prejudiced if the tribunal did not allow the change and why the Respondent would not be put to a disadvantage if the change was allowed.

12.7 Adding or substituting a new Respondent

Where you have brought a claim and then discovered that the Respondent you have named in the ET1 was not correct for some reason, for example because you were employed by a subsidiary company, you will need to apply to substitute the named Respondent for the correct one.

Under rule 37 Schedule 1 of the 2013 Employment Tribunal Regulations the tribunal may add any person as a party by way of substitution or otherwise if it appears that there are issues between that person and the existing parties, which is in the interests of justice to have determined. The tribunal may remove any party apparently wrongly included.

What this means is that the tribunal can add a party to the proceedings in addition to the existing parties or it can substitute an existing party for a new party. It can also remove a party who appears to have been wrongly included in the proceedings.

The tribunal will only allow such a change if certain conditions are met. These include satisfying the tribunal that the ET1 was otherwise correctly completed and submitted in time. If so the tribunal has a discretion whether to allow the change. You will need to satisfy the tribunal that putting down the wrong name was a genuine mistake. You will have to explain how the mistake occurred. The tribunal will also need to be satisfied that no prejudice would be caused to the new Respondent by allowing the change.

It is worth noting that even if you are applying to make the substitution outside the three month time limit you will not have to comply with the rules relating to late claims so long as you presented your ET1 in time, even though it named an incorrect Respondent.

Chapter 13

Additional information

An employment judge can order that a party provide further information or detail about their claim or their response (Employment Tribunal Rules 2013 Schedule 1 rule 10(2)(b)). A judge can do this either on his own initiative or following an application by the other party.

13.1   Additional information of the ET1

When you submit your ET1 to the tribunal it will be considered by an employment judge. The purpose of this is to confirm that the required details have been included, and also to check whether time limits or employee status are likely to be an issue that the tribunal will have to consider. The judge will also look to see whether you have included facts which support the allegations made. For example, if you have merely stated that you were unfairly dismissed without providing any detail of the way in which you think that the dismissal was unfair, then it is likely that the judge will ask you to provide details or further details of the facts you rely on.

If you state in your ET1 that throughout your employment you were subjected to comments that were discriminatory without giving any further details the judge might well ask you to provide a list of the remarks made, who made these remarks and when and where they were made.

If you state in your ET1 that you were dismissed because you made a protected disclosure without giving further details the judge is likely to ask you to provide information as to who you made the disclosure to, when and where you made the disclosure and what the subject of the disclosure was.

Even if the judge does not require further particulars of your ET1 the Respondent can apply to the tribunal for an order that you provide further details of the ET1. This will normally be requested on the basis that the Respondent is unable to respond to the allegations unless he is provided with them.

13.2   Additional information of the ET3

It is not sufficient for a Respondent merely to deny the claim that has been brought against him - he must provide details in his ET3 of the basis on which he is seeking to resist the claim.

If it appears to a tribunal judge, on reading through the ET3, that it contains inadequate details of your case he can ask you to provide further information. For example, it would not be sufficient just to say that the Claimant was dismissed for gross misconduct without specifying what the acts of gross misconduct were that you are relying on.

13.3   Importance of compliance

If the judge has made an order for you to provide certain information by a certain date, whether you are bringing a claim or responding to it, it is important that you make every effort to comply by the date given. If it becomes clear that you are going to have difficulty complying with the order by the date given you must contact the tribunal as soon as you become aware and ask for more time setting out the problems you are having complying with the order. Do not wait until the date has passed before contacting the tribunal because by then you will be in breach of the order and the tribunal may have already made certain sanctions against you.

There are various steps that a judge can take against a party who fails to comply with an order, the most serious of which are to strike out the claim or the response.

13.4   Written answers

An employment judge can order that a party provide further information or detail about their claim or their response (Employment Tribunal Rules 2013 Schedule 1 rule 10(2)(f)). A judge can do this either on his own initiative or following an application by the other party.

Until 6ᵗʰ April 2014 there was provision for a Claimant in a discrimination cases or an employee considering bringing a discrimination case to serve a questionnaire on their employer. This provision has now been removed but there remains a general right of a Claimant or a Respondent to ask questions of the other party. If that party does not answer the questions voluntarily the person asking the questions can write to the tribunal and ask that the tribunal make an order that the questions be answered. The tribunal will only agree to such an order if it considers that the questions are relevant to the issues in the case and are necessary for a fair disposal of the trial.

An employee, or even a job applicant who has not brought a claim but is considering doing so, can put questions to their employer if they consider that they have been discriminated against. The employer does not have to respond to these but the danger is that, if he does not, then a claim will be brought against him and the same questions will be put in a tribunal order. The benefit to the employer is that, if he does provide answers to questions, it might be that he will be able to satisfy the employee that there were good reasons for the decision made and it was not based on discrimination.

If the employee in a discrimination case, having put questions to his employer, is then singled out and subjected to some detriment because of this then he would be able to bring a claim of victimisation (see Chapter 4).

13.5   ACAS Guide

There is an ACAS Guide to *Asking and Responding to Questions of Discrimination in the Work Place*. This sets out useful information for an employee as to how to go about putting questions to his employer and the sort of wording that would be appropriate. It also provides guidance to an employer as to the benefits of answering questions and some tips about how the answers should be worded.

Now that the discrimination questionnaires have been abolished I suspect that this power to request written answers to questions will be used far more frequently. It remains to be seen whether tribunal judges will allow the same extent of questions, in particular regarding the race or sex of other employees or whether they were disabled and how they have been treated e.g. promoted, demoted or dismissed as would have been allowed in a discrimination questionnaire.

Chapter 14

Preliminary hearings

14.1   What is a preliminary hearing?

A "preliminary hearing" is a hearing conducted by an employment tribunal judge to deal with procedural matters before the final hearing takes place. The way the tribunal deals with these procedural matters is called "case management" and the orders or directions that a tribunal makes in respect of the procedural matters are referred to as "case management orders" or "directions".

When the Employment Judge considers the ET1 and ET3 he will decide if the case needs to be set down for a telephone hearing or whether it can be listed for a final hearing with standard directions being provided. If the case is a wages act claim or a straightforward unfair dismissal claim then the Judge will provide standard directions (see section 14.13) and have the case listed for a one hour or a one day trial. If the case includes a claim for discrimination or protected disclosure then the Judge will normally consider that a preliminary hearing will be appropriate - in these cases the tribunal will send to each party a questionnaire entitled *Agenda for Case Management at Preliminary Hearing*.

The *Agenda for Case Management at Preliminary Hearing* is a way of summarising the issues between the parties for the benefit of the Judge conducting the preliminary hearing. You will need to fill out this form and send a copy both to the other side and to the tribunal before the hearing.

This questionnaire deals with a number of points including whether the names of the parties are correct, whether any amendments are needed, whether any additional information is required, what remedy is sought, what the issues between the parties are and whether there are any preliminary issues to be decided. The form also asks about exchange of documents, whether medical evidence will be required (usually only for a disability discrimination case), how many witnesses are likely to be called and when their statements can be exchanged.

If you or any of your witnesses are likely to be on holiday or unavailable for any period over the next 12 months or so you need to specify the dates they will be unavailable so that the hearing is not listed on one of those dates.

Finally this questionnaire form deals with Judicial Assessment and Judicial Mediation, which I consider in further detail below (see sections 14.14 and 14.15).

When you have filled out the Agenda send a copy both to the other side and to the tribunal, and remember to keep a copy for yourself.

There are a variety of matters that can be dealt with at a preliminary hearing, including whether the tribunal has the legal power (or "jurisdiction") to hear the case. The most common matters which will be dealt with on this basis are whether the claim has been brought in time; in unfair dismissal cases, whether the Claimant was in fact an employee of the Respondent or whether he was self-employed; and, if he was employed, whether he had been employed for two years or whether it was an allegation of automatic unfair dismissal (which does not require a qualifying period).

The tribunal will usually decide these issues before letting the claim go ahead to a final hearing because if these points are decided in favour of the Respondent and against the Claimant, that will be the end of the case and there would be no need to have a final hearing.

A tribunal will usually hear some evidence on these points, but if the issue is whether the claim has been brought within the required time limit the tribunal will often only need to hear evidence from the Claimant. If the issue is whether the Claimant was an employee or self-employed, there will normally be a witness or witnesses for both the Claimant and Respondent dealing with this but the evidence will be restricted to this narrow issue.

14.2   Striking out and deposit orders

Another reason why a preliminary hearing might be ordered is that, having looked at the ET1, the judge might consider that the claim is so weak there should be a hearing to decide if the claim should be struck out or a deposit order made. To "strike out a claim" means to dismiss it without a full trial or hearing the evidence. Alternatively the judge might consider that the ET3 is so weak that he is considering striking it out or making a deposit order.

There are two orders a tribunal judge can make relating to a weak claim;

- If he considers that it has little reasonable prospect of success he can make a deposit order, which means that he can order the Claimant to pay a sum of money, up to a maximum sum of £1,000, if the Claimant wishes to continue his claim;

- If he considers that the claim has no reasonable prospect of success he can strike out the claim.

The same applies to the response;

- If the judge considers that it has little reasonable prospect of success he can make a deposit order, meaning that he can order the Respondent to pay a sum of money, up to a maximum sum of £1,000, if the Respondent wishes to continue to defend the claim.;

- If he considers that the response has no reasonable prospect of success he can strike out the response.

Both sides can apply to the tribunal requesting that a preliminary hearing be held on the basis that the other side's case is so weak that it should be struck out or a deposit order made.

14.3   Notice of preliminary hearing

When you receive a copy of the notice from the tribunal providing the date for the preliminary hearing the notice will also explain the reason for the hearing being held. If it is being held to consider whether to strike out the claim or make a deposit order the notice will say this. The notice will normally say why the judge considers that he feels the case is weak and should be listed for a preliminary hearing.

For example, if your claim is for unfair dismissal for gross misconduct and you are not denying the misconduct but claim that you should not have been dismissed, and the Respondent has explained in his ET3 that you were already on a final written warning for similar misconduct, a judge reading the papers might consider that you have little or no reasonable prospects of succeeding in your claim and set the case down for a preliminary hearing.

14.4   Respondent's application

If you are responding to a claim and consider that for some reason the claim is misconceived, has been wrongly brought or has little or no prospect of success, you can state this in your ET3 when setting out the facts you rely on in your response to the claim. A claim is said to be "misconceived" if the Claimant has not understood some legal basis on which he can bring a claim. For example, to bring a claim for unfair dismissal when you have been employed for less than two years and are not claiming automatic unfair dismissal (see Chapter 3), the claim would be regarded as misconceived because you have no legal right to bring the claim.

Alternatively once you have submitted your ET3 you can write to the tribunal and apply for the case to be listed for a preliminary hearing to consider the strength of the claim. You should also explain why you consider the Claimant has little or no prospect of success and that the claim should be struck out or a deposit order made.

14.5   Telephone hearing

It is quite common nowadays for the preliminary hearing to be conducted over the telephone, unless it is likely to be a hearing where the tribunal will need to hear evidence from the parties. If it is to be conducted by telephone the tribunal will give a date and a time when you will need to telephone the number provided. At this given time you will telephone that number and be put through on a conference call to the employment judge and the person representing the other party.

If it has been listed for a telephone hearing and you consider that you will need to call a witness or witnesses then you should contact the tribunal as soon as you get the notice and explain why you do not consider that a telephone hearing would be appropriate. If the tribunal accepts that this is the case it will list the preliminary hearing to take place at the employment tribunal and you will need to attend on the day given.

If the hearing is listed to be heard by telephone make sure you are somewhere where you can comfortably conduct the hearing - do not try to conduct it from your car or from somewhere noisy, because you will need to hear what is said and the judge will need to hear what you say. Ideally you will telephone from somewhere quiet where there are no distractions and you will have the papers set out on the desk or table before you. Remember that you will probably need to refer to what has been said in the ET1, the ET3 or any other documents the tribunal will have been sent.

14.6   Importance of preparing for the hearing

If you are the Claimant and receive a notice setting the case down for a preliminary hearing it is extremely important that you prepare fully for it, particularly if the judge has listed the case for such a hearing. This is because it means that the judge will have taken a view that there are problems with the claim and it will be for you to persuade the judge (which might be the same judge who listed it for hearing or a different judge) that in fact your claim does have reasonable prospects of succeeding. If the Respondent has requested the claim be listed for a preliminary hearing you will still have to persuade a judge that it does have a reasonable prospect of succeeding.

You need to be aware that when the judge initially reviews the case all he will have before him is the ET1 and the ET3 - he will not have any of the other relevant documents in the case nor will he have any witness statements. Therefore he might be making the decision to set the case down for a preliminary hearing on the basis that you have not fully set out or explained your case in your ET1. For this reason it is important that the judge is provided with any documents you rely on before the hearing. Do this by sending a copy of the documents to the judge and the other party explaining the significance of the documents to your case. If you feel you need to explain your case further or to clarify it to make it absolutely clear why you are alleging that you were unfairly dismissed or discriminated against, then you can do this in a statement, which you will need to send to both the tribunal and the other party before the hearing.

Whether it is a telephone hearing or a hearing conducted at the tribunal make sure you have all the papers you need to refer to and that you can put your hand on any document you might need. I find it helpful to keep all the documents in a ring binder and attach a post-it note to the important documents so that they can easily be found. If the judge refers to a document, such as the ET1, which you are unable to find, it is easy to get flustered, not to concentrate on what is being said and therefore unable to answer the point made. If you have to look for a document tell the judge you have not got it to hand and you will need a minute or so to find it; then tell him when you have found it.

Before the hearing make a list of those points you want to make. It is very easy, particularly with a telephone hearing, to forget a particular point that you wanted to make. It is important that you put all your strongest points before the judge at this stage otherwise you risk having the case struck out.

If there is a dispute on the facts then generally the judge will accept that the claim needs to go forward to a full hearing so that the tribunal can hear the evidence from both sides. This is particularly so in discrimination claims where often there will be two different versions of conversations or incidents or the Respondent will deny that a remark or conversation took place. In such cases the judge at the preliminary hearing cannot decide which side's version of events is more likely and therefore the case will be listed for a full hearing.

14.7   Making a deposit order

If the judge considers that the claim or the response has little reasonable prospect of success he can order the Claimant or the Respondent to pay a sum of money, not exceeding £1,000, as a condition of continuing to bring or defend a claim. If the money is not paid within 21 days of the order the claim or response will be struck out.

It is far more usual for deposit orders to be made against Claimants than Respondents. There are several reasons for this, including:

- the Claimant chooses whether to bring a claim or not but once a claim is brought the Respondent has to deal with it, and his only choice is to admit the claim or to resist it;

- a claim can be brought for a variety of different reasons - when an employee is dismissed he will often disagree with the reasons given by his employer and look for some other motive or hidden reason behind his dismissal even when the grounds for bringing a claim are weak.

In every case the Claimant will have to prove certain matters to satisfy the legal requirement necessary to succeed in his claim. For example, in an unfair dismissal claim he will need to prove that he was an employee, that he had been an employee for two years or that the dismissal was for an automatically unfair reason and he will need to prove that he was dismissed by his employer. It will then be for the employer to show that the dismissal was for a fair reason. If the employer's case is that the dismissal was for a fair reason it will be for the employee to show that in fact this was not the true reason for the dismissal or that the dismissal was somehow procedurally unfair.

If the judge, on reading the ET1, is doubtful whether the Claimant will succeed on proving one of these required legal elements then he might well make a "deposit order". The test is whether the Claimant has little reasonable prospect of succeeding. The judge will read both the ET1 and the ET3 and any other documents that are sent to him, but for the purpose of considering the strength of the case the ET1 is most important - if the case is weak even in this document then the Claimant will struggle to succeed.

If the Claimant can show that he has a reasonable prospect of proving the legal elements the judge can go on to consider whether the Claimant has a reasonable prospect of proving the facts that are necessary to succeed in his claim. If the judge considers that the facts set out are inconsistent or very unlikely to be true then he might well consider ordering a deposit to be paid, but generally, where there is a dispute of fact, the judge will consider that this is a matter for a full hearing, when the evidence on both sides can be tested in cross-examination. In these circumstances it would not be appropriate to order a deposit to be paid.

It is often the case that the Respondent in the ET3 will dispute the facts set out by the Claimant in their ET1. It is not the place of the judge at this stage to resolve a dispute of facts - this will normally be left for the full hearing. There might be some circumstances where the Respondent is able to provide a document that undermines the Claimant's case and on the basis of this document the judge could conclude that the Claimant has little reasonable prospect of success. For example, if the Claimant said that they had been dismissed but the Respondent said that they had resigned and showed a letter to the judge from the Claimant in which they said they were resigning, a judge might conclude that the Claimant has little prospect of succeeding in a claim of unfair dismissal and either strike the claim out or make a deposit order.

In the case of Hemdan v Ismail and Al-Megraby UKEAT/0021/16/DM the Employment Appeal Tribunal provided some useful guidance regarding deposit orders:

- Where there is a dispute about significant facts then it is unlikely that a deposit order should be made.

- Where a tribunal is minded to make a deposit order it should make enquiries into the claimant's ability to pay.

- The order to pay a deposit must be one that can be complied with. A party without the means to pay should not be ordered to pay a sum they are unlikely to be able to raise.

14.8   Amount of the deposit

If the judge decides that the Claimant or the Respondent has little reasonable prospect of succeeding and that a deposit order is appropriate, the judge will then go on to consider that party's ability to pay a deposit. The judge should only be ordering payment of an amount that the party can afford.

What this means is that you will need to have information about your financial position. If you are saying that you cannot afford to pay anything towards a deposit or only a very small sum, you will need to have those documents showing how much your income is every week or month and how it is spent. You should take your pay slip or, if you are in receipt of benefits, documents showing this; you should take recent bills showing the main expenses like mortgage or rent, gas and electricity, and any recent bank or building society statements or credit card statements.

14.9   Payment of the deposit

You have 21 days from the date of the order in which to pay the deposit, and if you fail to pay within this time your claim or response will be struck out. Payment can be by cheque but you must make sure that this reaches the tribunal by the date required. If possible it would be better to pay by electronic transfer.

If the judge does order a deposit you will need to seriously consider whether to proceed with your claim or with your defence. In the notice ordering a deposit the judge will specify why he considers that a deposit is appropriate. If you proceed with your claim and you lose on this point it is likely that the tribunal will make an order that you pay the Respondent's costs because you will be treated as having acted unreasonably by persisting with your claim. Similarly if you are the Respondent and a deposit order has been made against you and you lose on this point at the final hearing it is likely that a costs order will be made against you. The tribunal does not have to make a costs order and will not if you can convince it that it was reasonable to continue with your claim or defence.

There is power to ask for a reconsideration of the decision to make a cost order and you can ask for an extension of time in making the deposit payment. You will need to set out your reasons for asking for a review or an extension of time. You will also need to serve this application on the other side so that they can make any representations to the tribunal.

14.10   Striking out the claim or response

Schedule 1 Rule 37 of the 2013 Employment Tribunal Regulations deals with striking out a claim or response. The judge can strike out a claim or response at any stage of the proceedings. There are five specified grounds on which a claim or response can be struck out:

(1) When all or part of the claim or response is scandalous, vexatious or has no reasonable prospect of success;

(2) All or part of the claim or response can be struck out on the basis that the manner in which the proceedings have been conducted by or on behalf of the Claimant or Respondent is scandalous, unreasonable or vexatious;

(3) It can strike out a claim which has not been actively pursued;

(4) It can strike out a claim or response for non-compliance with an order or practice direction;

(5) A claim can be struck out if the tribunal considers that it would no longer be possible to have a fair hearing.

Before making a striking out order the tribunal must notify the party against whom it intends to make the order, giving him the opportunity to give reasons why the claim or response should not be struck out.

14.11   Grounds for striking out

Ground 1

The first ground appears to have three separate or different categories - that the claim or response is vexatious, scandalous or without reasonable prospects of success. In practice it is really only the third of these grounds that concerns the tribunals because generally, if a claim is vexatious or scandalous, it will have no reasonable prospects of success.

A vexatious claim

This is one that has no real prospect of success but is brought with the intention of harassing, annoying or embarrassing the Respondent. The same would apply to a response. It can also include a claim where the issues between the parties have already been decided but the Claimant is trying to bring the claim again. A vexatious litigant is someone who brings repeated claims, usually against the same Respondent, which have no merit but are brought just to cause annoyance to the other side.

A scandalous claim

This means one which is abusive or uses deliberately insulting terms to describe the other side. It would be regarded by the tribunal as being a misuse of the right to bring proceedings as it is intended to cause harassment or distress to the other party rather than to make a valid claim.

In practice if you do have a good claim and have been unfairly dismissed or discriminated against it is unlikely that you are going to be deliberately abusive or use foul language in your ET1 to criticise your employer. Equally it is unlikely that your employer will use foul language in their ET3 as this is likely to strengthen the Claimant's case.

Reasonable prospect of success

Where the claim appears from the documents to have a reasonable prospect of succeeding it is unlikely that it will be struck out by a tribunal - the same applies to a response. In such circumstances the tribunal could strike out those parts of the claim which are unnecessarily abusive or derogatory but leave other parts of the claim or response remaining which can then go on to be heard by a tribunal.

In my experience the main test which a tribunal will consider at a preliminary hearing is whether the claim or response has any real prospect of success. Where there is a dispute on the facts between the parties it is unlikely that a judge would strike out the claim or response before a full hearing unless there is some documentary evidence available which shows that the facts being put forward by a party are most unlikely to be correct.

The higher courts have said that discrimination claims and those involving whistle-blowing should not be struck out except in the very clearest of circumstances, since they tend to be fact sensitive and can involve public interest considerations.

Ground 2

The second ground applies where the way in which the case has been conducted either by the party themselves or their legal representative is scandalous, unreasonable or vexatious.

Again it does not seem to me that using the words "scandalous" or "vexatious" really add anything. I think that most tribunals would conclude that if a Claimant or Respondent was acting scandalously or vexatiously in court then they are acting unreasonably.

This rule covers cases where one of the parties conducts the hearing in a disruptive or unruly manner. It can include a situation where one party has tried to threaten or intimidate the other side who are then too frightened to continue with the case. The tribunal will have to consider first whether they find that the unreasonable conduct occurred and then go on to consider whether it would still be possible to have a fair trial. The claim or response should only be struck if the tribunal conclude that a fair trial is not possible. The tribunal must give the party against whom they are considering making the order an opportunity to say why such an order should not be made.

The conduct referred to will normally be behaviour in tribunal hearings but the rule covers any unreasonable behaviour in the way the proceedings are conducted - but again the conduct must be such that a fair trial cannot be possible.

Striking out a claim on such grounds will only be taken as a last resort and normally the tribunal will warn the offending party that if they persist with such behaviour a strike out is likely to be the result. In a case where a Claimant's lay representative accused the tribunal of race discrimination for refusing an adjournment, the Court of Appeal said that the tribunal was wrong to strike out the case on the basis that it had been conducted in a scandalous way. Instead the tribunal should have asked the representative to withdraw his remarks and warn him of the consequences if he did not do so and persisted with them. They should then have considered whether a fair trial was still possible (see *Bennett v London Borough of Southwark* [2002] EWCA Civ 223).

Ground 3

The third ground for striking out a claim is where it is not being actively pursued by the Claimant. What this means is if you have brought a claim and then for whatever reason do not pursue it by taking the appropriate steps to proceed with it the claim can be struck out.

In practice the third ground is likely to overlap with the fourth ground - failing to comply with a tribunal order or practice direction - although this applies to both the Claimant and Respondent.

Ground 4

In any proceedings there are various steps that both parties have to take and these will be set out by the tribunal early in the proceedings in the form of a "directions order". This order will set out the various actions each party has to take, the usual steps including the exchange of any relevant documents and witness statements. If one of the parties fails to comply with the order the other party will normally notify the tribunal who will make an "unless order" (see below). This will state that unless the party in default complies with the order by a stated date their claim or response will be struck out.

Even if a Claimant has not been in breach of any tribunal orders, if he deliberately fails to progress his claim and causes lengthy and inexcusable delays his claim can be struck out. Again a tribunal should only strike out the claim if they are satisfied that it is not possible to have a fair trial. If there is a good reason for the delay then the claim should not be struck out.

In practice one of the main reasons for lengthy delays in proceeding with a claim can be illness, either of the Claimant or of one of the main witnesses on either side. This can happen in cases where the Claimant is claiming disability discrimination under the Equality Act and his disability is an illness or connected with an illness which makes it too difficult for him to progress his claim.

If you face a problem progressing your case because of illness of either yourself or one of your witnesses it is important to let the tribunal know what the position is as soon as possible. You should also provide medical evidence - a letter from your GP should be sufficient but this letter will need to set out what the problem is, how it affects or prevents you from pursuing the claim and how long it is likely to be before you will be able to do so.

If you consider that the other side is unreasonably delaying progress of the case you can write to the tribunal, sending a copy to the other side, setting out your concerns and asking that the tribunal provide a date for the other side to take the next step in the proceedings.

Ground 5 (a fair hearing is no longer possible)

This tends to be catch-all ground and is often used together with one of the other grounds. For example, if the Claimant has delayed in pursuing the claim, the tribunal judge might well consider whether it is still possible to have a fair hearing or whether the delay has made it more difficult for the other party to call the evidence they would want to.

If you are making an application to the tribunal on any one of the first four grounds you can also add the fifth ground if you can show that in some way the other side's behaviour will make it more difficult to have a fair hearing.

14.12   Unless orders

If the tribunal has provided dates for various steps in the proceedings to be done by and other side has failed to comply with a direction, for example it has failed to provide a list of documents by the specified date, you should write to the tribunal informing them of the other party's failure and asking either for an order that the claim or defence be struck out or for an "unless order". An unless order means that the party will be given a new date by which to comply with the order and unless that party does comply the claim or response will be struck out.

If you are served with an unless order it is vitally important that you comply with the terms of the order by the date given, because if you do not your claim or response is automatically struck out. If you know that you will be unable to comply with the order then you must contact the tribunal as soon as you know this, explaining what the problem is, for example if you have not got a document that has been specifically requested. Do not just ignore the order because you have not got the document.

If you need more time to comply with the order, for example because a witness you need to take a statement from is on holiday, write to the tribunal and the other side to explain what the problem is and ask for further time to comply. It is worthwhile providing a date by which you will be able to comply but make sure you give yourself a bit of extra time to allow for unforeseen events. For example, if the witness is returning from holiday on 20th October ask that the date for providing the witness statement be extended to 27th October to allow for any difficulties in obtaining the statement.

If the order is unclear and you are not sure what you need to do to comply with it, for example you are not certain which particular documents are being requested, contact the tribunal and the other side and explain what the problem is, ask for clarification of the order and if necessary further time to comply.

14.13   Other directions

Once a tribunal judge has allowed the claim to proceed he is likely to make other directions to ensure that the case is ready for the final hearing. The usual directions will include:

- disclosure of relevant documents by a specified date;

- Claimant to provide the Respondent with a schedule of damages claimed;

- witness statements to be exchanged (in straightforward cases this will often be a week before the hearing);

- preparation of a bundle of relevant documents;

- hearing date with a time estimate i.e. one day or two days.

I will deal with each of these topics in the following chapters.

14.14   Judicial assessment

This is a free procedure introduced to try to encourage the parties to resolve their dispute by agreement. At the preliminary hearing the Employment Judge will provide an assessment of the strengths and weaknesses of each side's case, as well as the risks involved in continuing with the case and losing. This procedure will only take place where both parties agree to it. If you go to the Employment Cases Update website there is a helpful note on Judicial Assessments with a link to the Presidential Guidance. If you consider that your case might be suitable for judicial assessment and you are interested in judicial assessment then you should indicate this on the *Agenda for Case Management* questionnaire (at boxes 10.1 to 10.4) that you should have sent.

For a litigant in person the judicial assessment is a useful way of getting some judicial feedback as to the strengths and weaknesses of your case. The Judge might point out some problems that you had not considered or equally the Judge might refer to some of the problems that the other side have, which might make them more likely to want to settle the case. The Judge who conducts the judicial assessment will not conduct the hearing of the case. For a litigant in person I consider that there are no real disadvantages in having a judicial assessment and there can be real benefits. And of course it is a free service.

14.15   Judicial mediation

Boxes 10.3 and 10.4 on the *Agenda for Case Management* questionnaire refer to Judicial Mediation and ask whether you consider your case to be suitable for judicial mediation and whether you are interested in this.

Judicial mediation is also a free service (it used to cost £600 before tribunal fees were abolished) where both parties attend the employment tribunal, without their witnesses, and an Employment Judge tries to encourage the parties to settle their dispute. You and the Respondent's representative will be provided with separate rooms at the tribunal and the Employment Judge will visit each of you in turn, asking what you want from the tribunal process and how much you expect to be awarded if you are successful on all your claims. The Judge might point out certain problems with your case if these are evident or comment if he considers that your expectations are unrealistic. He will carry out a similar exercise with the other side. The Judge might encourage you to reduce the amount you are looking for and equally might encourage the other side to increase any offer they have made. The purpose is to try to get both parties to agree on a figure which they will both accept in settlement of the claim.

It is only worth entering into a mediation if you are prepared to negotiate on the amount you are seeking to recover. Equally if the Respondent is not prepared to consider offering any sum in trying to settle the case or only to offer an unrealistic figure then there would be no benefit in having a judicial mediation.

As with judicial assessments I consider that for a litigant in person there are no real disadvantages in having a judicial mediation and there can be real benefits, especially if it means that the case settles without the need for preparing for and undergoing a trial.

Chapter 15

Disclosure of documents

15.1   What is disclosure?

One of the usual requirements of both the Claimant and the Respondent in employment tribunal cases is to provide the other side with copies of all the documents they have which are relevant to the case. This is referred to as "disclosure" because the documents are being disclosed or shown to the other side.

Under rule 31 Schedule 1 of the Employment Tribunal Regulations 2013 a tribunal may order any person to disclose documents of information to a party (by providing photocopies or otherwise) or to allow a party to inspect such material as might be ordered by a County Court.

If you go to the Presidential Guidance on General Case Management you will find Guidance Note 2 on *Disclosure of Documents and Preparing Hearing Bundles.*

When a tribunal judge makes a case management order this will normally include an order for disclosure of documents. A common form of wording of such an order is:

> *"By 4.00pm on 20ᵗʰ October 2017 the parties must disclose to each other the documents in their control or possession that are relevant to any matter in the case"*

This disclosure can be done by sending photocopies of the documents to the other side. This will usually include any document relating to remedy as well as to liability. If you are sending photocopies of documents in your possession make sure these are "clean" copies; that is not documents that you have written comments on.

15.2   What documents should be disclosed?

In respect of liability the guidance document says that relevant documents may include those which record events in the employment history, for example a letter of appointment, contract of employment, notes of significant meetings such as disciplinary interviews, and a resignation or dismissal letter.

It is not only paper documents that must be disclosed - all relevant emails must also be disclosed. Although this will mainly affect the Respondent employer it also applies to the Claimant employee, who will need to provide disclosure of all relevant emails he might have on his computer whether at home or at work.

If you are a Claimant and you are aware that there is relevant email correspondence make sure that they have all been disclosed by the Respondent. If there is an email replying to a previous email make sure you have a copy of the earlier one. If there is an email with a query make sure you have a copy of the answering email. Text messages are also disclosable documents if these have been retained.

In respect of remedy the Claimant will want to provide any documents relating to his attempts to obtain a new job, while the Respondent might want to send documents such as newspapers showing suitable jobs being advertised.

The sort of documents that will be relevant in unfair dismissal cases will be:

- the contract of employment;

- the terms and conditions of employment, including any disciplinary policy;

- any documents relating to disciplinary meetings or hearings, including notes of any meetings or hearings;

- any documents relating to grievance meetings;

- the dismissal letter;

- any appeal letter;

- any previous disciplinary findings against the employee, particularly if they were still live and taken into account in the dismissal;

- any redundancy selection criteria;

- any documents relating to redundancy meetings;

- any appraisal documents if these were relevant to the redundancy selection;

- the Claimant's scores on the selection document;

- other employee's scores on the selection document;

- any documents relating to relevant alternative positions being advertised;

- in discrimination cases any documents relating to details of the employment or promotion of employees with the relevant protected characteristic that is sex, race, disability or age.

15.3   Sanction for failing to disclose documents

The tribunal has the sanction of striking out the claim or response of the party who fails to comply with the order to disclose documents, if this failure means that a fair trial cannot take place.

If you turn up to the tribunal hearing with a document which has not been disclosed, you might find that the judge will refuse to look at it unless you have a good explanation for failing to show it to the other side at the appropriate time. Even if the judge does allow the document in, the other side might need a postponement to deal with it, for example if it means calling another witness, and you might have to pay the costs of the adjournment.

15.4   Documents held by a third party

Where relevant documents are in the possession of someone or some organisation which is not a party in the case it is possible to apply to the tribunal for an order that this party provide disclosure of these documents. To succeed in such an application you will need to persuade the tribunal that these documents are necessary to dispose fairly of the case.

15.5   Standard disclosure

To start with the order for disclosure will be "standard disclosure". This will consist only of those documents that are relevant to the issues in the case. The test for what is relevant is any document that the party relies on in support of their case or any document that might support or assist the other party's case. This means relevant to both issues of the claim itself and as to the amount of damages. You cannot withhold a document because you know that it is damaging to your case.

15.6   Specific disclosure

If there are specific documents that you know exist, that are in the possession of the other party and have not been disclosed, and you consider them relevant to the issues you can ask for "specific disclosure" of these documents. This will also apply to any document mentioned in either the ET1 or ET3 or referred to by witnesses in their witness statement.

You should write to the other side and ask them to provide you with a copy of this document. If they refuse or do not answer your letter you will need to contact the tribunal for an order for specific disclosure. You will need to explain why you consider it relevant, why you think it is in the possession of the other side and explain that they have refused to provide you with a copy of it. As with orders against third parties the test will be whether the document is necessary to dispose fairly of the case.

A party is required to disclose documents that are within his control. This means not just documents that you have in your possession but also any relevant documents that someone else is keeping for you, which you can ask to be returned to you.

Each side must make a reasonable search for any relevant documents.

15.7   The overriding objective

The duty to provide disclosure of documents is subject to the overriding objective to enable the tribunal to deal with the case justly. The "overriding objective" means the basic principles that the tribunal must have regard to when considering an application. The rules give some further assistance as to what "dealing with a case justly" means - the tribunal must ensure both parties are on an equal footing, the case should be dealt with in ways which are proportionate to the complexity and importance of the issues and the case should be dealt with expeditiously and fairly and saving expense.

To put the parties on an equal footing includes preventing one party from using its superior financial resources to conduct the litigation in a way that puts the other party at a significant disadvantage. For example if, in a case of disability discrimination, the court had ordered a joint expert (this is a single expert witness who is jointly instructed by both the parties) but the Claimant could not afford to pay half his fees, the tribunal might order that his fees be paid in such proportion as the Claimant could afford, so that the Respondent would pay the majority. Another example is that, when preparing the bundle of documents for the hearing, it will be normal for the tribunal to order that the Respondent prepare this bundle because most employers will have the facility to photocopy documents.

Dealing with the case expeditiously means avoiding any unnecessary delays in proceeding with the case.

Dealing with the case in a way which is proportionate to the complexity and importance of the issues in the case means that the cost of taking a particular step in the case must not be so expensive or time consuming that it outweighs the benefit. For example, the tribunal might not agree to an order for disclosure of thousands of documents, which, although relevant to the claim, might only affect a small part of it. In this case the tribunal might restrict the disclosure to a small number of the more important of these documents.

15.8   Confidential documents

Where documents contain confidential information they must still be disclosed if they are relevant to the issues in the case but those parts that are confidential can be blanked out (or "redacted"). For example, if the Respondent has obtained witness statements from other employees but has promised those employees that their names will be kept secret then their names can be blanked out from the witness statements. If the other party objects to this the tribunal would have to decide whether the blanking out causes any unfairness.

It might be the case that even blanking out the names of the witnesses would not prevent them from being identified and the Respondent would not want to disclose the statement at all. In such circumstances the Respondent would have to make an application to the tribunal, explain the position and ask the tribunal that they be allowed not to disclose these statements. The statements would have to be shown to the tribunal and not to the Claimant, then the tribunal would have to assess the importance of the statements, and decide whether there could be a fair trial if the statements were not disclosed or what the possible consequences of disclosing the statements might be.

15.9   Privileged documents

There are some documents that do not have to be disclosed - these are documents that are called "privileged". All communications between a party and his legal advisor are subject to this privilege and need not be disclosed. The same applies to all communications between a party, his legal advisors and a third person as long as the communication or document has been made with reference to existing or planned litigation.

There is another category of documents that need not be disclosed - these are documents where disclosure would damage the public interest.

Chapter 16

Schedule of loss

16.1   What is a schedule of loss?

The schedule of loss is a document setting out the different claims that the Claimant is making, putting a figure to the amount claimed and showing how the figure is calculated.

As part of the preparation for the hearing the employment tribunal giving directions will often include a direction that the Claimant serve a schedule of loss on the Respondent by a certain date.

A normal order will be as follows:

> *No later than 4.00pm on 21ˢᵗ October 2017 the Claimant will provide the Respondent with a schedule of loss, which sets out the compensation claimed and how these sums have been calculated.*

When you are drawing up a schedule of loss you will need to set out the amount you will be asking the tribunal to award for the various parts of your claim.

I have set out a model schedule of loss at Appendix B.

16.2   Form of the schedule of loss

This document will need to have a heading with the name of the tribunal dealing with the case and the claim number. This is important because it will enable the tribunal to identify which case the schedule belongs to when it is sent to the tribunal. You will then need to add your name and the name of the Respondent. The document will be titled "Schedule of Loss". It is worth putting the date of the schedule on it so that if you change or update the schedule at a later date you will know immediately which is the most recent version.

16.3   Unfair dismissal claim

If you are claiming unfair dismissal your claim will be divided into a basic award and a compensatory award.

The basic award is calculated by reference to the number of years you have been employed by the Respondent and your age.

The compensatory award covers loss of earnings and various other claims.

If you have been dismissed without notice or payment in lieu of notice (sometimes called "PILON"), you can claim notice pay.

If your claim is discrimination in addition to unfair dismissal there will be a claim for injury to feelings.

If you are still employed and are claiming discrimination there will be no basic award but you can claim for injury to feelings and any other loss.

In the first part of the schedule it is helpful to set out the various relevant dates and figures which will form the basis of the calculations in your Schedule. You should set out the following information:

- The date on which your employment started and the date on which it terminated (if applicable);

- The number of full years you were employed;

- Your date of birth;

- Your gross annual salary;

- Your net annual salary;

- Your net weekly salary;

- Your employer's weekly pension contribution (if any).

If you have a new job you will need to set out:

- The date the new job started;

- Your new net weekly salary

16.4   Basic award

You should set out the date on which your employment started and the date on which it finished. This second date is called the "effective date of termination" (or EDT). The amount of the basic award is calculated on the basis of the number of full years of your employment with the Respondent. For example, if you started work on 1st January 2008 but were summarily dismissed on 20th December 2017 you will only have 9 full qualifying years. If you were dismissed on 2nd January 2018 you would have 10 qualifying years.

The maximum number of qualifying years is 20 even if you have been employed by the Respondent for more than 20 years.

The calculation of the basic award also takes into account your age at the date your employment finished. It is calculated by taking one week's gross pay and multiplying it by the number of full years you have been employed between the age of 22 and 40. It is multiplied by 1.5 weeks gross pay for each full year over the age of 41. The figure is half a week's pay under the age of 22.

So for example if you worked from 1ˢᵗ January 2004 to 7ᵗʰ July 2014 you would have 10 years' qualifying employment. If your 41ˢᵗ birthday was on 6ᵗʰ June 2009 then for 5 of these years (from 1ˢᵗ January 2004 to 6ᵗʰ June 2009) you would have been under 41 years old and for 5 of these years (between 6ᵗʰ June 2009 and 7ᵗʰ July 2014) you would have been over 41. In this case to calculate the basic award you would multiply one week's salary by 5 for the first 5 years employment and then 1.5 weeks salary by 5 for the second five years' employment.

If your gross weekly salary was £200 the basic award would be £2,500 (£200 x 5 = £1,000 plus £300 x 5 = £1,500).

In this example if your 41ˢᵗ birthday was after the 7ᵗʰ July 2014, say on 7ᵗʰ October 2009, the position would be different because you would have only worked for four full years over the age of 41 (from 7ᵗʰ October 2009 to 7ᵗʰ July 2014). In this case your basic award would be based on 6 years at one week's salary and four years at 1.5 weeks salary.

If your gross weekly salary was £200 the award would be £2,400 (£200 x 6 = £1,200 plus £300 x 4 = £1,200).

16.5   A "week's pay"

The amount of a week's pay is subject to a cap, which means the maximum amount that can be used in the calculation. The current cap is £538, and this figure is usually increased by a small amount each year. This figure of £538 has been in place since 6ᵗʰ April 2020, and before that it was £525. You can check what the figure is by going to ukpracticallaw.com, which has a helpful chart called "Current rates and limits for Employment Lawyers".

What this means is that you will have to limit your one week's pay to this figure of £538 even if you are earning more than this. This figure will not usually include overtime or bonuses but will include commission if this is part of your normal week's pay.

It is worth bearing in mind that if you received redundancy pay, this is calculated in the same way as the basic award and therefore you will not receive a basic award in addition to your redundancy pay.

The fact that you have found a new job after you have been dismissed by the Respondent does not affect your right to a basic award - you can still claim a basic award even if you started a new job on the same salary or a higher salary the day after you were dismissed.

16.6   Notice pay

If you were dismissed for gross misconduct you will normally have been dismissed summarily without any notice or notice pay. In these circumstances you can claim notice pay. This is something you are entitled to under your contract of employment and therefore the claim is for breach of contract.

There will normally be a provision regarding notice in the contract of employment but even if there is not you are entitled to a minimum period of notice as set out in section 86 of the Employment Rights Act 1996. This is not less than one week's notice if you have been employed for at least two years and then at least one week's notice for each year of employment for more than two years.

The amount of notice pay is based on the amount you would have been paid if you had been allowed to continue working until the end of your notice period. Therefore it will be a net sum, after deduction of tax and national insurance. It will include any bonuses, commission, overtime that you would have received in this period, and it will also include the monetary value of any benefits in kind, i.e. company car, use of company mobile telephone, healthcare etc.

16.7   Compensatory award

The compensatory award covers any sums that you have lost as a result of being unfairly dismissed or having been discriminated against.

The first element will normally be past loss of earnings.

This is based on your net loss of earnings between the date of dismissal and the date on which you are drawing up the schedule of loss. As with notice pay the figure will include any bonuses, commission, or overtime that you would have received in this period, and it will also include the monetary value of any benefits in kind.

When including a claim for benefits in kind it is helpful to show what figure you have taken for these. Thus if it is a company car you should set out how much in weekly or monthly figures you consider this benefit was worth to you.

If you started a new job the day after you were dismissed, earning the same or a higher salary, and you are unlikely to lose this job in the near future, then you will not be entitled to loss of earnings as you will not have incurred any loss. If you are paid less in your new job you can claim the difference between your new salary and your old salary.

If you have started a new job or have done some paid employment since you were dismissed you will need to set out your earnings from this work because the amount you are awarded will be based on the difference between the amount you would have earned if you had not been dismissed and the amount you received from your new job.

Since 29th July 2013 the maximum award is limited to the "statutory cap" or 52 weeks gross pay, whichever is the lowest. The statutory cap is currently £88,519 for any dismissal on or after 6th April 2020. So if your gross annual salary is £25,000 for example, the maximum compensatory award will be £25,000. If your gross annual salary is £100,000 the maximum compensatory award will be £88,519.

If you have claimed notice pay there will be an overlap with the compensatory award. For example if you have claimed one month's notice pay and are awarded this, you will not get your loss of earnings for the same period under the compensatory award as this would mean you were being compensated twice for the same period. But it is worth claiming for this period as notice pay rather than under the compensatory award because it means that if you have been out of work for a year or more you will still get a year's loss of earnings in addition to the notice pay.

16.8   Pensions

New guidance on the calculation of pension loss was published in August 2017 and this has been updated with a new revision in December 2019. This guidance is called "Principles for compensating pension loss" and broadly it says that for all defined contribution and most defined benefit schemes (sometimes called "final salary" or "career average" schemes), Claimants could be compensated for loss of employer pension contributions for a period of time the ET determines is appropriate. For Claimants who are members of defined benefit schemes, and who might be claiming career long loss for example, a more complex method can be used to calculate pension loss. However, it is expected that this type of calculation would be very rare in practice and expert actuarial advice may also be needed.

The guidance on pension loss can be accessed by typing 'Principles for compensating pension loss' into Google.

16.9   Job seeking expenses

You are entitled to recover the cost of any expenses incurred in looking for a new job, including travel expenses. You should keep any receipts as evidence of the sums spent.

16.10 Loss of statutory rights

This is a sum to compensate you for the loss of your right not to be unfairly dismissed. It is normally a figure of between £350 and £600 as it will now take you two years to build up these rights in a new job.

16.11 Future loss of earnings

The loss of future earnings relates to the expected loss of earnings from the date that you are drawing up the schedule of loss. If you have a date for the tribunal hearing it is easiest to divide this period up into the period up to the date of the hearing and the period after the date of hearing.

In theory a tribunal can award future loss of earnings up to retirement age, although in practice there are various limitations on future loss of earnings. There is the statutory cap giving the maximum award as limited to £88,519 or 52 weeks gross salary whichever is the lowest. If you are out of work the tribunal will consider when you are likely to get a new job which will depend on a variety of factors including your age, experience, the type of work you have done or are qualified to do and the job market.

The figure will include any bonuses, commission or overtime that you would have received in this period, and it will also include the monetary value of any benefits in kind.

If your claim for compensatory loss is likely to be over £30,000 you will be taxed on the sum above this amount and so you will need to gross up the figure claimed. What this means is that you will need to claim the gross amount which, when taxed, will leave you with the net amount you would have been paid if you had not been dismissed.

16.12 ACAS uplift

If you are alleging that the Respondent failed to follow the recommendations set out in the ACAS Code of Practice on Grievance and Disciplinary Procedures the tribunal can apply an uplift to the compensation it awards you. The ACAS uplift can be up to 25% of the compensatory award. The percentage uplift will normally be at the top end if the breach of Code of Practice was particularly serious, for example dismissal where no disciplinary procedure was followed. The uplift is likely to be lower if the breach was more minor.

It is normally worthwhile putting the uplift figure at 25% as the tribunal can reduce it if they do not consider the percentage should be as high as this. It is also worth explaining in a few words how the Respondent was in breach of the Code, for example they refused to allow a grievance hearing or failed to inform you of the right to appeal the decision.

16.13   Other claims

Holiday pay

If you are claiming holiday pay this should be included in the schedule. You should state how many days holiday you think you are entitled to and the daily amount claimed.

Failure to provide a statement of terms and conditions

If the Respondent has not provided you with a written contract of employment or a letter setting out the main terms and conditions of your employment you are entitled to an award of up to four weeks pay. This will be capped at £538 a week.

Injury to feelings

If you are bringing a discrimination claim or a claim that you have been subjected to detriment for whistleblowing (this only applies where the detriment in the whistle-blowing case is not dismissal but some other detrimental act), you can claim for injury to feelings.

You do not have to specify a figure for this but it is helpful if you set out which band you consider your case comes within. There are three bands, sometimes referred to as *Vento* bands from the case in which the guidelines bands were first set out.

The top *Vento* band covers awards from £27,000 to £45,000 and is appropriate in cases of serious discrimination where there has been a long campaign of harassment or discrimination and which has had a serious effect on the health of the employee. The most exceptional cases are capable of exceeding £45,000.

The middle *Vento* band is now from £9,000 to £27,000 and this will be appropriate for a serious one-off case of discrimination or harassment or where the Claimant has lost their job.

The low *Vento* band is from £900 to £9,000 and is appropriate for a minor act of harassment or discrimination.

16.14   Interest on awards

You are also entitled to interest on awards for discrimination both for the damages for injury to feelings and damages for other financial losses such as past loss of earnings. There is no need to set out the calculation in the schedule of loss - the tribunal will work out the appropriate interest on awards at the end of the case so long as you remind them. The current interest rate is 8% calculated on a simple interest basis.

The interest on the award for injury to feelings runs from the date of the discriminatory act to the date of judgment, but interest on awards for other financial loss such as loss of earnings runs from the mid-point being halfway between the date of the discriminatory act and the date of judgment.

Although there is no need to calculate the interest on the damages you have claimed in your schedule it could be a benefit if you are trying to negotiate a settlement, because it will increase the total amount of your claim and the Respondent will know how much you are claiming and how this is calculated.

Chapter 17

Settlement agreements

17.1   What is a settlement agreement?

A settlement agreement is a written agreement between an employer and an employee where they each agree the terms on which an employment claim brought by the employee should be settled. Normally this will include payment by the employer of an agreed sum of money and in return the employee agrees to discontinue his claim. The agreement will sometimes include various other terms such as a reference or a confidentiality clause which I will discuss later.

Before August 2013 settlement agreements were referred to as compromise agreements and if you are referring to books or documents printed before this date this is the term that will be used.

ACAS has published a Guide to Settlement Agreements which can be found on the ACAS website. There is also an ACAS Code of Practice dealing with settlement agreements and confidentiality.

The terms of the settlement agreement will normally be set out in one document that is signed by both parties. This document is a legally binding contract that can be enforced in the courts.

A settlement agreement will normally be entered into between the parties after a discussion and negotiation regarding the terms, and this will be either between the parties themselves, their legal advisors or with the help of an ACAS officer.

17.2   Early conciliation

Since May 2014 all claims have to be submitted to ACAS before the ET1 can be issued, which means that the question of settling the potential claim will usually have been raised before proceedings are started (see Chapter 8 on Early Conciliation).

The fact that no settlement was achieved before the claim was issued does not prevent the parties trying to settle the claim once proceedings have been brought. If you are acting for yourself in a claim you can contact your employer at any time before the tribunal hearing and ask whether he is prepared to consider settling the claim. He might be more willing to do so now that you have issued the claim and he has seen the way you set out your case in the ET1.

The settlement negotiations can take place in whatever format is most convenient for the parties, either by email, over the telephone or by arranging a settlement meeting. If a meeting is arranged and you wish to have a friend or colleague attending with you make sure that the employer is aware of this and has the opportunity to raise any objections they might wish to about this person's attendance. Because these meetings are voluntary, if you are not happy with the arrangements for the meeting you should make this clear.

17.3   Procedure

The normal way in which such negotiations proceed is as follows:

If you are the employee:

- you will put forward a figure that you consider is suitable compensation for your claim. You can begin with the absolute maximum that you could be awarded by a tribunal, although it is unlikely that your employer will agree to this sum, because he might as well take his chances in the tribunal as the award cannot be any higher. I would normally suggest starting perhaps 10% below the maximum possible award.

- it is usually worth starting high because as the negotiations continue you can bring this figure down, but it is not realistic for you as the Claimant to increase the figure.

If you are the employer you will either:

- accept the Claimant's figure;

- make a counter-offer (usually considerably lower than the Claimant's figure); or

- refuse to make any offer.

If your employer is not prepared to make any offer the negotiations will normally come to end. This happens when the employer thinks he is likely to win the tribunal case and he is prepared to put in the time and expense involved in defending the claim.

Often an employer believes that he is likely to win the case but is prepared to offer a small sum to try to settle the case; either because this will avoid spending time and money in defending the case, or because he is aware that in almost all cases, however strong, there is some risk that the case can be lost. This is called "litigation risk".

The employer will normally put forward as low a figure as he thinks might be acceptable. In some cases you might regard the offer put forward as insultingly small but, unless the employer makes it clear he does not intend to increase the offer, this does not mean the negotiations are at an end but ought to be seen as the employer trying to buy off the claim for as small an amount as possible.

Once the employer comes back with a figure it will then be for you to either accept this, or to reject it and put forward another figure, which will usually be rather lower than your previous offer. If you are not prepared to accept the employer's offer or put forward a lower offer then the negotiations will be at an end and the claim will proceed towards a hearing.

Negotiations will continue as long as one or both of the parties is prepared to move towards the other party's figure, but they will end when an agreement is reached or neither party is prepared to move and no agreement is reached.

17.4   Date for payment

If you are agreed on a figure it will then be necessary to agree when this sum will be paid. If it is a large sum and your employer has difficulty finding the amount in one lump sum it might become necessary to agree payment over two or more instalments. The normal period for payment of such a sum will be either 14 or 28 days. It is always worth specifying the actual date with the wording (see the model letter in Appendix B: Model letters and precedents), for example:

> *"Payment of the sum of £5,000 should be made by 4.00pm on 5th March 2021".*

If the payment is by instalments the date and amount of each instalment should be specified.

17.5   Reference

You will then need to consider any other terms you wish to be included in the settlement. Employees often want a reference included, but this can cause difficulties where the employee has been dismissed for misconduct. Even though the employee does not accept that he was guilty of the conduct alleged, the employer cannot put a different reason for dismissal in the reference as this would mislead future prospective employers.

The normal way around this problem is to set out the dates of employment and the job title and then agree on general phrases such as "hard working", "punctual", "trustworthy" "responsible" etc so long as these do not contradict the reason for the dismissal (see the model letter in Appendix B). An employer should only provide information or descriptions in the reference that they believe to be true.

17.6   Confidentiality clause

An employer will often want to keep the fact that he has settled the claim private and will therefore want included in the agreement a clause which prevents the employee from discussing the terms of the settlement with anyone apart from his immediate family and legal advisors. This is known as a "confidentiality clause" (sometimes referred to as a "non-disclosure agreement" or more informally as a "gagging clause"). There is no real disadvantage to the employee in agreeing to such a clause unless their main purpose in bringing the claim has been to expose their employer and they want as much publicity as possible. Most employees will be content to have obtained a financial settlement of the claim and will agree to such a confidentiality clause. If necessary it can be drafted so as to include both the employer and the employee (see the model letter in Appendix B: Model letters and precedents).

There has been recent criticism in the press regarding confidentiality clauses. The fact that an employee has agreed to a confidentiality clause does not prevent them making a protected disclosure under section 43A of the Employment Rights Act 1996 (the whistleblowing provisions) either to the appropriate regulatory body or to the police where a criminal offence is being reported. This right should be reflected in the wording of any settlement agreement which contains such a confidentiality clause.

17.7   Tax liability

It is important to be aware that where the compensation agreed is more than £30,000 tax becomes payable by the employee on any sums paid over this figure. This only applies to compensation for loss of earnings - it does not apply to an award for injury to feelings. If the amount of compensation you are claiming is likely to be more than this sum it will probably be worthwhile getting legal advice about your settlement.

17.8   Confidentiality of settlement negotiations

As a general rule the negotiations with your employer cannot be referred to in the tribunal proceedings. This is because of a legal principle referred to as the "without prejudice" principle. What this means is that when any two parties to a legal dispute try to settle this dispute by means of discussions and negotiations, what is said by the parties during these negotiations cannot be referred to in any subsequent court or tribunal proceedings.

The reason for this rule is to allow a full and free discussion between the parties which cannot then be used in later proceedings if the negotiations break down. For example where the negotiations have come to an end because your employer has not been prepared to offer you an amount that you regard as acceptable (let's assume he has offered you £5,000 but you will accept no less than £10,000), you would not be permitted to refer to the negotiations in your witness statement or to argue that the employer has accepted he was in the wrong because he offered

£5,000.

There is specific provision in relation to settlement negotiations between an employer and an employee before the employee is dismissed to prevent such negotiations being referred to in any subsequent claim for unfair dismissal. Under section 111A of the Employment Rights Act 1996 any evidence of pre-termination negotiations is inadmissible in any proceedings on a complaint for unfair dismissal.

17.9   Legal requirement for independent legal advice

Under section 203 of the Employment Rights Act 1996 an employee cannot agree to give up his rights to bring a claim in an employment tribunal unless certain conditions are met. These conditions are:

- the agreement must be in writing;

- the agreement must state all the claims, including potential claims, that it is intended to cover;

- the employee has received advice from a relevant independent advisor as to the terms and effects of the agreement and its effect on his ability to bring a claim in an employment tribunal;

- the advisor is insured to cover a claim by the employee arising from the advice;

- the agreement identifies the advisor;

- the agreement states that the conditions regulating settlement agreements under the Act are satisfied.

What this means is that unless the settlement agreement satisfies these conditions the agreement will not be legally binding on you, and it would not prevent you bringing a claim in the employment tribunal even though under the terms of the agreement you have settled your claim.

Because of the requirement your employer will want to ensure that you get legal advice on the agreement before signing it and most employers often pay the cost of having a lawyer look at the agreement and advise you on its terms. The normal charge for this advice is between £250 and £500.

17.10   Settlement agreement recorded by ACAS

When ACAS are involved and a settlement has been agreed between the parties the terms of the settlement agreement will be recorded by ACAS in a document called a "COT3". This document will be sent to each of the parties to sign. and it will be a binding agreement between the parties. ACAS will normally contact the employment tribunal to inform the tribunal that a settlement has been reached. The advantage for a litigant in person in having the agreement recorded in a COT3 is that the agreement does not have to satisfy the requirement of section 203 ERA.

17.11 Settlement agreement not honoured

Where you have entered into a settlement agreement with your employer and the terms of that agreement have not been kept by your employer i.e. he has not paid you the agreed amount of compensation, then your remedy is to bring a claim for breach of contract in the County Court.

Chapter 18

Witness statements

18.1   What is a witness statement?

A witness statement is a document which sets out the evidence that the witness wishes to put before the employment tribunal. It will usually be type written and set out in numbered paragraphs. The person making the statement will confirm that the contents of the statement are true.

It is a standard direction in employment cases that any witness to be called by either side provides a witness statement setting out the evidence that the witness will give. This will apply to the Claimant and any witness the Claimant wishes to call to give evidence to support his case, as well as to the Respondent and any witnesses they wish to call.

18.2   Evidence in chief

At the tribunal hearing the judge will have been provided with a copy of all the witness statements, and he will have read these before the hearing. These statements will be taken as the "evidence in chief" of that witness. What this means is when the witness (and if you are the Claimant this will include you giving evidence in your own case) gives evidence at the tribunal hearing, he will be asked whether the contents of the statement are true. He will then be cross-examined on this statement.

Because the witness statement will normally constitute the evidence in chief of that witness, it is therefore important that all relevant facts and matters are included in that witness statement. It is not sufficient for you just to include the basic facts and hope to be able to expand on these when you give evidence. The judge hearing the case might not allow you to give any additional evidence (see Chapter 20). You need to include as much detail as you can about the facts that you rely on. You will generally expect to go into rather more detail in your witness statement than you put into your ET1.

In Chapter 10 I considered what should be included in section 8 of the ET1 and much of what I said in respect of the ET1 will apply to your witness statement. It is worth having a copy of your ET1 available when you draft your witness statement. If you set out the facts of your case in detail in the ET1 then this should form the basis of your witness statement. It is important that there should not be any inconsistencies between what you have said in your ET1 and in your witness statement, since such inconsistencies are likely to be picked on by the other side when they are cross-examining you and will be used to suggest that your evidence is unreliable.

Guidance document on witnesses and witness statements

If you go to the Presidential Guidance on General Case Management you will find Guidance Note 3 on *Witnesses and Witness Statements.*

18.3   Format of the witness statement

The format of the witness statement is to have the case number at the top of the document, then the names of the parties. The document should be entitled "Witness Statement of ....."and give the full name of the person making the statement. The statement should be set out in numbered paragraphs - do not make the paragraphs too long, since short paragraphs tend to be easier to read. See Appendix B: Model letters and precedents for an example of a witness statement.

The witness statement will normally start with the words "I John Smith do say as follows" and then start with paragraph 1. In the first paragraph you should set out the date you started working for the Respondent company and the date of dismissal or, if you have not been dismissed, state that you are still working for the Respondent. You should give your position with the Respondent company and then set out the facts upon which your claim is based.

I suggest that the best way to set out your case is to set out a history of the complaint using the main dates when something significant happened, starting with the earliest incident and then deal with each incident in chronological order as it happened. If are you are able to remember the date on which an event occurred or something was said put down that date as this will make the narrative more convincing. If you cannot remember the exact day include the month if you can.

18.4   Challenging the Respondent's case

If there are facts or matters that are raised in the ET3 which either contradict what you have said or perhaps were not dealt with in your ET1, you should deal with these points in your witness statement. For example, if in the ET3 it states that on a particular date you were given a verbal warning by your manager and you accept that you had a conversation with your manager on that date but were not given a verbal warning, you will need to deal with this conversation in your witness statement. You will agree that on that date you spoke to your manager but deny that you were given any warning and give details of the conversation as you remember it.

18.5   Referring to documents

By the time you make your witness statement you should have received copies of the relevant documents in the case (see Chapter 15: Disclosure of documents). You should refer to any relevant documents, and, if there is an agreed bundle of documents with page numbers you can refer to the page number. Otherwise you will want to identify the document by giving its date and describing the document, for example the contract of employment or the disciplinary procedure etc. If it is a letter or email give the date displayed on the document and who it was sent by and who it was sent to. For example:

> *"On 15ᵗʰ June 2020 Mr Smith sent Mr Jones an email which contained a verbal warning about his behaviour."*

You can summarise what the letter or email is about but do not bother setting it out in detail as the tribunal can read the letter for themselves.

If the documents include notes of a meeting or disciplinary hearing and you consider that these notes are incorrect or have left out relevant parts you will need to refer to this and give the correct version in your witness statement. Again identify the notes by giving the date and state who the meeting was conducted by. For example you will say:

> *"On 15ᵗʰ June 2020 I attended an investigation hearing conducted by Mr Smith, my line manager. Notes of this meeting were made by Mr Jones of the HR department. I do not accept these notes are an accurate reflection of what was said at this meeting. In particular I do not agree with the statement recorded on the first page of these notes where I accepted that I had been wrong to leave work early. In fact what I said was ....".*

If you were not given a copy of the notes at the time of the meeting you should say so, since this explains why you did not correct the notes at the time they were made.

It is preferable to limit the facts to those things that you have seen and heard. Where necessary you can include things that you have been told but this is regarded by tribunals and courts as second hand or "hearsay" evidence.

18.6   Facts supporting your claim

You will need to put down all the facts that support your claim. If you are claiming unfair dismissal and you had been dismissed for misconduct you will need to set out the factual circumstances leading up to your dismissal explaining the misconduct you were accused of. You will need to explain why you say you did not do the thing you were accused of, and why your employer should not have believed that you were guilty. If you consider that your employer had some other motive for wanting to dismiss you, you should set that down and explain what evidence you have for believing he had that motive.

If you were dismissed for redundancy you will need to explain why you consider that you were not redundant and whether there were other jobs available that you could have done. If you consider that the selection procedure was unfair you will need to explain why you consider it was unfair. For example, if you are alleging that the marking of the selection matrix was wrong you will need to explain why but also that if had been marked correctly you would not have been made redundant. If there was someone else you say should have been included in the selection pool you will need to explain why and also why that person would probably have been selected before you.

If you are alleging discrimination you should try to set out all the examples of discriminatory conduct that you rely on. You should set out the incidents in chrono-logical order; that is starting with the earliest one and listing them in date order until you set out the most recent incident. It does not matter that the earliest incident might have occurred a number of years earlier because a tribunal might accept that it is part of a series of events. Try and give as much detail as you can about the date the incident occurred, where it occurred and who it was that said the thing or did the thing complained of.

If you are alleging disability discrimination you will need to explain your disability and how it limits your ability to carry out everyday tasks.

18.7   Remedy

At the end of your witness statement you will need to deal with the remedy you are asking for. If it is reinstatement or re-engagement (see Chapter 21: Remedies) you will need to explain why you want to be reinstated or re-engaged by the Respondent.

If you are asking for an award of compensation you will need to explain whether you have obtained a new job, when you got this job and how much you are paid. If you have not got a new job you will need to give details of all the efforts you have made to find work. If there are particular problems finding work you should give details of these problems.

If it is a discrimination case or a whistleblowing case and you are claiming injury to feelings you will need to give details of the effect of discrimination or the detriment on you, how it made you feel, whether you suffered any psychiatric injury such as depression and what treatment you received.

Chapter 19

Preparation for the hearing

19.1   Introduction

Thorough preparation plays a vital part in maximising your chances of a successful outcome in your tribunal hearing. It is no good leaving this preparation until the last minute; if you find you have not got all the documents you need or have been unable to contact the witness you were relying on, it might well be too late to do anything about this.

You will have been notified by the tribunal of the day of the hearing well in advance. This date is usually included in the letter sent by the tribunal setting out the timetable for the action with the dates for various steps to be undertaken. These normally include the day on which disclosure should take place and the day on which the witness statements should be exchanged.

There are two key elements that you will need to ensure are ready for the hearing - the witnesses and the documents. You will need to make sure that any witnesses you intend to call are aware of the date of the hearing and are available to attend on that date. You will also need to make sure that you have all the documents you wish to rely on during the tribunal hearing.

19.2   Witnesses

You can normally only call evidence from witnesses when you have served a copy of their witness statement on the other side. If you are the Claimant this will apply to you as a witness - even though it is your case you will still have to make a witness statement. I have considered witness statements in Chapter 18. You need to make sure that any other witness you want to call has provided you with a witness statement. Often witness statements will be exchanged by the parties a week before the hearing date, which means each side sends a copy of their witness statements to the other side.

19.3   What is the position if you cannot get a statement?

There are some circumstances when you want to call evidence from a person who does not wish to attend the tribunal or is not prepared to make a witness statement.

If you are the Claimant it can be the case that you wish to call someone to give evidence who is still employed by the Respondent but they do not wish to get involved or to give evidence because they believe that it might harm their employment prospects or make life more difficult for them at work.

If you consider that it is important to your case for the tribunal to hear evidence from a person who does not wish to attend the hearing you will need to obtain an order from the tribunal ordering that person to attend to give evidence. Under Employment Tribunal Regulations 2013 Schedule 1 Rule 32 the tribunal may order any person to attend a hearing to give evidence or to produce documents or information.

Do not leave this until the last minute but contact the tribunal well in advance of the hearing date. You will need to write to the tribunal:

- giving the name and address of the person you want to attend the hearing;

- setting out what the evidence is that you expect them to give and explain how this will help your case;

- stating that the witness is not willing to attend the tribunal voluntarily. If the person has given you a reason why they do not wish to come you will need to put down this explanation.

If the claim you are bringing is a claim under the Equality Act it is worth pointing out to the witness you want to call that, if they are subjected to detrimental treatment by their employer because they have been supporting a discrimination claim, then this would constitute victimisation under section 27 of the Equality Act. Under section 27(2)(b) of this Act giving evidence or information in connection with proceedings under the Equality Act is a protected act.

If the claim is not under the Equality Act and the person is subjected to a detriment as a result of giving evidence in a claim against his employer then this is likely to constitute a breach of contract which would entitle that person to resign and bring a claim for constructive dismissal.

There is always a risk in calling a person as a witness if you do not have a witness statement from them because you can never be certain what that person is going to say in their evidence. So you will need to be fairly confident that the witness will be able to give evidence that will assist your case, otherwise you would be better not calling them as a witness at all.

Where a witness is brought to court under a witness order the tribunal can order that the parties bear the costs of bringing that witness to the tribunal i.e. travel expenses and lost wages and then order that the losing party pays those costs.

For those witnesses who agree to come to the tribunal voluntarily there is no longer any provision for their expenses to be paid by the tribunal.

Where the witness is willing to attend the tribunal but is not prepared to make a witness statement you will need to consider carefully whether it is worth calling them to give evidence. Ask them why they are unwilling to make a statement, since if they do not have a good reason it might be that they would not give evidence that was favourable to your case.

If you do decide to call that witness you will need to explain to the tribunal that they were not prepared to make a statement, and you will probably have to explain why you wish to call that person, and what evidence you think they can give that will be relevant to the issues in the case.

19.4 At what time will the witness need to attend the hearing?

You will need to warn your witnesses that it will not be possible to say when they will be called on to give evidence. Therefore they will need to turn up before 10.00am but it might be that they will be at the tribunal until the afternoon before they get called on to give evidence. The tribunal will assist where it can to allow a witness who needs to get away for some urgent reason to give their evidence as soon as possible, but this can depend on whether the Claimant's case or the Respondent's case is heard first (for the likely order in which the cases will be heard see Chapter 20).

19.5 Witness unable to attend the hearing

If there is a problem with one of your witnesses attending on the day listed for the hearing you have several options. If the witness is important to your case and their evidence is likely to be disputed by the other side you should contact the tribunal as soon as you become aware of the problem. It would be helpful to send a copy of their witness statement with your letter or email so that the tribunal is aware of what the witness's evidence is, explaining why the witness cannot attend the hearing and asking for it to be postponed to another date on which the witness can attend.

If the witness does not give very significant evidence or the evidence is unlikely to be disputed or challenged by the other side you can contact them and ask them to agree the evidence. If the other side is willing to agree this evidence then the witness statement can be put before the tribunal without calling that person on the basis that it is agreed evidence.

If the other side is unwilling to agree to this you will have to decide whether you wish to go ahead without that witness. If you have a witness statement from the person you can put this before the tribunal but because that witness is not present to be cross-examined this evidence will not carry as much weight as if they had attended at the tribunal hearing.

19.6   Postponing the hearing

The tribunal will be unlikely to postpone a hearing that has been fixed for a set date unless the witness has a good reason for being unable to attend. For example if the person has booked a holiday abroad, you will need to find out when this was booked because, if it was booked before the dates were fixed for the trial, you should have found this out and notified the tribunal that, when fixing the trial date, they should avoid this date. If it was booked after the trial date was fixed you will have to show that you had notified the witness of the trial date and therefore it was not your fault that they booked the holiday. If you failed to notify the witness of the trial day you will have to explain why.

If you or one of your witnesses is unable to attend the tribunal hearing because of illness you will need to satisfy the tribunal that the illness is sufficiently serious to prevent attendance at the tribunal. Clearly if the illness or condition means that you or the witness is in hospital the tribunal will be likely to accept that it is a serious condition. If it is not such a serious illness, the fact that you or your witness has a sick note for work will not usually be sufficient to satisfy the tribunal that you or he cannot attend to give evidence. What you need is a note from a doctor confirming that you or your witness is too ill to be able to give evidence.

A postponement of a hearing is sometimes referred to an "adjournment", which means that the hearing is put off until another day.

19.7   Documents

In every case there will be some documents that are relevant to the issues that the tribunal will have to decide, and it is for both parties to ensure that all the relevant documents are brought before the tribunal for the hearing.

The starting point is the disclosure of documents (see Chapter 15). Once the parties have agreed which are the relevant documents and which they each wish to rely on, copies of these documents will be collected together to make the bundle of documents that will be put before the court.

It is normally the case that the Respondent will prepare the bundle because they usually have the use of office and photocopying facilities. If neither side has a photocopier and the documents have to be photocopied commercially it would be normal for this cost to be split between the parties. The bundle will include both the Claimant's and the Respondent's documents. The bundle will need to be marked with page numbers so that these can be easily referred to in the tribunal hearing. This page marking should not be done on the original documents but should be done on the first copy and further copies can be taken from this.

It is important that all the documents you wish to rely on are included in the bundle.

If you produce a document at the hearing which has not been disclosed and is not in the bundle then the tribunal can refuse to allow it to be produced in evidence. You will have to explain why it was not disclosed at the proper time, and you will have to satisfy the tribunal that it is important to your case that the document is allowed in as evidence. It is equally important that any documents referred to in your own witness statement, the statements of your witnesses, the other side's witnesses and in the ET1 and ET3 are included in the bundle of documents.

If you are preparing the trial bundle you will need to make sure that it contains the ET1 and the ET3. These should be the first documents. Then you should include the Schedule of Loss and any documents sent by the tribunal containing directions or orders. Finally you will include all the relevant documents that have been disclosed by the parties - these should normally be included in chronological order with the earliest documents first and the latest documents at the end. Witness statements are not included in the trial bundle.

If you are providing the bundle of documents for the tribunal you will need to make sure that, in addition to the bundle for yourself and the other side, there is a bundle for witnesses giving evidence and a bundle for the judge (or, if there are to be three judges, three bundles, one for each judge). The tribunal will normally have informed you if the case is going to be heard by one judge sitting alone or by three judges. Nowadays most straightforward unfair dismissal claims, contract claims and working time claims will be heard by a judge sitting alone, whereas discrimination claims will normally be heard by three tribunal judges.

You will need copies of your witness statement, one for yourself, one for the judge (or three if there are to be three judges), and a spare one just in case a further copy is needed. You will also need copies of the statements made by your witness, and again ensure that there is one for each judge and the witnesses.

19.8   Vulnerable parties and witnesses

Giving evidence in an employment tribunal can be a daunting prospect. This is particularly the case for parties or witnesses who might be regarded as vulnerable, possibly because of some mental or physical disability or health condition. In order to facilitate participation by such individuals the employment tribunals are instructed to make appropriate directions. These can be found in the *Presidential Guidance: Vulnerable parties and witnesses in Employment Tribunal Proceedings*, which can be found online. It sets out a list of criteria under which a person might be regarded as vulnerable and appropriate measures such as giving evidence by video link.

If you consider that either you, or one of your witnesses, might fall within the category of a vulnerable witness this should be raised with the tribunal who can be asked to make appropriate directions.

19.9   Impact of coronavirus

Because of the coronavirus pandemic it might become more difficult to obtain a witness statement from someone you consider can provide helpful evidence. If this is the case and there is a specific date on which the witness statements must be exchanged then it is important to contact the tribunal and explain what the problem is. The tribunal can then consider whether it is appropriate to extend time if you are able to give a specific date by which you expect to be able to obtain the statement or otherwise the tribunal might list a case management hearing to consider the matter.

Similarly if it becomes apparent that a witness you wish to call to give evidence will be unable to attend a tribunal hearing because they or a member of their family is a vulnerable person then you should contact the tribunal as soon as you become aware of this problem. It might be that the other side will agree the statement without the need for the person to be called to give evidence. Alternatively it might be possible to make arrangements that the witness gives evidence by way of a video link.

Chapter 20

The hearing

20.1   Visiting an Employment Tribunal

One of the best pieces of advice I can give to prepare you for the hearing of your case is to visit an employment tribunal and sit in on a hearing. This will familiarise you with the layout of the tribunal rooms, which tend to be set out in a similar fashion. You will be able to see where the parties sit, how the parties or their representatives address the judge, how witnesses give their evidence and in particular how cross-examination is carried out.

Tribunal hearings are almost always public hearings and if you explain at the office that you would like to sit in on a hearing because you have your own case coming up, the staff should be able to direct you to a tribunal where a contested hearing is due to take place. You will need to sit on one of the chairs provided at the back of the tribunal room.

Worrying about the procedure can distract you from putting your case at its best and from making the points that you want to. Familiarity with the tribunal set up and the procedure should reduce this worry and allow you to concentrate on your case.

20.2   Length of hearing

Most simple claims which do not include more than a couple of witnesses will be listed for one day. Many people attending the tribunal for the first time are surprised at how long the proceedings actually take - they expect to be there for an hour or two and in fact they are there all day.

The number of days which have been allocated for the hearing of your case will have been included on the letter from the tribunal setting out the hearing date. If you are the Claimant, the Respondent or representing the Respondent you will need to be present for the whole of the hearing. If you are in work you should make arrangements with your employer to enable you to attend each day.

20.3   Tribunal hours

The tribunals normally sit from 10.00am to 4.30pm with an hour for lunch at 1.00pm. It is always worth getting to the tribunal early - I would recommend aiming to get to the tribunal by 9.00am as this will give you time to spare if there are traffic difficulties.

Make sure your witnesses know where the tribunal building is and ask them to get to the tribunal at about 9.00am. This will give them an opportunity to read through their witness statement and for you to let them know what the procedure will be.

If the case is a full hearing and listed for one day expect to be there until 4.00pm or 4.30pm. If you are leaving your car in a car park get a ticket for the full day, as you do not want to have to worry about getting a parking ticket when you should be concentrating on your case.

20.4   Appearance

I would recommend dressing smartly for the hearing as it shows a proper respect for the tribunal and that you are taking it seriously.

20.5   Pre-hearing discussions

The tribunal hearing itself will usually start at 10.00am or 10.30am. Before this it is normal for a discussion to take place between the representatives to see whether it is possible to try to reach a settlement. It is quite usual for cases to be settled at this time, since both sides know what they stand to lose if the case goes against them. The representatives will also discuss whether there are any procedural problems with the documents or witnesses, which would need to be raised with the judge at the beginning of the hearing and they will exchange any law reports they intend to rely on.

At the tribunal offices there will be separate waiting rooms for the Claimants and their witnesses and the Respondents and their witnesses. I would recommend that you introduce yourself to the other side's representative if they have one or if not the main person acting for the Respondent. Ask if they have any proposals to make towards settlement or alternatively you can put forward a figure that you would be prepared to accept by way of settlement.

If you need more time to negotiate with the other side to try to reach a settlement you should contact the clerk who has been assigned to your case and get them to ask the judge if you can have a bit longer. The tribunal will normally allow this although it will usually put a time limit on discussions so that if by, say 11.00am, it did not look as if agreement was going to be reached then the case would have to start.

Even though you are at the tribunal there are still benefits in settling the case. You can agree a reference and the wording of the reference, there will be no recoupment (see below) of any benefits received and for the Respondent a confidentiality clause can be agreed and there is no risk of a financial penalty.

"Recoupment" means that state benefits you have received between the date of your dismissal and the date of the tribunal hearing are paid back to or "recouped" by the Department of Work and Pensions. The reason for this is you will not get an award for loss of earnings as well as state benefits for the same period. I have set out in more detail at section 21.9 (Compensatory award: Deduction of benefits) how the recoupment provisions work.

20.6   Postponement of the hearing

The tribunal has a complete discretion to postpone the case to another day (this is sometimes referred to as an "adjournment"). This can be done either at the request of one of the two parties or of its own volition. The overriding principle is that the case must be dealt with justly and fairly to both sides but the tribunal must also be mindful to avoid delay and to save expense.

The tribunals are always reluctant to postpone a case on the date set for hearing and will only do so if proceeding with the case would result in an injustice to one or other party.

If one party applies for a postponement the tribunal must give the other party an opportunity to state whether they agree to or oppose the postponement and to explain why.

If the Claimant is unable to attend through no fault of his own then the tribunal will normally allow a postponement. The same will apply if the Respondent is acting in person or if a witness whose evidence is crucial to the case cannot attend.

If you or one of your witnesses is unable to attend the tribunal hearing because of illness you will need to satisfy the tribunal that the illness is sufficiently serious to prevent you from attending the tribunal. Clearly if the illness or condition means that you or the witness is in hospital the tribunal will be likely to accept that it is a serious condition. If it is not such a serious illness the fact that you or the person has a sick note for work will not usually be sufficient to satisfy the tribunal that you or he cannot attend to give evidence. What you need is a note from a doctor confirming that you or your witness is so ill they cannot attend the tribunal to give evidence.

Where the party requesting the postponement has been at fault the tribunal might allow the postponement but order that that party should pay the costs caused by the wasted hearing. This will normally be restricted to the costs of legal representatives attending the hearing. For example, if you are applying to postpone the case because of the illness of one of your witnesses and you have known for several weeks that they are unlikely to be able to attend the hearing but you failed to inform the tribunal of this until the day of the hearing, it is likely that you will have to pay the costs of the hearing.

20.7   Other proceedings

One situation in which the tribunal will normally postpone the hearing is if there are either high court proceedings or criminal proceedings going on at the same time which cover the same or very similar issues as those which are relevant in the tribunal proceedings. For example, if an employee was dismissed for stealing from his employer and was then charged with theft by the police, any hearing for unfair dismissal might well be postponed until the criminal proceedings had been concluded.

If there is a possibility of such other court proceedings you should contact the tribunal as soon as you are aware of these so that the tribunal can consider whether to postpone the employment case.

20.8   One judge or three?

Most unfair dismissal cases will be heard by a tribunal judge sitting alone. This also applies to other straightforward cases such as breach of contract claims or claims for holiday pay. Where the claim is for discrimination there will usually be three judges hearing the case. The judge in the middle will normally be a full time employment judge and the people sitting on either side of him are "lay members" (these are people with experience of employment practice).

Where there are three judges you will address the main employment judge unless specifically asked a question by a lay member. You should address the judge as "Sir" or "Madam".

20.9   Summarising the issues

At the outset of the hearing the judge will introduce himself and the two lay members if he is sitting with them. He will summarise the issues that the tribunal needs to decide and ask both parties if they agree that these are the issues and whether there are any others the tribunal will need to decide. He will also let the parties know if he intends to deal with liability and damages altogether or whether he intends to give judgment on liability and then deal with damages if the Claimant is successful. The tribunal normally takes this second course if the issue of damages is likely to be complicated or involve consideration of a significant amount of further evidence.

The judge will also deal with any other preliminary matters including applications for a postponement or applications to amend the claim or the response. He will also consider which party should call their evidence first.

20.10   Who gives evidence first?

The standard rule is that the person who is making the allegation has the burden of proving it and they will go first. So, if you are bringing a discrimination case, claiming that the Respondent has discriminated against you, it will be for you to prove the discrimination and therefore you will go first.

The exception to this rule is in cases of unfair dismissal, where, even though you are claiming that the Respondent has unfairly dismissed you, the law says that it is for the employer to show that he has dismissed the employee for a fair reason. Therefore the Respondent will go first in unfair dismissal cases and call their evidence to try to show that the dismissal was fair.

This exception only applies where the Respondent admits that there was a dismissal. If he does he will need to prove that the dismissal was a fair dismissal. If the Respondent does not agree that there was a dismissal, for example if he says that the Claimant resigned, then the Claimant will go first as he will have to prove that there was a dismissal.

Similarly, if it is a constructive dismissal case the Claimant will go first because he will need to prove that the Respondent was in breach of contract which entitled him to resign.

If the case involves both unfair dismissal and discrimination my experience is that generally the Claimant will go first because they will be putting forward the discrimination claim that the Respondent has to meet.

If the Claimant goes first he will call his witnesses before the Respondent calls theirs.

20.11   Order of witnesses

There is no specific rule about the order in which witnesses will be called, although generally if you are the Claimant you will give evidence before you call your witnesses. If you have witnesses that need to get away as soon as possible the tribunal will usually be sympathetic to this and will allow them to be called first. It would then be normal to call witnesses in the order in which they deal with events, so those witnesses giving evidence about the earlier events will be called to give evidence first. The same will apply to the Respondent's witnesses - if there is one witness who deals with the bulk of the Respondent's case it would be usual to call them first and then call witnesses in the order in which they deal with events.

20.12   The evidence

The questioning of each witness falls into four separate stages:

- The first stage is "examination in chief", which is where one party asks questions of its own witnesses. This is normally in the form of his witness statement.

- The second stage is "cross-examination". This is when one party asks questions of the other party's witnesses.

- The third stage is "judge's questions". Although the judge can ask questions of a witness at any stage to clarify a point, it is usually after cross-examination that the judge will ask questions of a witness, although in some cases the judge will not feel the need to ask any questions.

- The fourth stage is "re-examination" when the witness will be asked questions by his own representative. This is limited to dealing with points raised in cross-examination or by the judge's questions.

There is a difference between the type of questions you can put in examination in chief and in cross-examination. In examination in chief you are not allowed to put a leading question to your witness. What this means is that you cannot suggest the answer you want and ask the witness to agree with it. You must ask questions in a neutral way which does not suggest the answer that you want. With cross-examination you can put the answer you want to the witness and ask them to agree it.

20.13   Procedure for the Claimant

I will consider the procedure on the basis that you are the Claimant acting in person and that you are putting your case first.

The oath

You will be called to the witness desk, which will usually be beside the bench or desk where the representatives are sitting. You will need to take the oath, which will be on the Bible if you are a Christian or, if not, you will be given the option of swearing on another holy book. If you are not religious you can affirm.

Evidence in chief

The procedure in the tribunal is that your witness statement is taken to be your evidence. This is why it is so important that you have included everything you want to say about the facts of the case in your statement. The tribunal judge will have read the statement before the hearing. The judge can allow you to give additional or supplemental evidence but you will need to have a good reason for doing so if it was something you should have included in your witness statement.

Sometimes you will wish to deal with a point that has arisen from the other side's statements that was not included in their ET3, and which you have not dealt with in your witness statement. The tribunal will normally allow you to deal with this but remember that you are giving evidence of facts and things that happened so this is not the time to make general comments about the other side's case.

If there are documents referred to in your witness statement, for example notes of a disciplinary hearing or a dismissal letter, it is helpful to refer the judge to these at this time so that he can read them. These documents should be in the witness bundle.

Once you have finished giving any additional evidence you will then be cross-examined by the other side's representative or, if they are acting in person, whoever is representing the company.

You will also need to deal with any evidence you rely on in relation to the amount of damages you are claiming. This will include efforts to find an alternative job or, if you have found one, what the difference in salary is between your old job and the new one. In some cases the employment judge will indicate that he does not wish to hear any evidence in relation to the damages at this stage but that he will decide the question of liability first and then, if the Claimant is successful, he will go on to hear evidence in relation to the appropriate remedy.

Purpose of cross-examination

One purpose of cross-examination is to test the other side's case and where possible to undermine it. This will be done for example by highlighting inconsistencies between the witness statement and documents. If the witness is giving evidence of facts that you disagree with and you are able to show that the witness is untruthful then it is likely that your version of events will be preferred to theirs. Similarly if you can show that the witness is a person who makes mistakes about dates or facts then again you will be able to say to the tribunal at the end of this case that this person was not a reliable witness and the tribunal should not accept their version of events.

If the person asking you questions in cross-examination is a lawyer and possibly even if he is acting in person but has experience of legal procedure, he will be putting questions to you in such a way as to get the answers that he wants. The question will put in the form of a suggestion such as

> *"Do you agree that on the 24th December such an event occurred?"*

Another purpose of cross-examination is to put your case to the other side's witnesses. What this means is that if they say that an event happened on a certain day and your case is either that this did not happen at all or that it happened in a different way or on a different day, then you have to put your case to that witness. Similarly when the other side is cross-examining you they will need to put their case to you to give you the opportunity to agree or disagree with it.

I will give an example.

You are a female employee and are bringing a claim for sex discrimination and the allegation is that on 3rd September at the main offices where you work your Manager called you into his office and asked you to sit on his knee. If the Respondent's case is that this incident never occurred and that the Manager never said this to you then the Respondent will need to put this to you in cross-examination. If there is a diary entry or some other evidence showing that either you or the Manager was not in work that day, the Respondent will ask you to look at the diary entry and suggest that you are either lying or mistaken about the incident.

If the Respondent's case is that you have taken the comment out of context and that what the Manager actually said to a group of people coming into a meeting in his room was "can you all bring chairs with you - I don't want anyone to have to sit on my knee", and that this was said in a joking way and not just to you but to a group of both men and women, then the Respondent would need to put this to you in cross-examination. The way they would do this would be by a series of questions:

- do you agree that this was a weekly department meeting?

- do you agree that this meeting was attended by Mr Smith, Mr Jones and Mrs Clarke as well as yourself?

- do you agree that all these people were present when the comment was made?

- do you agree that what the manager actually said was: "can you all bring chairs with you - I don't want anyone to have to sit on my knee"?

- do you agree that this was said in a joking way and that everyone laughed?

All these questions are asked in such a way that they can be answered with a "yes" or a "no" but it might be the case that answering in this way might not provide the full picture, in which case you will need to expand on your answer to explain this. For example, in answer to the question above: "do you agree that all these people were present when the comment was made?" your answer might be "yes, but they were all talking amongst themselves and did not hear what the manager said as he was speaking to me".

If you have referred to an event in your ET1 as occurring on one date and in your witness statement you give a different date you would have to expect to be cross-examined on this point and it might be suggested that you are not telling the truth about the date or that you are mistaken. You can usually get an idea from the Respondent's ET3 or the witness statements as to which facts are going to be challenged and can prepare yourself to be asked questions on these points.

Where your case relies on an allegation of some mistreatment you have suffered, for example a discriminatory remark or behaviour, it is likely that you will be asked whether you made a complaint about this at the time and if you did not it might well be suggested that the fact that you did not complain means the incident did not occur. You need to be prepared for such a question and be able to give an explanation as to why you did not complain at the time.

If the question of damages is being dealt with the Respondent will need to cross-examine the Claimant about this and this will often be with regards to his efforts to obtain alternative employment.

Judge's questions

The tribunal judge can ask questions of a witness at any stage of the proceedings. He will be making a note of all the evidence given and will want to clarify any answers. He might ask the witness to clarify an answer they have just given to a question put in cross-examination or re-examination.

Once the cross-examination has finished it will normally be for the judge or judges to ask questions of the witness. It is important to listen carefully to these questions as they will often give some indication of what the judge is thinking about those issues he is asking questions about and which he considers to be important.

Re-examination

Once the judge has finished his questions there will be an opportunity for you to ask questions in re-examination. You can only ask questions about matters that have arisen in cross-examination and this is your opportunity to correct any misleading impression that might have been given by your answers in cross-examination.

If you are representing yourself the re-examination will consist of statements about matters raised in cross-examination. Taking the example given above, if in answer to the question: "do you agree that all these people were present when the comment was made?" you had answered just "yes", in re-examination you could explain that the other people present were all talking amongst themselves and did not hear what the manager said as he was speaking to you alone.

If in cross-examination you had been shown a diary entry or document which appeared to suggest that a date you had given in your witness statement was incorrect you can, in re-examination, refer the tribunal to a different document which shows that the diary entry was wrong or was changed at some later date.

20.14 Your witnesses

Examination in chief

Once you have finished your evidence you will need to call any witnesses you have. They will have to take the oath or affirm. Their witness statement will have been read by the judge. If there are any documents referred to by this witness which have not already been read by the tribunal, the tribunal should be told where these are in the bundle of documents and invited to read them.

If you have any additional questions you wish to ask the witness this can be allowed by the tribunal, although if it is something important which should have been included in the statement you might be asked to explain why this was not dealt with there. You might want to deal with any new points raised by the Respondent in their witness statements which were not referred to in the ET3. It is important to remember that you cannot ask leading questions, which is a question in which you are suggesting the answer to the witness. For example:

> *"Is it right that you were at the factory on the morning of 24th December?"*

is a leading question.

> *"Where were you on the morning of 24th December?"*

is not a leading question because it is not suggesting an answer.

Cross-examination

Your witnesses will then be cross-examined by the other side. Again the purpose of cross-examination will be to discredit or undermine the witness by suggesting their evidence is unreliable and putting the Respondent's case to that witness.

Judge's questions

The judge might put questions to the witness if there are points on which he wants clarification. Again it is important to note these questions as they might well give some indication of how the judge views the case.

Re-examination

You then have the opportunity of re-examining your witness. You can only ask questions about points that arose in cross-examination. You cannot ask leading questions. This is your opportunity to correct any misleading impressions that might have been given by answers in cross-examination.

Statements of witnesses not being called to give evidence

Once you have called all your witnesses you will then refer the tribunal to any statements of your witnesses that have been agreed by the other side and also to any witness statements which the tribunal have allowed you to put in because that witness was unable to be present, even though they were not agreed by the other side. Such a statement will not have the same force that actually calling the witness would have because the other side has not had the opportunity of cross-examining them.

20.15   The other side's case

When you have concluded all your evidence it will then be for the other side to put their case. The procedure will be exactly the same in that each witness will give evidence in chief in the form of a witness statement, they will then be cross-examined, the judge may then ask questions and the witness can be re-examined.

Preparation is a key ingredient in successful cross-examination. Time spent working on the documentation will be most important in enabling you to cross-examine the other side's witnesses successfully. Compare what is said in the ET3 to what is said in the witness statement to see if there are any differences or discrepancies. Then compare what is said in the ET3 and the witness statements to what is said in the documents, for example whether the account given in the witness statement is the same as the account given in the notes of a disciplinary hearing.

What you are looking for is differences or discrepancies between these documents. The key dates and facts ought to be referred to in both the ET3 and the witness statements. In cases of dismissal for misconduct or capability you will need to compare what was said in the disciplinary or capability hearings and the dismissal letter to what is said in the witness statements. In redundancy cases you will need to consider what is said in the consultation meetings with what is said in the witness statements.

I find it helpful to put a cross by anything in the witness statements that is to be challenged as incorrect, plus a note as to what the correct statement or fact ought to be. If there is something in the witness statement that is contradicted by a document, make a note of the document page in the bundle of documents next to the point in the witness statement.

It is also worthwhile writing down a summary of all the points you want to make in cross-examination and then ticking them off as you go through them. When you are asking questions in the tribunal it is very easy to forget all the points you have intended to make and once the witness has given evidence you will not normally be allowed to recall them to put points that you intended to make but forgot to do so.

Make sure that you challenge the witness on all the important parts of his witness statement that you do not agree with, even if it is to do no more than stating to the witness that he was wrong about a fact or a date and that the correct date was the one you say it is. The danger, if you do not challenge the witness on all the disputed facts, is that you might be taken as having agreed this fact.

20.16   Submissions

After hearing all the evidence, both parties have an opportunity to summarise their case in what are called "closing submissions". This is your opportunity to comment on and criticise the other side's evidence and to put forward the arguments in favour of your case. This is also the time when you will refer the judge to any relevant law and provide him with copies of any law reports or legal decisions on which you wish to rely. You will need an additional copy of the law report for yourself and the other party.

It is helpful to make some notes before the hearing of the points you will want to make. You will then go through these points in your closing submissions and refer to the evidence where it supports your case or undermines the other side's case.

The order in which you make the closing submissions will depend on who called their evidence first. The standard rule is that the party that calls their evidence first goes second when making submissions.

In addition to the main issue of liability you must also remember to deal with issues of contributory fault or any *Polkey* reduction (see Chapter 21) if these points are being raised by the other side. Also you will need to deal with the question of damages if the judge is deciding these at the same time as liability. The best way of doing this is going through the schedule of loss (see Chapter 16) and justifying the figures you have put down there.

If you are going first the other side will have the opportunity to make submissions after you and to answer the points that you have made. If the other side have made their submissions first it will then be for you to make your submissions and you should try to deal with all the points made by the other side in addition to setting out the case and law that you rely on.

The Respondent will need to remember to put forward its arguments to support a reduction for contributory fault or a *Polkey* reduction if this is being alleged. The Respondent will also need to deal with the question of damages again and this can best be done by going through the Claimant's schedule of loss, setting out which amounts are agreed and which are not agreed. Where a figure is not agreed the Respondent will need to suggest an alternative figure or say that no damages should be awarded for that item, putting forward the argument supporting their figures.

Finally, the party that made the first closing submissions will have the opportunity to respond on any points of law raised by the second party in their submissions.

20.17   Video hearings

At the start of the coronavirus pandemic in March 2020 the President of the Employment Tribunals ordered that all hearings listed to take place in an employment tribunal would be converted to a preliminary hearing in which the Judge could give directions for the future progress of the case. This was later changed to cover only those hearings listed to take place before 26th June 2020. It was hoped that after that date hearings could take place as planned.

Whether hearings after 26th June 2020 would take place in person with the parties attending at the employment tribunal would depend to a large extent on the personal circumstances of the parties, their witnesses and their family members. Where such persons were vulnerable or shielding it might not be possible for the hearings to take place in person and would therefore have to take place by means of a video link. It is likely that such hearings will be increasingly used in the future.

The President of the Employment Tribunals has provided an on-ine document of FAQs (Frequently Asked Questions) arising from the Covid-19 pandemic. As well as helpful guidance regarding litigants in person having difficulty preparing their case because of a lack of access to witnesses and the impact on time limits, this document has several sections on video hearings.

Question 15 deals with technology available for use in a video hearing. This is something that should be discussed at the preliminary hearing when directions are being made for the future progress of the case. There are a range of video platforms available including Skype for Business. For access via Skype an account is not needed but it might be necessary to download an app, free of charge, to connect. Make sure it is compatible with your computer well before the hearing - if it is not you will need to contact the tribunal.

Question 16 sets out the etiquette which applies to video hearings which includes:

- Identify a quiet location from which to call;

- Ask family members or colleagues not to disturb you;

- Join the meeting at the start and wait for the judge;

- Turn off your mobile phone or switch to silent;

- Place your mobile phone away from audio speakers to limit interference;

- Avoid sitting with bright light behind you;

- Consider using a headset to avoid echoes, feedback etc;

- Mute your microphone when not speaking and remember to unmute when speaking;

- If the facility is available to blur the background, use this;

- Do not enter "mirror screen" or "share screen" or send a document without the judge's permission;

- Use the side panel (chat facility) if available, to signify a wish to speak;

- Re-join on the same invitation link if you are cut off;

- Most important of all **do not record the hearing without permission**.

It is important to remember that these video hearings are formal tribunal proceedings and should be treated as such. Therefore you should dress smartly as if attending the tribunal in person. If live evidence is being given by yourself or your witnesses ensure that the appropriate holy book is available if the oath is being sworn. Make sure each party is working from the same bundle of documents with the same page numbers - this includes a bundle for the judge and for each of the witnesses. Any additional documents will need to be provided in advance of the hearing - it will be difficult to do this whilst the hearing is underway. Ensure that your internet connection is strong enough to enable the hearing to proceed without being cut off and ask family members not to download from the internet whilst the hearing is ongoing. If the bundle of documents is in electronic form and not a hard copy and you have a 2nd computer available to you it is helpful to have the documents on the 2nd computer so that you can refer to them whilst the hearing is proceeding. You are not allowed to eat during the hearing but make sure you have some water available to you. When giving evidence you must not communicate with anyone else in the room, nor can you refer to any document that is not in the agreed bundle unless you have permission from the judge. Obtain a telephone number for the tribunal so that you can contact them if there is a problem with the connection.

Chapter 21

Remedies

21.1 Introduction

I now consider the different remedies available for each of the main claims that you are likely to bring in the tribunal. This will cover the possible remedies for unfair dismissal, wrongful dismissal, breach of contract, discrimination, working time and holiday pay claims. I have also included awards for various breaches of the employment law that an employer might commit, such as the failure to provide particulars of employment and the failure to allow an employee to be accompanied to a disciplinary meeting. I have not included claims related to membership of trade unions or equal pay claims.

21.2 Documents

If you go to the *Presidential Guidance on General Case Management* you will find Guidance Note 6 on Remedy. This guidance provides a useful checklist of documents that the parties might need to refer to when considering remedy. These documents include:

- contract of employment including details of any pension scheme;

- copy pay slips for the last 13 weeks;

- evidence of payments made by the Respondent such as redundancy pay or pay in lieu of notice;

- document showing the last day the Claimant worked, such as the P45;

- document showing how many days/hours a week the Claimant worked;

- any document explaining how overtime is paid;

- any document showing when the holiday year starts;

- any document recording holiday taken and holiday pay;

- any documents showing the Claimant's attempts to find new job;

- copy contract of employment and pay slips for new job;

- medical reports or "Fit" notes if unable to work since dismissal;

- any documents showing job availability in the locality for which Claimant could have applied.

21.3   Breach of contract claims

The most common breach of contract claim is a failure to pay notice pay. This will usually arise where an employee is dismissed summarily for gross misconduct. To be dismissed "summarily" means to be dismissed immediately without any notice.

Failure to pay notice pay is a breach of the contract of employment because most contracts will include a clause or paragraph dealing with termination of employment. A typical paragraph will state:

> *"The employer can terminate the contract of employment by giving the employee one month's notice in writing."*

In addition to the amount of notice stated in the contract there is provision in the Employment Rights Act 1996 ("ERA") regarding minimum periods of notice. Section 86 of the ERA states that an employee who has been employed for at least two years is entitled to not less than one week's notice and then at least one week's notice for each year of employment for more than two years up to a maximum of 12 years. This is called "statutory notice" as distinct from "contractual notice".

The statutory provision relating to minimum periods of notice overrides any contractual provision which would provide a shorter period of notice. Therefore if the contract of employment refers to one month's notice, this will be the minimum period of notice for the first four years of employment, but once you have worked for the Respondent for five years or more then you will be entitled to the statutory minimum period of notice.

If you have worked for five full years you will be entitled to five weeks notice; if you have worked for ten full years you will be entitled to ten weeks notice. The maximum length of statutory notice is 12 weeks, so if you have worked for 20 full years you will be entitled to 12 weeks notice and this remains the same even if you have worked for 25 or 30 years.

Although I have referred to claims for notice pay for summary dismissal you can claim notice pay in any case where you have been dismissed without the Respondent having given you the full amount of notice you are entitled to, either under the contract or under statute, whichever is the longer period.

If you succeed in your claim that the Respondent has dismissed you without notice or without giving you the full amount of notice to which you are entitled, you will be awarded damages in respect of the amount of notice pay to which you are entitled. The amount of damages will be the amount you would have been paid if you had been allowed to continue working until the end of your notice period. Therefore it will be a net sum, after deduction of tax and national insurance, and will include any bonuses, commission or overtime that you would have received in this period. It will also include the monetary value of any benefits in kind, i.e. company car, use of company mobile telephone, healthcare etc.

Even if you obtain a new job immediately after your dismissal you will be entitled to recover any notice pay you should have received - this is not subject to the duty to "mitigate your loss". This is a legal phrase which means you must make reasonable efforts to try to find an alternative job (see section 21.9 for a full explanation of mitigation of loss).

21.4   Other contract claims

You can bring a claim for breach of contract in respect of any benefit to which you were entitled under the contract of employment and which you have not received from your employer. This will include claims for commission you should have been paid or other contractual benefits that you did not receive or non-payment of expenses to which you are entitled to be reimbursed.

You can only bring such a claim on the termination of your employment - if you are still employed you would need to bring the claim in the County Court. The limit an employment tribunal can award for a breach of contract claim is £25,000. So if your claim is likely to be more than this you will need to consider bringing the claim in the County Court and you should consider getting professional advice on the advantages and disadvantages of bringing the claim in the County Court rather than the employment tribunal.

It is also worth remembering that the limitation for contract claims is three months from the date on which the contract of employment is terminated and this will apply even where the breach of contract has occurred many years earlier.

A breach of contract claim will not normally include a claim for failure to pay holiday pay, because unless the contract of employment specifically provides for the payment in respect of any untaken holiday, there is no implied term that an employee is entitled to be paid. In these circumstances the claim must be brought as a claim for breach of the provision of the Working Time Regulations or a deduction from wages claim.

21.5   Deduction from wages claim

You can bring a claim for non-payment of wages as a breach of contract claim but these claims can also be brought under section 13 of the Employment Rights Act 1996 (ERA) as unlawful deductions of wages.

Under section 13 an employer cannot make a deduction from the wages of a worker unless certain circumstances apply as follows:

- he is allowed to do so by law, for example he can deduct tax and national insurance payments;

- the worker has previously agreed in writing to the deduction being made;

- and in certain circumstances the employer can recover sums which have been over paid to the worker.

A claim for unlawful deduction of wages will include the basic pay you receive plus any bonuses you are entitled to (but not discretionary bonuses) and any commission or holiday pay you have accrued. It will not include payment of a sum in place of notice - this will have to be brought as a breach of contract claim. One of the benefits of bringing a claim for unlawful deduction of wages is that such a claim can be brought whilst you are still employed by the Respondent.

If you have been dismissed and are claiming that you are owed wages you can bring your claim both as a claim for breach of contract and a claim for unfair deductions.

A claim for failure to pay Statutory Sick Pay ("SSP") cannot be dealt with by the tribunal under section 13 but an application must be made to HM Revenue and Customs who have exclusive rights to adjudicate an issue regarding entitlement to SSP.

You need to be careful when calculating the time limit for bringing a claim under section 13 ERA because where there is a shortfall in the pay packet, the time limit (i.e. three months) starts to run from when the reduced payment is made. However, when no payment at all is made, the time limit starts to run from the time the obligation under the contract to make the payment arose.

21.6   Unfair dismissal

Reinstatement

Under section 9 of the ET1 form (see Chapter 9) which you filled in to bring your claim you will have stated what remedy you want.

The first box applies only to unfair dismissal, and should be ticked if you want your old job back plus compensation. Getting your old job back is called "reinstatement". The second box, which again only applies to unfair dismissal, should be ticked if you want another job with your employer or an associated employer plus compensation. Getting a different job with the same employer is called "re-engagement". The third box should be ticked if you just want compensation.

If the tribunal orders reinstatement it will be as if you had not been dismissed so that all the rights under your contract of employment will be returned to you, including any pay owing. If, in between the time you had been dismissed and the order for reinstatement, you would have been awarded a pay rise or some other improvement in your conditions of work, your employer will need to provide you with this benefit.

Re-engagement

This means that the tribunal will order that you be given a different job with either the same employer or an associated employer. The job must be comparable to the job from which you have been dismissed. The tribunal will need to state the nature of the job, the amount of pay and any other benefits you will get and the date that the job will start.

There are three main factors that the tribunal will take into account when considering an employee's request for reinstatement or re-engagement:

- whether the employer agrees;

- whether it is practicable; and

- whether the employee caused or contributed to his dismissal.

The tribunal will only consider an order for reinstatement or re-engagement if, at the end of the case, the employee states that this is something he still wants. It sometimes happens that although the employee stated in his ET1 he wants to be reinstated, the relationship between himself and his employer has broken down further during the course of the litigation process or the hearing and he no longer wants his job back or to work for the Respondent.

In my experience it is unusual for an employer having dismissed an employee to agree to take him back. If in your case the Respondent is willing to take you back in your old job or find a new position for you then the tribunal will normally agree to this.

Where the tribunal takes the view that it is evident from the proceedings that the relationship between the employer and the employee has broken down to such an extent that no real trust or confidence exists between them, it will be unlikely to make an order for reinstatement or re-engagement.

The fact that the Respondent has replaced the employee will not prevent an order for reinstatement from being made unless the employer can persuade the tribunal that:

- the only practicable arrangement for him to get the Claimant's work done was by employing a permanent employee; or

- he had engaged the replacement after a reasonable period without having heard from the Claimant that he wished to be reinstated or re-engaged, and it was no longer reasonable to arrange for the Claimant's work to be done except by a permanent employee.

If the employee has caused or contributed to his dismissal this will be a factor taken into account by the tribunal when considering re-engagement or reinstatement.

Orders for reinstatement or re-engagement are unusual orders for the tribunal to make. One of the main problems is that the process of bringing a claim and having it heard in the tribunal often aggravates the breakdown in trust between the parties. For example where an employee has accused his line manager of having lied or acting in bad faith when conducting disciplinary proceedings a tribunal will be reluctant to make an order reinstating the employee which would mean having to work with the same line manager.

Where an employer fails to comply with a re-engagement or reinstatement order and is not able to show that it was not practicable to comply with the order, the tribunal can make an additional award of between 26 and 52 weeks pay.

21.7   Compensation

In unfair dismissal cases the damages awarded by the tribunal fall into two categories - the basic award, which is essentially compensation for losing your job; and the compensatory award, which is compensation for all the losses you have suffered as a result of losing your job (mainly this will be loss of earnings).

21.8   Basic award

The basic award is intended to compensate you for the loss of your job and so the longer you have had the job the higher the amount of compensation is. It is calculated on exactly the same basis as a redundancy payment. If you were dismissed for redundancy and have received a redundancy payment from the Respondent, you will not be awarded a basic award in addition to this.

The amount of the basic award is calculated on the basis of the number of full years of employment and your age at the effective date of termination of your employment. For example if you started work on 1st January 2010 but were summarily dismissed on 25th October 2019 you will only have 9 full qualifying years. If you were dismissed on 2nd January 2020 you would have 10 qualifying years.

The maximum number of qualifying years is 20 even if you have been employed by the Respondent for more than 20 years.

The basic award is calculated by taking one week's gross pay and multiplying it by the number of full years you have been employed between the age of 22 and 40; it is multiplied by 1.5 weeks gross pay for each full year over the age of 41; the figure is half a week's pay under the age of 22.

So for example if you worked from 1st January 2010 to 7th July 2020 you would have 10 years' qualifying employment. If your 41st birthday was on 6th June 2015 then for 5 of these years (from 1st January 2010 to 5th June 2015) you would have been under 41 years old and for 5 of these years (between 6th June 2015 and 7th July 2020) you would have been over 41. In this case to calculate the basic award you would multiply one week's salary by 5 for the first 5 years employment and then 1.5 weeks salary by 5 for the second five years' employment.

If your gross weekly salary was £200 the basic award would be £2,500 (i.e. £200 x 5 = £1,000 plus £300 x 5 = £1,500).

In this example if your 41st birthday was after the 7th July 2015 (say on 7th October 2015) the position would be different because you would have only worked for four full years over the age of 41 (from 7th October 2015 to 7th July 2020). In this case your basic award would be based on 6 years at one week's salary and four years at 1.5 weeks salary.

If your gross weekly salary was £200 the award would be £2,400 (£200 x 6 = £1,200 plus £300 x 4 = £1,200).

Limit to a week's pay

The amount of a week's pay is subject to a cap, which means the maximum amount that can be used in the calculation. The current cap is £538 and this figure is usually increased by a small amount each year. This figure of £538 has been in place since 6th April 2020 and before that it was £525. You can check what the figure is by putting Employment Rights (Increase of Limits) Order 2020 into Google search and a number of different websites will come up showing the increase in the limit.

What this means is that you will have to limit your weekly pay to this figure of £538 even if you are earning more than this. This figure will not usually include overtime or bonuses but will include commission if this is part of your normal week's pay.

You can claim a basic award even if you started a new job on the same salary or a higher salary the day after you were dismissed, unless you have unreasonably refused an offer by the Respondent to reinstate you - I will consider this and other ways in which the basic award might be reduced in more detail below.

There are some circumstances where there is a minimum figure for the basic award - this figure is currently £6,562. These circumstances include a dismissal where the tribunal finds that the reason for the dismissal is connected with the fact that you have been designated to carry out certain health and safety activities or are a worker's representative on health and safety matters.

Reduction in the basic award

There are certain circumstances, which are set out in section 122 Employment Rights Act 1996, in which the basic award can be reduced.

Unreasonable refusal of offer of reinstatement

The first of these circumstances is that your employer has offered to reinstate you on the same basis as you were employed and the tribunal considers that you have unreasonably refused this offer of reinstatement. The tribunal can reduce the award if it considers it is just and equitable to do so. This phrase "just and equitable" essentially means whether it is fair to do so in the circumstances. If the tribunal finds that your refusal of the offer was unreasonable it is likely to reduce the amount of the basic award.

Contributory fault

The second ground on which the tribunal can reduce the basic award is where it considers any conduct of the Claimant before the dismissal was such that it would be just and equitable to reduce the basic award. This is usually referred to as "contributory fault". The basic principle is where you have done something that led to or contributed to your dismissal and this can be taken into account by the tribunal in reducing the award if it thinks it would be fair to do so.

A typical example of contributory fault is where the employee has been dismissed for an act of gross misconduct but the employer has not carried out a fair procedure. The tribunal has decided that the dismissal was unfair because of the procedural failings but it has also concluded that there was good evidence you were guilty of the misconduct alleged and in the circumstances it would be fair to reduce the amount of the basic award. The tribunal can reduce the award by up to 100% so that you would get no basic award if it considered that, in the circumstances of the case, your conduct was so serious that you did not deserve anything.

There will not normally be a reduction in respect of contributory fault in a redundancy case.

The conduct that is taken into account can be conduct that is not discovered by the Respondent until after the dismissal. For example, if you are dismissed for fighting and your employer discovers after your dismissal that you had been stealing from the company then, even if the tribunal concludes that you were unfairly dismissed for fighting, it can still reduce the basic award if it finds there was good evidence that you had been stealing.

If you were dismissed for redundancy and have received a redundancy payment from the Respondent you will not be awarded a basic award in addition to this.

21.9   Compensatory award

The compensatory award covers any sums that you have lost as a result of being unfairly dismissed or having been discriminated against. The main provisions in relation to the compensatory award are set out in section 123 of the Employment Rights Act 1996.

Section 123(1) says that the amount of the compensatory award

> *"must be an amount that the tribunal considers is just and equitable in all the circumstances having regard to the loss sustained by the Claimant as a result of the dismissal insofar as that loss is attributable to action taken by the employer".*

What this means is that the tribunal must consider whether it is fair to make an award of compensation in all the circumstances of the case.

The award is for loss sustained by the Claimant and includes any expenses he has incurred because of the dismissal and any benefits he would have been awarded if the dismissal had not taken place.

Maximum award

Since 29th July 2013 the maximum award is limited to the "statutory cap" or 52 weeks gross pay, whichever is the lowest. The statutory cap is currently £88,519 for any dismissal on or after 6th April 2020. So if your gross annual salary is £25,000 for example, the maximum compensatory award will be £25,000. If your gross annual salary is £100,000 the maximum compensatory award will be £88,519. This limit does not apply if the dismissal was for whistleblowing or connected to health and safety activities, nor does it apply in discrimination claims under the Equality Act 2010.

The statutory cap will apply where you have not been able to find a new job and have been or are likely to be out of work for 12 months. If you have found a new job but on a lower salary you will be able to claim the difference between your old salary and the new salary. If you can satisfy the tribunal that you are unlikely to get a better paid job in the next couple of years they can award the difference in salary for these future years so long as the amount does not exceed the figure for your gross one year's salary.

For example if you are being paid £2,000 a year less in your new job than in your old job, and this is likely to be the case for the next five years, the tribunal can award you loss of earnings over this five year period, i.e. £10,000, so long as this is less than your gross annual salary.

Loss of earnings

The main element of the compensatory award will normally be past loss of earnings.

This is based on your net loss of earnings between the date of dismissal and the date of the award. It is important to remember that it is the *net* loss after deduction of tax and national insurance because this represents the amount you would actually have been paid if you had not been dismissed.

The figure will include any bonuses, commission or overtime that you would have received in this period. It will also include the monetary value of any benefits in kind, including such things as use of a company car or company mobile phone. You will need to put forward some evidence as to how much, in weekly or monthly figures, you consider this benefit was worth to you. For example you could obtain a figure from a phone shop showing how much it would cost to rent an equivalent mobile phone. The AA on their website has a table showing the cost of running a car privately.

The award is to compensate you for earnings that you have lost, therefore if you started a new job the day after you were dismissed earning the same or a higher salary and are unlikely to lose this job in the near future, then you will not be entitled to loss of earnings as you will not have incurred any loss.

If you have started a new job or have done some paid employment since you were dismissed you will need to set out your earnings from this work. The amount of compensation you are awarded will be based on the difference between the amount you would have earned if you had not been dismissed and the amount you received from your new job.

If you have started a new job but have then been dismissed through no fault of your own, this will not prevent you claiming a continuing loss of earnings against the Respondent but you will need to give credit for any sums you have been paid in the other job.

Overlap with notice pay

If you have claimed notice pay there will be an overlap with the compensatory award. For example if you have claimed one month's notice pay and are awarded this, you will not get your loss of earnings for the same period under the compensatory award as this would mean you were being compensated twice for the same period. But it is worth claiming for this period as notice pay because it means that if you have been out of work for a year or more you might still get a year's loss of earnings in addition to the notice pay.

Pension

There are two main types of workplace pension schemes. One is a defined contributions scheme, sometimes referred to as a "money purchase" scheme. The other is a defined benefit scheme, sometimes referred to as a "final salary" scheme.

If your pension is a money purchase scheme you are entitled to claim the amount that your employer contributed to your pension as part of your compensatory award. You should be able to find this sum on your pay slip.

If your pension is a final salary scheme the amount of the pension will be based on your final salary and length of service. Because of the cost to the employer these schemes have become less popular and your potential loss can be much greater than the amount of the employer's contributions as it is based on the reduction in the value of the pension that has been caused by your dismissal.

New guidance on the calculation of pension loss was published in August 2017 and updated in December 2019. This guidance is called "Principles for compensating pension loss" and broadly it says that for all defined contribution and most defined benefit schemes (sometimes called "final salary" or "career average" schemes), Claimants could be compensated for loss of employer pension contributions for a period of time the ET determines is appropriate. For Claimants who are members of defined benefit schemes, and who might be claiming career long loss for example, a more complex method can be used to calculate pension loss. However, it is expected that this type of calculation would be very rare in practice and expert actuarial advice may also be needed.

The guidance on pension loss can be accessed at: https://www.judiciary.uk/wp-content/uploads/2013/08/Principles-Second-Revision.pdf.

Job seeking expenses

You are entitled to recover the cost of any expenses incurred in looking for new work, including travel expenses. You should keep any receipts as evidence of the sums spent.

Loss of statutory rights

This is a sum to compensate for the loss of the right not to be unfairly dismissed. It is normally a figure of between £350 and £600 as it will now take you two years to build up these rights in a new job.

Future loss of earnings

The loss of future earnings relates to the expected loss of earnings from the date that you are drawing up the schedule of loss (see Chapter 16). If you have a date for the tribunal hearing it is easiest to divide this period into i) the period up to the date of the hearing and ii) the period after the date of hearing.

In theory a tribunal can award future loss of earnings up to retirement age, but in practice there are various limitations on future loss of earnings. There is the statutory cap giving the maximum award as limited to £88,519 or 52 weeks gross salary whichever is the lower. If you are out of work the tribunal will consider when you are likely to get a new job. This will depend on a variety of factors in particular the availability of work which you are qualified to do in the region that you are able to work.

If your claim for compensatory loss is likely to be over £30,000 you will be taxed on the sum above this amount and so you will need to gross up the figure claimed. What this means is that you will need to claim the gross amount which, when taxed, will leave you with the net amount you would have been paid if you had not been dismissed.

Deductions from the compensatory award

Any sums that you have been paid by your employer for the dismissal will be deducted from the compensatory award.

The loss of earnings must be caused by the dismissal i.e. it must be the dismissal that has caused your loss of earnings rather than some other cause. For example if you were off sick at the time of your dismissal your compensation would be limited to the amount of sick pay you would have received, which might be less than your usual pay (it is your illness that has caused you to receive sick pay and not the dismissal). This will not apply if it is the actions of your employer in dismissing you that caused you to become sick.

Polkey deduction

One of the most common areas of deduction, particularly in cases of dismissal for gross misconduct and redundancy dismissals, is what is referred to as a "*Polkey* deduction". This is because it comes from a well-known legal case of *Polkey v AE Dayton Services Ltd* [1987] UKHL 8 which was heard in the House of Lords.

This principle will apply in cases where the employer has been found to have unfairly dismissed the employee because of some defect in the procedure, for example by not giving the employee an opportunity of putting his case, or not carrying out a fair procedure when selecting the employee for redundancy. Having made a finding of unfair dismissal the tribunal will then go on to consider what would have happened if a fair procedure had in fact been followed. If they find that there was a 100% chance that the employee would have been dismissed in any event then the compensatory award will be limited to the period between when the employee was actually dismissed and the date by which it would have taken a fair procedure to have taken place, possibly a month or two.

Where the tribunal finds that, if a fair procedure had been followed, the employee definitely would not have been dismissed then there would be no *Polkey* reduction.

Alternatively the tribunal can find that there was some percentage chance of a dismissal, possibly 50%, and reduce the compensatory award by that percentage.

Mitigation of loss

The phrase "mitigation of loss" means acting so as to limit the amount of your loss. With respect to loss of earnings this means that you would be expected to make reasonable efforts to find a new job.

If you have not been able to find a new job it is important to show the tribunal the efforts you have made to get one. One of the best ways of doing this is to keep a note or a diary entry of all the efforts you have made to look for work, attending the job centre, looking online, registering with agencies, and looking in trade journals or the jobs section of local papers. Make a note of all the jobs you have applied for with details of the date, who the job was with and other details about the job. Keep a note of all the replies you got and any interviews you attended.

Although it is for the Respondent to persuade the tribunal that the Claimant has not mitigated his loss by looking for work, if the Claimant has no evidence of trying to find alternative position and has no good excuse for this, he will normally be considered not to have mitigated his loss. In these circumstances the tribunal would probably limit the amount of loss of earnings he would be awarded.

The most usual position is that the Claimant will have made some attempts to find a new job but the Respondent will seek to persuade the tribunal that he has not made a reasonable effort to do so. Often the Respondent will obtain lists of job vacancies that they argue the Claimant could have applied for within his region. It will then be for the Claimant to explain to the tribunal why the jobs shown were not suitable or why he did not apply for them. The Claimant has to show that he has made reasonable efforts to obtain alternative work, including taking a job on lower wages if he is unable to find a job on the same pay as his previous job.

Contributory fault

The Employment Rights Act 1996 at section 123(6) states that where the tribunal finds that the dismissal was to any extent caused or contributed to by the Claimant it shall reduce the amount of the compensatory award by such proportion as it considers just and equitable.

What this means is if the tribunal finds that you have done something that led to or contributed to your dismissal this can be taken into account by the tribunal in reducing the amount of the compensatory award if it thinks it would be fair to do so. The degree of fault will be given in percentage terms. For example the tribunal will state that you were 50% to blame for the dismissal and so will reduce the award by 50%.

There are three elements to contributory fault:

- you must have done something wrong or failed to do something that you should have done, and the tribunal will need to specify what it is that you have done wrong. You need to have been at fault, so for example absence from work through sickness would not normally be regarded as being your fault.

- this act must have contributed to the dismissal, which means that the Respondent must have been aware of the act at the time of the dismissal and it was part of the reason that you were dismissed. This will exclude something that the Respondent later finds out about after the dismissal. So for example if you were dismissed for fighting and afterwards the Respondent finds out that you had been stealing, the compensatory award could not be reduced for contributory fault but it could be reduced under the provisions of section 126 (1) if it did not consider it was fair in the circumstances to allow you to have compensation.

- finally the tribunal must consider that it would just and equitable i.e. fair to reduce the amount of the compensatory award.

Once the tribunal concludes that all three elements are present it will then consider by what percentage the award should be reduced, which can be up to 100% when you would receive no compensatory award at all. It will only be as much as 100% if the tribunal were to conclude that the dismissal was totally your fault.

Deduction of benefits

When a Claimant receives an award for loss of earnings he will have to give credit for state benefits received during the period in which he claims loss of earnings. The reason for this is to avoid what is referred to as "double recovery" where the Claimant gets both state benefits and loss of earnings for the same period.

If the benefit received was Employment and Support Allowance (formerly Incapacity Benefit), the amount of benefit received is calculated by the judge and this is deducted from the award for loss of earnings. It is important for the Claimant to provide the correct figure and he should bring along to the tribunal hearing any documentation he has showing the receipt of benefits. This will apply where the inability to work has been caused by the dismissal.

If the Claimant has been paid income support or jobseekers allowance during the period covered by the claim for loss of earnings the procedure is slightly different. The judge will calculate the amount of lost earnings up to the date of the tribunal hearing. This figure is referred to as "the prescribed element". It will not include any future loss of earnings. The Respondent will not pay this prescribed element until he has been contacted by Department of Work and Pensions who will provide him with "a recoupment notice". This notice will set out the amount that the Respondent has to pay to the DWP in respect of income support or jobseekers allowance that the Claimant has received. The difference between this sum and the amount of prescribed element will then be paid by the Respondent to the Claimant.

ACAS uplift

If you are alleging that the Respondent failed to follow the recommendations set out in the ACAS Code of Practice on Grievance and Disciplinary Procedures the tribunal can increase the compensatory award (but not the basic award) by up to 25%. The percentage uplift will normally be at the top end if the breach of the Code was particularly serious, for example dismissal without following any disciplinary procedure. The uplift is likely to be lower if the breach was more minor.

The tribunal can reduce the award by up to 25% where the Claimant has failed to raise a grievance before bringing the claim and the tribunal finds that the Claimant has unreasonably failed to comply with the provisions of the ACAS Code of Practice on Disciplinary and Grievance Procedures.

21.10   Other claims

Holiday pay

If you are claiming holiday pay, this will based on the number of days holiday the tribunal finds that you were entitled to.

Failure to provide a statement of terms and conditions

If the tribunal finds that the Respondent has not provided you with a written contract of employment or a letter setting out the main terms and conditions of your employment, you are entitled to an award of at least two weeks and up to four weeks pay, which will be capped at £538 a week.

It is important to note that you only get this award if you have succeeded on another substantive claim such as unfair dismissal, wrongful dismissal or discrimination.

Breach of right to be accompanied to a disciplinary or grievance hearing

The maximum award is two weeks pay capped at £538 a week.

Injury to feelings

If you are bringing a discrimination claim you can claim for injury to feelings. You can also claim injury to feelings if your claim is that you have been subjected to detriment for whistleblowing, but this only applies where the detriment in the whistleblowing case is not dismissal but some other detrimental act.

You do not have to specify a figure for this but it is helpful if you set out which band you consider your case comes within. There are three bands, sometimes referred to as "*Vento* bands" (from the case in which the guidelines bands were first set out).

The top *Vento* band covers awards from £27,000 to £45,000 and is appropriate in cases of serious discrimination where there has been a long campaign of harassment or discrimination and which has had a serious effect on the health of the employee. The most exceptional cases are capable of exceeding £45,000.

The middle *Vento* band is now from £9,000 to £27,000 and this will be appropriate for a serious one-off case of discrimination or harassment or where the Claimant has lost their job.

The low *Vento* band is from £900 to £9,000 and is appropriate for a minor act harassment or discrimination.

Psychiatric injury

In addition to an award for injury to feelings in a discrimination claim, a Claimant is also entitled to damages for any psychiatric illness they have suffered as a result of the Respondent's discrimination. If you are intending to bring a claim for psychiatric illness it will be necessary for you to have a medical report, preferably from a qualified psychiatrist or psychologist, confirming both you are suffering from a psychiatric illness and that this has been caused or contributed to by the Respondent's behaviour.

Recommendations in discrimination cases

In discrimination cases the tribunal make recommendations. This recommendation will normally be that the Respondent must, within a specified time, take certain specified steps which would have the effect of removing or reducing any adverse effect of any matter to which the proceedings relate might have on the Claimant. For example if, in a disability discrimination case, one of the effects is that the Claimant's disability means that he is particularly sensitive to the cold the recommendation would be that the Claimant be provided with a heater within a certain period.

Interest

You are entitled to interest on awards for discrimination both for the damages for injury to feelings and damages for other financial losses such as past loss of earnings. There is no need to set out the calculation in the schedule of loss since the tribunal will work out the appropriate interest on awards at the end of the case (as long as you remind them).

The interest on the award for injury to feelings runs from the date of the discriminatory act to the date of judgment; interest on awards for other financial loss such as loss of earnings runs from a mid-point being halfway between the date of the discriminatory act and the date of judgment.

Summary of adjustments that the tribunal can make to the compensatory award

The first thing the tribunal must do is assess the total amount of the loss that you have suffered as a result of the dismissal. In a discrimination case this will include any award for injury to feelings.

The tribunal will make the following deductions or additions where appropriate:

- The tribunal will deduct from the figure any payments the Respondent has made to you for the dismissal and this can include a payment in lieu of notice or a termination payment;

- The tribunal will then deduct any sums you have earned from other employment since your dismissal;

- The tribunal will then factor in any *Polkey* deduction, so if they consider there was a 50% chance you would have been dismissed in any event, the amount of the compensatory award would be reduced at this stage by 50%;

- The tribunal will then consider whether there should be any uplift or reduction to the award on the basis that the employer or employee failed to follow the ACAS guidelines. Again this will be given as a percentage figure up to 25% and the award will at this stage be increased or decreased by this percentage;

- The tribunal will then consider any reduction for contributory fault and will at this stage reduce the award by the percentage by which it finds you contributed to the dismissal;

- The tribunal will make any deduction for income support etc;

- If the compensatory award is over £30,000 and therefore liable for taxation any grossing up (see Chapter 16) to take account of tax will be done before the statutory cap is imposed;

- Finally the tribunal will limit the award to the amount of any statutory cap if this applies. For example if the claim is for unfair dismissal and the compensatory award is still above the statutory cap of £88,519 or 52 weeks gross salary it will reduce the award to this figure. If the claim is for discrimination or for unfair dismissal because of whistleblowing or health and safety activities there is no statutory cap.

Chapter 22

Judgments

22.1 Reserved judgment

After the tribunal has heard all the evidence and the parties' submissions it can either give a decision the same day or it can give a "reserved judgment". A reserved judgment means that the decision is not given on the day of the hearing but will be sent to the parties in writing at a later date.

As a general rule if the matter is complex either factually or because of the law the tribunal will give a reserved judgment. Also if the tribunal hearing finishes late in the day and there is insufficient time to give a judgment the tribunal is likely to give a reserved judgment.

If the judge dismisses the claim in the written judgment and there is no counter-claim, or if the judgment deals with both liability and the amount of damages, then there will be no need for the parties to return to the tribunal unless there is an application for costs to be dealt with.

22.2 Judgment on liability only

If the judgment deals only with liability and it is in favour of the Claimant then the parties will have to return to the tribunal to deal with the amount of damages, unless this can be agreed between them.

If you are bringing a claim and have succeeded on liability then you can either try to negotiate a settlement for damages with the other side or you can let the tribunal decide the amount. You will be in a significantly stronger position negotiating at this stage than before the hearing because you are no longer at risk of losing your claim.

The tribunal should have considered in their judgment issues of contributory fault and *Polkey* reduction (see Chapter 21) but if it has not dealt with the amount of damages, it will probably not have dealt with the issue of whether you have miti-gated your loss.

As with settling the case before the hearing the benefit of agreeing the amount of damages with the other side is that you can negotiate for a reference to be part of the settlement agreement. You will also not suffer a reduction of damages under the recoupment provisions for job seekers allowance.

22.3   Reasons for the decision

When giving judgment, whether orally at the end of the hearing or in writing by way of a reserved judgment, the tribunal must give reasons for their decision. If the tribunal judge gives his judgment orally at the end of the hearing you can request either at the time or within 14 days that this judgment be given in writing.

Rule 62(5) of Schedule 1 of the 2013 Employment Tribunal Regulations states that the reasons shall:

- identify the issues which the tribunal has determined;

- state the findings of facts made in relation to those issues;

- identify the relevant law;

- state how the law has been applied to the findings in order to decide the issues;

- where a financial award is made the reasons shall identify how the amount to be paid is calculated.

The judgment will normally summarise the evidence that the tribunal regarded as relevant to the issues it had to decide. Where there is a dispute of fact based on the evidence from different witnesses and it is a fact that is important to the issues, the tribunal will make a finding of fact based on the evidence they have heard and will state which of the witnesses they consider to have given more reliable evidence. Sometimes tribunals are reluctant to find that a witness lied when giving evidence and will either say that that witness was mistaken or just that they preferred the evidence of the other witness.

It is important that the tribunal identifies the issues on which they have to make a finding. For example, in a case of unfair dismissal where the Claimant was dismissed for misconduct, the issue that the tribunal has to decide is whether the dismissal was fair and reasonable. The tribunal must not consider whether it would have dismissed the employee but whether dismissal was within the band of reasonable responses that was open to an employer.

In unfair dismissal claims, whether the Claimant or the Respondent is successful, the tribunal should identify what it has found to be the reason for the dismissal, unless it finds that there was no dismissal.

When a tribunal decides to reduce an award for contributory fault or on the basis of a *Polkey* reduction it must set out the facts on which it has based this decision and explain why it is making the reduction.

22.4   Inferences

In discrimination cases the law has recognised that it will often be very difficult for employees to prove that their employer was motivated by discrimination. For example if a female employee is not promoted the employer is unlikely to say that the reason she was not promoted was because she was female. In these circumstances if the female employee can show that she was better qualified for the new position than the male employee who was actually promoted, this could raise an "inference" that the employer discriminated against her because of her sex. It will then be for the employer to satisfy the tribunal that there was some other non-discriminatory reason for the promotion of the male employee.

Where the tribunal makes an inference like this it is important that it sets out all the facts that it relies on to make the inference and if the employer puts forward different reasons for his decision the tribunal will need to explain why it does not accept the employer's reasons.

22.5   Remedy

If the judgment deals with remedy and this includes an award to be made to the Claimant by the Respondent, the judge will set out the amount that the Respondent has to pay and how this has been calculated. If there are deductions to be made, including reducing the award for contributory fault or on the basis of the *Polkey* principle or any uplift, the judge will include these in his calculation. He will set out the amount that the Respondent will have to pay the Claimant and the time by which this amount should be paid, which will usually be 14 or 21 days.

If it is a discrimination claim and the tribunal finds that the Claimant has been subjected to discrimination, it can make recommendations. These will be included in the judgment and will usually be that the Respondent must, within a specified time, take certain specified steps, which would have the effect of removing or reducing any adverse effect that any matter might have on the Claimant.

22.6   Reconsideration of judgments

In certain circumstances a tribunal can be asked to "reconsider" a decision or judgment it has made. This was formerly referred to as a "review" of a judgment and means that the tribunal is asked to look again at the decision it has made and see if it was correct.

Under rule 70 of Schedule 1 of the 2013 Employment Tribunal Regulations a tribunal may, either on its own initiative or on the application of a party, reconsider any judgment where it is necessary in the interests of justice to do so.

A reconsideration is different from an "appeal" because there are very limited circumstances in which a tribunal will reconsider a decision. I will set out these circumstances below.

When the tribunal does carry out a reconsideration of its judgment it can confirm, vary or revoke the original decision:

- If it "confirms" the judgment this means that the tribunal is satisfied that the right decision was made and it will not change that decision.

- If it "varies" the judgment the tribunal accepts that the decision was incorrect and it will give a new, different decision.

- To "revoke" the judgment means to withdraw the decision and if this is done the judgment can be given again.

The application for a reconsideration can be made at the hearing or within 14 days from the day the judgment was sent out. Unless the application is made at the hearing it must be made in writing and sent to the tribunal with a copy being sent to all the other parties.

The rules state that, where practicable, the reconsideration of a judgment is made by the same judge as made the decision. The judge will look at the application and if he considers that there is no reasonable prospect of the judgment being varied or revoked the application will be refused. Otherwise the tribunal will send the parties a notice giving the other party, who did not make the application, an opportunity to respond to the application.

If the tribunal judge agrees to a reconsideration this will done at a hearing, unless the judge considers that a hearing is not necessary, but in this case both parties must be given an opportunity to make further written representations.

22.7 Circumstances in which a judgment will be reconsidered

A judgment can be reconsidered in the following circumstances:

- if the decision was wrongly made as a result of an error on the part of the tribunal staff;

- if one of the parties did not receive notice of the proceedings;

- if the decision was made in the absence of a party who was entitled to be present. This will apply if the absence was for a genuine reason and not merely because the party chose not to attend;

- new evidence has become available since the decision, which was not or could not reasonably have been available at the original hearing;

- the interests of justice require that a reconsideration be undertaken.

If you are trying to get a reconsideration of the judgment on the basis that you did not receive notice of the proceedings, it will not usually be sufficient just to inform the tribunal that you did not receive that notice - you will have to give some explanation as to why you never received notice of the proceedings. This is because the tribunal will have sent out a notice of the hearing date at least 14 days before the date fixed. This notice will have been sent out by post to the address that the tribunal have for you from the ET1 or ET3. The law says that where a notice has been sent by post it is presumed or "deemed" that there has been valid service of the notice. In these circumstances you will have to persuade the tribunal that for some reason you did not get the letter, for example because the address they sent it to was incorrect.

If you are trying to get a reconsideration on the basis that the decision was made in your absence you will need to persuade the tribunal that you had a good reason for this absence. This reason will normally need to include an explanation as to why you were unable to contact the tribunal before the decision was made to let them know that you would be unable to attend.

If you are trying to get a reconsideration on the ground of new evidence it is not just sufficient to show that you have evidence that was not put before the original tribunal. You have to show that this evidence was not available before the hearing and that you could not reasonably have known that it existed before the hearing.

The last ground for a reconsideration is that it is in the interests of justice that you should be allowed one. This general ground is often included as well as one of the other specific grounds. When considering the interests of justice the interests of both parties must be taken into account by the tribunal.

An example is where the tribunal makes a finding such as contributory fault or a *Polkey* reduction without warning the party that it was considering this issue and had not given them an opportunity to address the tribunal on this point.

Another example is where an event which occurs soon after the decision has the effect of undermining that decision. For example, if the Claimant was awarded a sum for loss of future earnings on the basis that he was unlikely to get another job in the near future and in fact he gets a new job very shortly after the decision, then the Respondent could apply for a reconsideration.

When making an application for a reconsideration make sure you include as much detail as you can, not only giving the reasons why you want a reconsideration, but also why it would be unfair if you were not allowed a reconsideration.

Chapter 23

Costs

23.1   Costs orders

The question of costs has become increasingly important in employment cases as tribunals appear to be more willing to make costs orders.

One of the risks that a Claimant faces when bringing a tribunal claim is that he not only loses the case but he has to pay some or all of the Respondent's legal costs, which can amount to many thousands of pounds. In a recent case the Employment Appeal Tribunal upheld an £87,000 costs award against an unrepresented Claimant of limited means (*Vaughan v London Borough of Lewisham & Ors* UKEAT/0534/12/SM). It was said in this case that the threshold test for costs was the same whether the party was acting in person or was professionally represented.

A costs order will only be made in favour of a party who has been legally represented and the word "costs" covers any fees, charges or expenses incurred by that party for the purpose of or in connection with a tribunal hearing.

The party paying the costs is called the "paying party". The party to whom the costs are being paid is called the "receiving party".

23.2   Preparation time orders

Where the receiving party is unrepresented the order is referred to as a "preparation time order". A preparation time order is an order that the paying party make a payment to the receiving party in respect of their time spent working on a case.

If you are representing yourself and you consider that the other side, whether it is the Claimant or the Respondent, has acted unreasonably you can apply for a preparation time order. This will only apply to time spent by yourself or anyone helping you prepare your case in the preparation for the hearing and not to time spent in the hearing itself. The current hourly rate allowed by the tribunals is £40 per hour and increases each year on 6th April by £1 an hour.

It is worthwhile noting down the time spent on preparing different aspects of the case as you go along so that you will have a record to present to the tribunal when making your application for a preparation time order.

The rules relating to costs orders and preparation time orders are set out in Schedule 1 of the Employment Tribunal Rules 2013 from rule 74 to rule 84.

I will refer to costs orders in this chapter but the same principles will apply to preparation time orders.

23.3 When can a costs order be made?

The rules say that a tribunal may make a costs order where a party or a party's representative has acted vexatiously, abusively, disruptively or otherwise unreasonably in either bringing or conducting the proceedings or the claim or response has no reasonable prospects of success.

A vexatious claim

This is one that has no real prospects of success but is brought with the intention of harassing, annoying or embarrassing the Respondent, and the same would apply to a response. It can also include a claim where the issues between the parties have already been decided but the Claimant is trying to bring the claim again. Vexatious conduct is behaviour that is intended to cause harassment or annoyance to the other side. It is an abuse of the tribunal system in that the motive in bringing the claim is to cause harassment.

An abusive claim

This means one in which abusive or deliberately insulting terms are used to describe the other side. It would be regarded by the tribunal as being a misuse of the right to bring proceedings to cause harassment or distress to the other party rather than to make a valid claim.

Disruptive behaviour

This means behaviour which is intended to prevent or disrupt the proper progress of proceedings. This is likely to refer to behaviour during the course of a hearing which has the effect of preventing the hearing continuing.

No reasonable prospects of success

The most common basis for a costs order is that one of the parties has behaved unreasonably in either bringing a claim which had no reasonable prospects of success or defending a claim on a basis that had no reasonable prospects of success. In effect this one category includes all the other categories, as any behaviour which is vexatious, abusive or disruptive is likely to be found to be unreasonable behaviour.

23.4 Deposit

Under rule 39 Schedule 1 of the Employment Tribunal Rules 2013 the tribunal has the power to make a "deposit order" against a party as a condition of continuing the claim or response (see Chapter 14). If a deposit order has been made and that party has then lost on the allegation or argument for which the deposit was made, that party shall be treated as having acted unreasonably in pursuing the argument. That party is likely to have a costs order made against him unless he can show that it was not unreasonable to pursue that argument. If costs are ordered, the payment of the deposit shall go towards the amount of costs to be paid.

23.5 Costs warning

Even where the tribunal has not ordered a deposit be paid it is open to either party to notify the other side that they consider either the claim or response as a whole, or a specific point or argument, to be unreasonable and warn the other side that if they persist with this point and lose they will have to face an application for costs.

The fact that a costs warning has been given by a party is a factor that a tribunal can take into account when considering whether the other party has acted unreasonably and whether a costs order should be made.

This is a tactic that is in my experience often used by one side's representative, normally the Respondent, against the other side, the Claimant. What it means is that the losing party cannot say to the tribunal that they were not warned of the risk of having a costs order made against them. Although a costs warning from the other side does not have the significance of a costs warning made by the tribunal it is still a factor that tribunals tend to take into account.

When making a costs warning to the other side it is important to specify why you consider their case to be misconceived or unreasonable.

The fact that there has been no costs warning from either the tribunal or the other side does not prevent a tribunal from making a costs order at the end of the case if it considers that party has acted unreasonably.

23.6 Untruthful allegations

One of the most common ways a tribunal will conclude that a Claimant has acted unreasonably is if they consider the allegations, normally of sex or race discrimination, against the Respondent have been made up. If the tribunal concludes after the hearing that the Claimant has deliberately lied about the allegations, they will normally go on to consider making a costs order.

23.7 Withdrawal of the claim

If you withdraw your claim there is a risk that the other side will apply for a costs order against you. The later you make your application to withdraw the more likely it is that the tribunal will find that you have acted unreasonably. You will need to explain why it is that you are withdrawing the claim and why you did not withdraw the claim earlier.

The tribunal can make an award of costs if it considers that you acted unreasonably in delaying the application to withdraw but it should only award those costs that have been caused by the delay - it should not award all the costs in respect of bringing the claim unless the tribunal concludes that it was unreasonable to have brought the claim at all.

23.8   Postponement of a hearing

If, at the tribunal hearing, one party asks that the hearing be postponed, the tribunal will normally consider making a costs order against that party unless it is satisfied that the party asking for the postponement was not at fault, for example if they or one of their witnesses was ill and unable to attend the hearing. The costs order will not be for all the costs but only in respect of those costs that have been wasted as a result of the postponement.

23.9   Breach of an order

A tribunal may also make a costs order where a party has been in breach of any order or direction.

23.10   Reinstatement or re-engagement

The tribunal must make a costs order if, in an unfair dismissal case, the Claimant has indicated that he wishes to be re-engaged or reinstated and the Respondent has failed, without a special reason, to produce evidence as to the availability of a job and there has to be an adjournment (postponement) for the Respondent to produce this evidence.

23.11   Amount of costs order

When a tribunal has decided to make a costs order (this does not apply to preparation time orders) it can either make an order that a specified amount of costs up to a limit of £20,000 be paid or order that the amount to be paid be determined by a judge by way of a detailed assessment, in which case the amount of the costs ordered can be over £20,000.

A "detailed assessment" is a procedure where the party in whose favour the order has been made sets out a detailed list of all the time their legal advisors have spent preparing the case, as well as the hourly rate they have charged. This can differ depending on who it was that was working on the case - a partner in a firm of solicitors will have a higher hourly rate than a trainee or legal executive.

23.12   Wasted costs order

This is a costs order that is made against a party's representative rather than the party themselves. The tribunal may make a wasted costs order against a representative in favour of any party if they have incurred costs as a result of an improper, unreasonable or negligent act or omission by the representative.

23.13   Ability to pay

In deciding whether to make any costs order, including a preparation time order, the tribunal must have regard to the paying party's ability to pay. What this means is that before making a costs order the tribunal must make some enquiry into the party's ability to pay, which will mean looking at their current income, whether this is likely to change in the future and whether any savings or capital are available. As long as the tribunal has regard to the ability to pay they do not have to take this into account but if they do not they will have to explain why. Even where the paying party has no current means to satisfy a costs order the tribunal can make the order on the basis that it was likely that the party would be able to pay at some time in the future.

Chapter 24

Appeals

24.1   Who can appeal?

Either side can appeal a judgment, decision, direction or order of the employment tribunal but you will have to show that there has been an error of law. The appeal will be to the Employment Appeal Tribunal ("EAT"). Generally you will have 42 days from the date of the decision in which to bring your appeal.

A Practice Statement on Notice of Appeals and Skeleton Arguments was published by the President of The Employment Appeal Tribunal in 2015 and can be accessed at www.judiciary.gov.uk/publications/practice-statement-notices-of-appeal-and-skeleton-arguments. The guidance stresses the importance of keeping Notice of Appeals short and to the point. It also provides guidance on what they should look like.

24.2   Grounds of appeal

It is not enough to bring an appeal on the basis that you disagree with the tribunal's decision or you disagree with their findings of fact - you will need to show that the tribunal made an error of law.

In general terms an error of law will mean that the tribunal has made a mistake about the legal principles to be applied to the case but in certain circumstances this can apply to the evidence. The tribunal will have heard the witnesses give evidence and they will decide which witnesses they believe or prefer - the Employment Appeal Tribunal will not usually interfere with these findings. But if you can show that there was no evidence to support the findings that the tribunal made or that no reasonable tribunal could have made these findings and the decision was perverse, this can form the basis of an appeal.

The party bringing the appeal, whether this is the employee or the employer, is referred to as the "appellant" and the party opposing the appeal is the "Respondent".

24.3   Procedure

In order to bring an appeal the appellant must send various documents to the EAT:

* the "Notice of Appeal";

* the judgment or decision you wish to appeal;

- a copy of the written reasons given for the judgment or decision;

- a copy of the ET1;

- a copy of the ET3.

Unless these documents are sent to the EAT, or an explanation is provided as to why they are missing, the appeal will be regarded as "invalidly lodged".

24.4   Time limit for appealing

The Notice of Appeal and supporting documentation must be lodged within 42 days of the date of the judgment or decision you are appealing against. The 42 days start from the date the judgment was sent to the parties and not the date on which you received it. You will need to use one of the Notice of Appeal forms that can be found at the government EAT website. If you wait until the last day of the 42 day period you need to bear in mind that a Notice of Appeal served on the EAT office after 4.00pm will be considered to be served the following day and therefore out of time.

It is important to note that this 42 day time limit applies even if you have applied to the employment tribunal for a reconsideration of the decision. If your application for a reconsideration is successful you can withdraw the appeal.

If you have applied to the tribunal for a reconsideration of their decision you should include a copy of your application for a reconsideration with your notice of appeal.

24.5   Where the response had been struck out

Where the appellant is an employer who was refused leave by the employment tribunal to extend time to enter his response, he will need to send a witness statement with his Notice of Appeal explaining the circumstances in which he failed to send his response in time and why he considers he has a good defence to the claim. He will need to draft an ET3, send a copy of this with his Notice of Appeal and include any other documents he would wish to rely on in support of his appeal.

24.6   Extension of time

If your appeal is out of time, that is the 42 day time period has passed, you can apply for an extension of time. You will need to make your application for an extension of time when you lodge your Notice of Appeal or after lodging it - you cannot make the application before lodging your appeal. You must give full reasons for the delay.

24.7   Contents of Notice of Appeal

The Notice of Appeal must identify the point of law on which the appeal is based, and it should also state the order that the appellant wishes the EAT to make at the hearing. As long as the Notice of Appeal identifies the point of law on which the appeal is based there is no need to set out any detailed argument supporting the grounds of appeal nor to set out any extracts from decided cases unless this is essential to understanding the grounds of appeal.

The position is rather different if the grounds of appeal are based on the argument that there was no evidence to support the findings that the tribunal made or that no reasonable tribunal could have made these findings and the decision was perverse - these are referred to as "perversity appeals".

If you are basing your appeal on perversity it is not enough simply to state that the judgment or order was contrary to the evidence or that it was perverse. You will need to set out full particulars of why you say that the judgment was perverse. This means that you will probably have to refer to specific passages in the judgment and explain why there was no evidence to support such a finding or why the finding was contrary to the evidence and therefore perverse. If necessary you can attach copies of witness statements that were before the employment tribunal in support of your argument.

24.8   Preliminary consideration by a judge

All grounds of appeal and the supporting documents are considered by an EAT judge who will consider whether there are reasonable grounds for bringing an appeal. There are various decisions that the judge can make:

(1) If the judge does not consider that there are reasonable grounds for bringing the appeal then leave will not be given for the appeal to proceed. You can request an oral hearing before an EAT judge to request that this decision be reconsidered;

(2) If the judge considers that further clarification of the grounds of appeal are needed the EAT will contact the appellant to provide this further clarification;

He can decide that the whole or only parts of the grounds of appeal should go to a full hearing.

24.9   Where the appeal will be heard

The oral hearing for leave to appeal, like any full hearing, will take place at the EAT at:

5th Floor, 7 Rolls Building

Fetter Lane

London

EC4A 1NL.

24.10   Preliminary hearing

If the judge considers there are, or might be, reasonable grounds of appeal he will then decide whether to allocate the case for further consideration at a preliminary hearing or for determination at a full hearing. He will also give appropriate directions for the hearing. If there is a pending application for a reconsideration of the decision in the tribunal the judge might postpone (or "stay") any further steps in the appeal until this reconsideration is decided.

The purpose of the preliminary hearing is to determine whether any of the grounds in the notice of appeal have reasonable prospects of success, or if there is some other compelling reason why the appeal should be heard.

If the judge considers that the case should be listed for a preliminary hearing the Notice of Appeal will be sent to the other side, the Respondent to the appeal. The Respondent will have 14 days to provide written submissions in response to the Notice of Appeal and to put forward any points to show that the appellant has no reasonable prospects of success. The Respondent also has the opportunity to put in a cross-appeal, but this must be done within 14 days of receiving the Notice of Appeal.

24.11   Cross-appeal

A cross-appeal is where an appeal is put in by the Respondent. For example the employer might appeal against a finding that the dismissal was unfair and the employee might put in a cross-appeal against the amount of damages he was awarded.

The Respondent will need to indicate if the cross-appeal is conditional on the appeal being successful, in which case if the appeal fails either at the preliminary or full hearing stage there will be no need for the EAT to consider the cross-appeal. Consider this example:

- The employer appeals against a finding that the dismissal was unfair on the basis that there was a suitable alternative post that the employee, dismissed for redundancy, should have been offered; and

- The employee cross-appeals against the finding that the redundancy selection procedure was fair;

- If the employer loses their appeal there would be no point in the employee proceeding with the cross-appeal.

Alternatively the Respondent will need to indicate if the cross-appeal is unconditional, that is it will proceed even if the main appeal fails. Consider this example:

- The Respondent/employer appeals against a finding of unfair dismissal; and

- The Claimant/employee cross-appeals against a finding of contributory fault;

- If the employer fails on his appeal the employee might well want the cross-appeal to go ahead in any event.

The preliminary hearing will be listed for a hearing at the EAT at the address given above. Normally only the appellant or his representative will attend but if the Respondent has lodged a cross-appeal or if the judge considers it desirable they will also be invited to attend. The hearing will not be expected to last more than an hour and any submissions should be limited so that they do not take longer than this.

Where a cross-appeal is heard at the preliminary hearing the judge will consider whether that cross-appeal shows reasonable grounds of bringing an appeal.

If the appellant chooses not to attend, the preliminary hearing can proceed on the basis of written submissions put in by the appellant.

24.12   Full hearing

Where the judge is satisfied that the appeal, and any cross-appeal, shows reasonable grounds it will be listed for a full hearing. If the appeal, but not the cross-appeal, has reasonable grounds then leave will only be given for the appeal to go to a full hearing. If the appeal does not have reasonable grounds then the Judge will only consider the cross-appeal if it is an unconditional cross-appeal, and whether it should go to a full hearing.

It is only when leave has been given for the appeal to go to a full hearing that the Respondent will be required to submit an answer to the Notice of Appeal. He will have 14 days to do this. The answer should be in Form 3. The Respondent must set out the grounds on which he intends to resist the appeal.

A Notice of Appeal can be amended but leave will need to be obtained from the EAT to do so. This can be done at the preliminary hearing.

If the appeal is sent for a full hearing it will be assigned to one of three categories:

- Category P is where it is recommended that it be heard in the President's list.

- Category A will apply if the appeal is complex and raises a point of public importance.

- Category B applies to all other appeals.

If the judge decides that the case should go to a full hearing he will give the appropriate directions.

The EAT will send the Notice of Appeal with any permitted amendments and any submissions to the Respondent. Within 14 days the Respondent must send to the EAT and serve on the appellant the Respondent's answer. The appellant must then serve a reply.

24.13   Listing the appeal

The case will then be listed for an appeal hearing. The parties should give a time estimate of how long they expect the case to last. The parties will also have to provide a "skeleton argument" prior to the hearing. This is a document which sets out the main submissions in summary form and will also include references to any reported cases the party will refer to and the principle of law or the passage in that case that they rely on. These skeleton arguments should be lodged not less than 14 days before the full hearing. The parties will also have to agree a bundle of relevant documents to be used for the hearing and these should be lodged with the EAT no later than 28 days from the date of the directions order.

The hearing will normally be heard just by a single appeal judge or an appeal judge sitting with two lay members. It is very unusual for the EAT to hear any evidence. The rule in relation to calling new evidence, whether in the form of a document that was not before the employment tribunal or a new witness, is that it is for the party wishing to use this new evidence to show that it could not reasonably have obtained this evidence before the tribunal hearing. They must also show that the evidence is relevant, believable and would have had an important influence on the outcome of the decision.

The appellant will present his argument first. The Respondent will then go next and the appellant will reply on points of law.

24.14   The decision

There are various ways in which the EAT can dispose of an appeal;

- it can dismiss the appeal;

- it can allow the appeal and substitute its own decision;

- it can allow the appeal and send the case back to be heard again by the same or a different tribunal where there can either be a complete re-hearing or just a re-hearing on a particular point.

The EAT will normally give a full reasoned judgment at the time that its makes the final order disposing of the case.

24.15 Costs

The successful party at the EAT does not automatically recover their costs. He will only be allowed his costs if he can show that the proceedings brought were unnecessary, improper, vexatious, misconceived or there was unreasonable delay or other unreasonable conduct in the bringing or conducting of the proceedings.

An application for costs can be at the end of the hearing or in writing within 14 days from the date of the order. It must state the grounds on which costs are sought and show how the costs have been incurred. When considering an order for costs the EAT may have regard to the other side's ability to pay.

Where the party applying for costs is a litigant in person the EAT can make a costs order, which can include costs for the same categories of work and disbursements which would have been allowed if he had had legal representation, although the amount allowed can be no more than two-thirds the amount that would be allowed if legally represented. It can also include any legal expenses incurred which relate to the conduct of the proceedings and any other expenses incurred in relation to the proceedings.

The EAT can also make a wasted costs order against the other party's legal representative in respect of any costs incurred as a result of improper unreasonable or negligent acts or omissions on the part of any representative.

Word or phrase	Definition
ACAS	Advisory, Conciliation and Arbitration Service which provides free and impartial information and advice to employers and employees on all aspects of workplace relations and employment law.
ACAS Code of Practice on Disciplinary and Grievance Procedures	Code of Practice issued by ACAS, the most recent version of which was published in March 2015.
ACAS Guide to Discipline and Grievances at Work	Guide by ACAS providing good practice advice for dealing with discipline and grievances in the workplace.
ACAS uplift	If the employer has failed to comply with the ACAS code of practice, some tribunal awards can be uplifted (or reduced if the employee has failed to comply) by up to 25%.
Acts of Parliament	Laws, enforced in all areas of the UK where it is applicable.
Additional award	An award where the employer has not complied with a court order to reinstate or re-engage the employee.
Adjournment	Postponement, where the tribunal hearing is postponed to a new date.
Age discrimination	Less favourable treatment because of the person's age.
Agency worker	A worker employed by an employment agency. Agency workers are often called 'temps'.
Amending a claim	Altering or changing a claim.

Word or phrase	Definition
Appeal	Application to a higher court or tribunal for a reversal of the decision of a lower court or tribunal.
Automatically unfair dismissal	Dismissals for a reason which are classed as 'automatically unfair', regardless of the reasonableness of the procedure and how long the employee had been employed.
Basic award	One of the awards available for unfair dismissal. It is calculated by multiplying a week's pay by the number of years employed (this is 1.5 weeks pay for each year of employment over the age of 41, 1 week's pay for each year of employment between the ages of 22 and 41 and 0.5 week's pay for each year of employment under the age of 22).
Bias	Where the tribunal unfairly favours one side against the other side for reasons not connected with the case.
Breach of contract	Legal cause of action if any of the agreed terms and conditions of an employment contract are broken by the employer or employee.
Bundle	Also referred to as the trial bundle, all the relevant documents and evidence in a case are collected together given page numbers and put in a lever arch file for use at the tribunal hearing.
Burden of proof	This is the duty on a party, usually the Claimant, to convince the tribunal of the necessary facts and issues to give judgment in their favour.
Capability	Ability to perform your job.
Capability procedure	Procedure which is designed to support employers in dealing with problems regarding the performance of employees.
Caselaw	Law based on decisions in other cases.
Claim	Formal application to have a complaint heard.

Word or phrase	Definition
Claimant	The party who brings a claim.
Comparators	Person or people against whom another person can compare themselves when trying to prove that they have been discriminated against.
Compensation	Monetary award.
Compensatory award	One of the awards available for unfair dismissal and is calculated on the basis of loss of earnings and other benefits.
Compromise agreement	The old name for settlement agreement.
Conciliation	An alternative dispute resolution process whereby the parties to a dispute use a conciliator, who meets with the parties both separately and together in an attempt to resolve their differences.
Confidentiality clause	A provision in a settlement agreement which prevents one or both parties from disclosing certain information to anyone else.
Constructive dismissal	Dismissal where the employee resigns as a result of the employer's breach of contract.
Continuing act	Continuous discriminatory state of affairs.
Contract of employment	Agreement between an employer and an employee which sets out their employment rights, responsibilities and duties.
Contributory fault	Where the Claimant is partly or wholly responsible for their dismissal.
Coronavirus Job Retention Scheme	A scheme to prevent extensive redundancies during the coronavirus crisis when many businesses were ordered to close. The employees remain at home and are paid 80% of their salary which their employer can recover from the government.

Word or phrase	Definition
Costs	Amount paid in lawyers' fees, court fees or other costs to bring or defend a claim.
COT3	A form used by ACAS to record the terms of settlement of an employment tribunal case.
Counterclaim	Where a Claimant has brought a breach of contract claim in the ET1 against the Respondent, the Respondent can bring a counterclaim for breach of contract against the Claimant in the ET3.
County Court	This is the lower level civil court, below the High Court, and it is where most civil claims will be brought.
Cross-appeal	Appeal brought by the Respondent after the appellant has appealed the original decision.
Cross-examination	Asking questions of the other parties' witness.
Damages	An award of money to compensate the party bringing the claim.
Default judgments	Judgments without trial which can occur where the Respondent has failed to file a defence or a party has failed to comply with an order.
Defence	Argument opposing the other party's allegation.
Deposit order	Amount of money, up to a maximum of £1,000, to be paid by the Claimant before the tribunal will hear the claim where the tribunal judge considers that the claim has little reasonable prospect of success. It can also be made in respect of a response.
Direct discrimination	When an employee is treated less favourably than other employees because that employee has one or more of the 9 protected characteristics. See also 'Indirect discrimination'.

Word or phrase	Definition
Directions	Orders that a tribunal judge gives for the procedural steps that each side must take to ensure that all the appropriate evidence is available for the hearing.
Disability discrimination	Discrimination where a disabled person is treated unfavourably because of something arising in consequence of that person's disability and it cannot be shown that the treatment was a proportionate means of achieving a legitimate aim.
Disciplinary hearing	Hearing conducted by an employer to consider an allegation of misconduct against an employee.
Disciplinary procedure	The procedure carried out by an employer in cases of misconduct. It will usually be a 3 stage process: investigation, hearing and decision.
Disclosure	Showing the other party all those documents that you have which you consider to be relevant to the case to be heard by the tribunal.
Discrimination	Unfavourable treatment because the employee has one of the 9 protected characteristics.
Dismissal	Ending of an employee's employment contract by the employer.
Double recovery	A Claimant should only be compensated once for his losses. If he has already received state benefits for a period, then to be awarded loss of earnings for the same period would be double recovery.
Early conciliation	A requirement on an employee to contact ACAS before bringing a claim to try to settle the dispute with the employer.
Effective date of termination	Date on which the employment contract came to an end.
Employee	Someone who is employed under a contract of employment.

Word or phrase	Definition
Employment Appeal Tribunal	The tribunal which deals with appeals from the Employment Tribunal.
Employment Rights Act 1996	The main Act of Parliament setting out the basic employment law including the law relating to dismissal and compensation.
Employment Tribunal	The tribunal dealing with employment claims.
Equality Act 2010	An Act of Parliament setting out the basic discrimination law.
ET1	The form filled out by the Claimant in order to bring the claim in the employment tribunal.
ET3	Respondent's response form.
Evidence in chief	Your own witnesses evidence.
Examination in chief	The questioning of your own witness in support of your case.
Express term	The actual terms contained within a contract of employment, such as rate of pay.
Extension of time	Extra time granted by the tribunal if a claim or appeal is brought outside the time limit or for additional time to comply with a tribunal order.
Final written warning	The last warning, that is in writing, before dismissal might be considered.
Fixed term contract	Contract of employment with a defined end date.
Fundamental breach of contract	Serious breach of contract.

Word or phrase	Definition
Furlough	A temporary layoff from work. Normally the employee will not be paid their salary but during the coronavirus crisis the government have agreed to pay the employer 80% of the employee's salary up to £2,500 a month.
Future loss of earnings	Loss of earnings after the tribunal hearing.
Garden leave	The employee does not have to work their notice period but is still bound by their employment contract during this time. It is not the same as payment in lieu of notice.
Grievance	Formal complaint.
Gross misconduct	Serious misconduct including theft, fighting and bullying that would justify immediate dismissal without notice.
Gross up	Add on an amount to an award to take into account the amount of tax the recipient will have to pay.
Harassment	Unwanted conduct, related to a protected characteristic, which is designed to, or has the effect of, violating that person's dignity, creating an intimidating, hostile, degrading, humiliating or offensive environment. It also includes unwanted conduct of a sexual nature and less favourable treatment of a person because they have refused to submit to conduct of a sexual nature.
Holiday pay	Payment of normal wages while the employee is on holiday.
Human Resources	The department which deals with employee issues such as disciplinary matters, payroll, recruitment etc. Sometimes called the Personnel Department.
Hypothetical comparator	Theoretical person with whom an employee can compare themselves if an actual comparator is not available.
Illegal contract	A contract whose terms are illegal, for example non payment of tax and national insurance.

Word or phrase	Definition
Immediate loss of earnings	Loss of earnings between the dismissal and tribunal hearing.
Implied term	Terms not specified in a contract of employment, for example the implied term of trust and confidence.
Indirect discrimination	Where a rule or policy applies to everyone, but it has a worse effect on some people who have a protected characteristic than others and which has the effect of putting those people at a particular disadvantage.
Inference	Conjecture or assumption based on known evidence and facts.
Injury to feelings	Damages awarded in discrimination cases for hurt, distress or injury resulting from the discriminatory act.
Investigation	Search for the facts and evidence after a complaint or accusation has been made.
Itemised pay slip	Pay slip detailing gross and net pay and any deductions such as tax, NI and pension contributions.
Joint and several liability	If two Respondents are held to be jointly and severally liable the Claimant can recover all his damages awarded to him from either one of the Respondents.
Judge	The person who presides over court or tribunal proceedings.
Judgment	Decision of the court or tribunal.
Judicial Assessment	A free procedure introduced in October 2016 to try to encourage parties to resolve their dispute by agreement at the preliminary hearing where the Employment Judge will provide an assessment of the strengths and weaknesses of each side's case, as well as the risks involved.
Judicial Mediation	A free process where both parties attend the employment tribunal without their witnesses, and an Employment Judge tries to encourage the parties to settle their dispute.

Word or phrase	Definition
Just and equitable	Fair to both sides.
Lay member	A person sitting with a judge hearing a tribunal claim who has no legal qualifications.
Leave	Permission.
Legitimate aim	A good reason or purpose for the discrimination.
Limitation period	Maximum length of time that can elapse between the act complained of and making a claim to the ET.
Litigant in person	A Claimant or Respondent representing themselves.
Lodging a claim	Taking a claim to court.
Mediation	Process where an independent mediator attempts to settle a claim or complaint without going to court.
Misconduct	Behaviour that is regarded as unacceptable by the employer.
Mitigating circumstances	Circumstances or reasons which would lessen the degree of blame.
Mitigation of loss	Acting so as to limit the amount of loss.
Mutuality of obligation	Employer's obligation to provide work and employee's obligation to do it.
National minimum/living wage	The lowest wage that an employer can pay employees.
Notice pay	Earnings during a period of notice.

Word or phrase	Definition
Notice period	The period of time between the date an employee is informed of his dismissal or the date of his resignation and the date when the contract of employment comes to an end.
Overriding objective	The basic principles that the tribunal must have regard to, to deal with a case justly.
Payment in lieu of notice	Payment instead of working out the period of notice. It is sometimes abbreviated to PILON.
PCP	Acronym for "Provision, Criterion or Practice" (see Indirect discrimination).
Polkey deduction	The case of *Polkey v AE Dayton Services Ltd* [1987] UKHL 8 provides for a reduction in any award for compensatory loss to reflect the chance that an unfairly dismissed employee would have been dismissed fairly in any event.
Pre-action conciliation	Early conciliation before a tribunal claim is brought.
Precedent	a) Model letter or template; b) Principle or rule established in a previous legal case that is either binding on or persuasive for a court or other tribunal when deciding subsequent cases with similar issues or facts.
Preliminary hearing	Hearing conducted by an employment tribunal judge to deal with procedural matters before the final hearing takes place.
Preparation time order	An order that the paying party make a payment to the unrepresented receiving party in respect of their time spent working on a case.
Privilege	The principle that some documents or evidence need not be disclosed, for example correspondence between a solicitor and a client.

Word or phrase	Definition
Prohibited conduct	Conduct that constitutes discrimination as set out in Chapter 2 Equality Act 2010.
Proportionate means	A fair balance between the discrimination and the reason or purpose for it.
Protected act	An act done in relation to the Equality Act 2010, for which they are protected from being victimised.
Protected characteristic	Characteristic, such as race or sex, for which the person with that characteristic is protected from discrimination (see Chapter 1 of the Equality Act 2010).
Protected disclosure	Sometimes known as 'whistleblowing', where a person reports suspected serious wrongdoing at work.
Protective award	An award of up to 90 day's pay where the employer has failed to consult properly when making more than 20 employees redundant.
Qualifying period	The length of continuous employment before an employee can make a claim at the tribunal.
Race discrimination	Unfavourable treatment because of the employee's race.
Reasonable adjustments	Changes to a disabled employee's working practices which are reasonable for the employer to implement.
Reasonable belief	Genuine belief.
Reasonable grounds	Proper reasons.
Reasonable investigation	Full and proper search for the truth of the allegation.
Reasonably practicable test	Reasonably feasible or reasonably possible. The test applied when bringing a discrimination claim out of time.

Word or phrase	Definition
Recommendations	Instruction by the tribunal to the employer to change some aspect of the employment that has resulted in discrimination.
Reconsideration of judgment	Review.
Recoupment notice	Document sent by the DWP to the Respondent, detailing the amount of state benefits that Claimant has received, and the amounts the Respondent must pay to the DWP and the Claimant.
Redundancy	Dismissal as a result of a decision by the employer to reduce the workforce.
Re-engagement	Getting a different job with the same employer.
Re-examination	Where a witness will be asked questions by his own representative dealing with matters raised in cross-examination of that witness.
Reinstatement	Getting your old job back.
Re-labelling	Where you seeking to add or substitute a new cause of action or claim but one which is linked to or arises out of the same facts as you have already included in your existing claim.
Remedy	This is what you want from the tribunal if you are successful in your case. It is usually compensation but can include re-engagement or reinstatement.
Repudiation of contract	Where the employer has committed a serious breach of contract, the employee is regarding himself as no longer bound by the terms of the contract and is, in effect, treating the contract as ended.
Reserved judgment	Where the decision is not given on the day of the hearing but will be sent to the parties in writing at a later date.
Resignation	Where the Claimant chooses to leave their employment.

Word or phrase	Definition
Respondent	The party responding to a claim.
Review	Reconsideration of a decision.
Sanction	Penalty usually imposed by a tribunal where one party has failed to comply with an order.
Schedule of loss	Document listing the remedies that the Claimant is asking for.
Selection pool	Group of employees out of which redundancies will be made.
Self-employment	Working for yourself.
Service provision change	Where a service which was previously done by one organisation is now being done by another.
Settlement agreement	A written agreement between an employer and an employee where they each agree the terms on which an employment claim brought by the employee should be settled.
Sex discrimination	Less favourable treatment on the grounds of sex.
Sham redundancy	Where a redundancy situation does not really exist but the employer makes someone redundant because they do not want them in employment any longer.
Sick pay	Payment whilst off sick. This could be statutory sick pay, which is the minimum sum an employer is required to pay for up to 28 weeks, or contractual sick pay.
Skeleton argument	A document setting out the main submissions in summary form and will also include references to any reported cases the party will refer to and the principle of law or the passage in that case that they rely on.

Word or phrase	Definition
Some other substantial reason	A reason for dismissal which does not come with any other specified category.
Specific disclosure	Disclosure of certain documents they are known to exist and that are in the possession of the other party.
Standard disclosure	Disclosure of documents that are relevant to the case.
Statutes	Acts of Parliament.
Statutory Instruments	Secondary legislation such as Working Time Regulations 1998.
Statutory rights	Rights that an employee has by virtue of a statute.
Stay	Where proceedings are halted or suspended by the tribunal either indefinitely or for a specified period.
Striking out	Dismissal of a claim without a full trial or hearing the evidence.
Submissions	Summary of each party's argument made after the evidence has been heard.
Summary dismissal	Dismissal without giving notice.
Supreme Court	The highest court in the UK (formerly known as the House of Lords).
Suspension	Where the employee is not allowed to attend work for a period of time because of a disciplinary investigation but remains employed on full pay.
Tax liability	For awards in respect of loss of earnings made in excess of £30,000, the Claimant may have to pay tax on the excess.

Word or phrase	Definition
Termination of employment contract	Ending of an employee's employment contract.
Third party	Someone or some organisation which is not a party in the case.
Time limits	Period of time within which a claim must be made.
Trade Union and Labour Relations (Consolidation) Act 1992	TULR(C)A 1992: The Act of Parliament dealing with trade unions.
Transcript	Written record of a hearing or meeting.
Transfer of undertakings	If one organisation acquires another, qualifying employees of the first organisation will transfer to the second organisation and retain all their existing employment rights.
Transferee	The organisation which acquires another, or the 'new' business.
Transferor	The organisation which sells to another, or the 'old' business.
TULR(C)A	Trade Union and Labour Relations (Consolidation) Act 1992.
TUPE	Transfer of Undertakings (Protection of Employment) Regulations 2006.
Unfair dismissal	Termination of employment by the employer which is not for a fair reason.
Union representative	A person from a trade union who supports a union member.
Unlawful deductions	Amounts of money which have been unlawfully deducted from the employee's pay.

233

Word or phrase	Definition
Unless order	A tribunal order which tells one party to do something and if they don't, the claim or response will be struck out.
Upholding a grievance	Agreeing with the party who brought the grievance.
Vicarious liability	Where the employer is liable for the discrimination or wrongful act carried out by one of his employees in the course of his employment.
Victimisation	Where an employee is treated less favourably because they have made a complaint, or helped someone else make a complaint, in connection with the Equality Act 2010.
Wasted costs	Costs order that is made against a party's representative rather than the party themselves.
Week's pay	Gross weekly pay of the Claimant, which is used to calculate the basic award but subject to a cap (currently £538).
Whistleblowing	Making a protected disclosure.
Withdrawal of claim	Decision not to pursue the claim further.
Witness order	An order compelling someone to attend a tribunal hearing as a witness.
Witness statement	A document which sets out the evidence that the witness wishes to put before the employment tribunal.
Worker	A "worker" includes employees but also covers people who work under a contract to perform personally some work or service but could not be classed as an employee.
Working Time Regulations	Regulations governing such things as rest periods, holidays and weekly hours.

Word or phrase	Definition
Written grievance procedure	Process by which employees can make a formal complaint.
Written reasons for dismissal	Under section 92 of the Employment Rights Act 1996 an employee who is dismissed is entitled to written reasons for the dismissal. If these have not been given the Claimant could be entitled to compensation.
Written statement of particulars	Contract of employment.
Written warning	The second stage of warning, after a verbal warning. The third stage is a final written warning.
Wrongful dismissal	Where the employer has dismissed the employee in breach of the terms of the contract of employment, usually where the required notice has not been given.
Zero-hours contracts	Contract of employment where there are no guaranteed hours or payment.

Grievance letter 1

A.N. Smith
123 Hillside Road
Bigtown

Mr Jones
Bigtown Manufacturing Limited
100 High Road
Bigtown

12th October 2019

Dear Mr Jones,

I am writing to ask for your help with a problem I am having at work.

I work on the production line at the factory in Bigtown. I do the evening shift, working from 2.00pm to 10.00pm. I have been working this shift for the last three years.

Since last May when Mr Brown became the Production Line Manager he has been trying to get me to change my shift so that I work alternate morning and evening shifts on different weeks. I have explained to him that because I take the children to school in the morning it is not possible for me to work the morning shift. Since I refused to agree to change my shift Mr Brown has made life difficult for me at work - he has stopped my overtime and he continually criticises my work in front of other members of the production team.

When I spoke to Mr Brown about this he said that overtime was limited but I know that other members of the production team have been getting overtime.

I have tried raising this matter informally but this has made no difference in Mr Brown's behaviour towards me. I would be grateful if you could treat this letter as a formal grievance and have the matter considered under the company's grievance procedure.

I look forward to hearing from you as soon as possible

Yours sincerely

A.N. Smith

Grievance letter 2

T.R Hunter
125 Hillside Avenue
Bigtown

Mr Jones
Bigtown Manufacturing Limited
100 High Road
Bigtown

12th October 2019

Dear Mr Jones,

I work as a secretary to Mr Brown the Production Line Manager at the Bigtown Factory Premises. I have worked full time for Bigtown Manufacturing for five years. I am currently on maternity leave and due back on 1st September 2020. I would like to come back to work on a part-time basis so that I have more time with my baby.

I spoke to Mr Brown about this last week but he said it would not be possible as I was needed full time. I suggested that I could work part-time on a job share basis with his current secretary who is covering my maternity leave period but Mr Brown said that this would cause too many difficulties as customers would have to deal with two different people on different days.

I know that other secretaries work on a part-time or job share basis for other Managers and this does not cause problems.

I have raised this matter informally with Mr Brown but he clearly was not prepared to consider the matter at all. I am not satisfied with the reasons he gave for refusing my request and I would now like the matter to be dealt with under the company's formal grievance procedures.

I look forward to hearing from you.

Yours sincerely

T.R Hunter

Grievance letter 3

A.N. Smith
123 Hillside Road
Bigtown

Mr Jones
Bigtown Manufacturing Limited
100 High Road
Bigtown

18th October 2019

Dear Mr Jones,

I am writing to ask for your help with a problem I am having at work.

I work as a team leader on the production line at the factory in Bigtown. Last week the conveyor belt got stuck as some of the larger items got jammed in it. Mr Brown, the Production Line Manager, told me to clear the jam without switching the conveyor belt off. I told him this was dangerous and I might get my hand caught. He told me it would waste far too much time to shut the machine off and then have to start it up again. I refused to clear the jam unless the conveyor belt was turned off and Mr Brown got someone else to do this. Mr Brown said that he did not want me as team leader if I was not prepared to do what he told me.

I have been a team leader now for two years and have had no complaints about my work. I consider it most unfair to lose my position as team leader because I was not prepared to risk an injury by clearing the jam whilst the conveyor belt was still switched on.

I would be grateful if you could treat this letter as a formal grievance and have the matter considered under the company's grievance procedure.

I look forward to hearing from you as soon as possible.

Yours sincerely

A.N. Smith

Grievance letter 4

C Ferguson
125 Fellside Road
Bigtown

Bigtown Manufacturing Limited
100 High Road
Bigtown

12th October 2019

Dear Mr Jones,

I am writing about a matter that has been of considerable concern to me for some time. I am a black female employee working as an Administrator in the Distribution Section at the Bigtown factory. I have been employed in this position for four years and in that time I have gained a considerable amount of experience of the procedures in Distribution department. On several occasions when one of the Supervisors has been off sick I have been asked to carry out various supervisory tasks.

In the last year I have been for two interviews for the post of full time Supervisor and on each occasion I have been unsuccessful. On both occasions the position has been given to a white male. On one of these occasions the post went to someone from outside the company who had applied for the post. On the last occasion the job was given to another administration clerk who had been employed by the company for a considerably shorter period than I have.

I have heard comments that the company would not want a female supervisor in the Distribution section.

I consider that I have been denied promotion because I am black or alternatively because I am female.

I have raised this matter informally with Mr Smith, my Line Manager, but he clearly was not prepared to consider the matter at all. I would now like the matter to be dealt with under the company's formal grievance procedures.

Yours sincerely

Ms C Ferguson

Invitation to grievance meeting 1

Mr Jones
Bigtown Manufacturing Limited
100 High Road
Bigtown

Mr A N Smith
123 Hillside Road
Bigtown

21st October 2019

Dear Mr Smith,

Thank you for your letter of 18th October 2019. I can confirm that your complaint will be dealt with under the company's formal grievance procedure. This is set out in section 10 of the Terms and Conditions of Employment. The grievance meeting will be held by Mr Ford, the Head of Production and Mr Davis from the H.R. Department will be present.

The meeting will take place in the conference room in the Administration Building at 10.30am on 25th October. If this date is not convenient for you can you please let me know as soon as possible and provide alternative dates on which you will be available.

You are entitled to be accompanied to this meeting by a trade union official or a work colleague. I would be grateful if you could let me know if you would like to be accompanied and who it would be so that we can make the necessary arrangements.

Yours sincerely

Mr A Jones

Outcome of grievance meeting 1

Mr Ford
Bigtown Manufacturing
Limited
100 High Road
Bigtown

Mr A N Smith
123 Hillside Road
Bigtown

26th October 2019

Dear Mr Smith,

On 12th October 2019 you wrote to me with a number of complaints. These were that:

- Mr Brown was trying to get you to change your shift pattern;

- when you refused he stopped your overtime; and

- he criticised you in front of your work colleagues.

Before the grievance meeting on 25th October 2019 I spoke to Mr Brown about your complaints. He said that he had asked you to change your shift patterns because the company was trying to introduce a more flexible shift system. He said that you had refused but had not given any reason.

Mr Brown said that overtime generally had been reduced because of a downturn in production and this applied to all the members of the production line team not just to you.

Mr Brown said that there had been several occasions when he had to point out to you that your work was below standard.

At the grievance meeting on 25th October 2019 you explained that because you had to take your children to school in the morning you would have difficulty doing a morning shift. I explained that we were trying to introduce a more flexible working pattern and if you were able to make other arrangements for your children getting to school it would be helpful if you could change your shift but that this was not something we were going to insist on.

You accepted that there had been a downturn in production but still insisted that other members of your team were getting overtime. I looked at the time sheets for all the members of your team and was able to satisfy myself that in fact there had been no overtime for any members of your team for several months. Your grievance regarding overtime was therefore not upheld.

You have accepted that Mr Brown was justified in speaking to you about your performance but you found it humiliating to be told this in front of your work colleagues. I have spoken to Mr Brown about this and if he has occasion to speak to you in future about your performance he will do so in private. To this extent I uphold your grievance on this point.

I hope you are satisfied with the outcome of this grievance procedure but if you are not satisfied you can appeal by writing to Mr Black, the H.R Manager within 7 days.

Yours sincerely

Mr Ford

Head of Production

Outcome of grievance meeting 2

Mr Jones
Bigtown Manufacturing Limited
100 High Road
Bigtown

Ms C Ferguson
125 Fellside Road
Bigtown

26th October 2019

Dear Ms Ferguson

On 12th October 2019 you wrote to me complaining that you considered you have been discriminated against and that you have been refused a promotion on two occasions because you are black and female.

At the grievance meeting on 25th October 2019 I heard from both you and Mr Smith, who had conducted the interviews and made the two appointments that you have complained about.

Mr Smith explained that both positions were advertised internally and externally. On each occasion there were between 20 and 30 applicants, of these five were invited to come for an interview. You were one of the five who were short-listed for interview but unfortunately you were unsuccessful on each occasion.

Mr Smith said that he selected the person that he considered was best suited for the position irrespective of race, colour or sex. He explained why the persons he selected were better qualified or suited for the position than you were. Having heard both from your self and from Mr Smith I am satisfied that this was the case and that you were not discriminated against. I therefore do not uphold your grievance.

I hope you are satisfied with the outcome of this grievance procedure and that you will not be deterred from applying for other positions in the future. If you are not satisfied you can appeal by writing to Mr Ford, the Head of Production within 7 days.

Yours sincerely

Mr Jones, Head of Distribution

Invitation to disciplinary investigation meeting

Mr Jones
Bigtown Manufacturing Limited
100 High Road
Bigtown

Mr A N Smith
123 Hillside Road
Bigtown

23rd October 2019

Dear Mr Smith,

You have been signed off sick from work for the last week with back ache yet we have been informed that you were seen in town on several occasions last week. One of these occasions was at a football match, and you did not appear to be injured. We have tried contacting you at your home on several occasions and there has been no answer.

Your current sick certificate ends on 25th October 2019 and when you return to work on 26th October you will required to attend a disciplinary investigation meeting at 10.30am.in order for you to explain your actions and why you have not been at home when certified off sick.

I should remind you that, under the disciplinary procedure in the Terms and Conditions of your Contract of Employment, dishonesty can constitute an act of gross misconduct meriting summary dismissal.

You have the right to be accompanied by a trade union official or a work colleague.

If you are unable to attend that meeting please contact me as soon as possible so alternative arrangements can be made

Yours sincerely

A Jones

Invitation to disciplinary hearing

Mr Jones
Bigtown Manufacturing Limited
100 High Road
Bigtown

Mr A N Smith
123 Hillside Road
Bigtown

28th October 2019

Dear Mr Smith,

I am writing to you about an incident that apparently occurred yesterday at work. The Production Line Manager, Mr Brown, says that he saw you fighting with another team member, John White. You were both sent home.

Please find attached to this letter a statement made by Mr Brown setting out details of the incident.

You will required to attend a disciplinary investigation meeting on 30th October 2019 at 10.30am. in order for you to explain your actions. You are entitled to bring any witnesses you would like to give evidence on your behalf.

I should remind you that, under the disciplinary procedure in the Terms and Conditions of your Contract of Employment, fighting can constitute an act of gross misconduct meriting summary dismissal.

You have the right to be accompanied by a trade union official or a work colleague.

If you are unable to attend that meeting please contact me as soon as possible so alternative arrangements can be made

Yours sincerely

A Jones

Dismissal letter

Mr Jones
Bigtown Manufacturing Limited
100 High Road
Bigtown

Mr A N Smith
123 Hillside Road
Bigtown

31st October 2019

Dear Mr Smith,

At the disciplinary hearing yesterday you admitted that you had been fighting with another member of the production team, John White. You said that he had provoked you and had been constantly making abusive and derogatory comments towards you.

You accepted that you were aware that fighting at work was a serious disciplinary matter. You said that this had never happened before and that in the three years you had worked for the company you had a good disciplinary record.

I do not accept that the provocation from Mr White was an excuse for you to attack him and your behaviour was not acceptable. In spite of the fact that you have a good disciplinary record we regard fighting on the shop floor as a very serious matter. It constitutes gross misconduct and in the circumstances we have no option but to dismiss you with immediate effect.

You have the right to appeal against this decision. Your appeal must be submitted in writing within seven days of today.

Yours sincerely

A Jones

Appeal against dismissal

A.N. Smith
123 Hillside Road
Bigtown

Mr Jones
Bigtown Manufacturing Limited
100 High Road
Bigtow

1st November 2019

Dear Mr Jones,

I wish to appeal against the decision to dismiss me. I admitted that I had been fighting with John White but I explained that I had put up with weeks of provocation from him by way of abusive and derogatory remarks. I had complained about this to the Production Line Manager on a number of occasions but nothing had been done and the provocation had continued.

I explained that on the day of the fight I was upset because of problems at home and this caused me to react to Mr White's comments.

I have worked for the company for three years without any previous disciplinary problems. I do not consider that I should be dismissed for this first offence particularly as Mr White was not dismissed but only given a final warning.

Yours sincerely

A Smith

Resignation letter 1

A.N. Smith
123 Hillside Road
Bigtown

Mr Jones
Bigtown Manufacturing Limited
100 High Road
Bigtown

30th October 2019

Dear Mr Jones,

At the grievance hearing on 25th October 2019 you said that you would speak to Mr Brown and advise him not to criticise me in front of my work colleagues. I had hoped that Mr Brown's attitude towards me would improve but in fact it has got worse. He has continued to pressurise me into accepting morning shifts and makes sarcastic and derogatory comments when I explain that I can't.

He has continued to criticise me in front of my work colleagues and has made it clear that he does not want me working as part of his team.

I cannot put up with his bullying behaviour any longer as it is starting to affect my health. I regard this behaviour as a breach of the implied term of trust and confidence. In these circumstances I have no alternative but to resign.

Yours sincerely

A N Smith

Resignation letter 2

C Ferguson
125 Fellside Road
Bigtown

Bigtown Manufacturing Limited
100 High Road
Bigtown

30th October 2019

Dear Mr Jones,

On 12th October 2019 I wrote to you complaining about the fact that I considered that I had been discriminated against and had been refused promotion because of my sex and/or colour. There was a grievance hearing on 25th October 2019 and my grievance was rejected.

I do not consider that my grievance was fairly dealt with. You did not take into account the fact that on several occasions I had actually been asked to carry out supervisory duties. You did not explain why it was necessary to advertise the position externally when there are people employed by the company who perfectly capable of carrying out the position. You ignored the fact that several people had told me that the company did not want a female supervisor in the Distribution Section.

Since the grievance hearing I have been subjected to harassment and sarcastic comments from Mr Smith and employees in the Distribution section.

I consider that I have been discriminated against because I am black and a female, I do not consider that my complaints have been taken seriously and I have been subjected to harassment and victimisation because I have complained. I regard this behaviour as a breach of the implied term of trust and confidence. In these circumstances I have no alternative but to resign.

Yours sincerely

Ms C Ferguson

ET1 Section 8.2: Details of claim - unfair dismissal (1)

1. I have been employed by the Respondent since 1st October 2011 as a Production Line Worker at the Respondent's factory in High Road, Bigtown.

2. I work as part of a team of four. One of the other team members is John White. Because Mr White has worked at the factory for longer than me he feels that he is entitled to order me around. He will often make abusive and threatening remarks to me.

3. On 5th June 2019 Mr White raised his fist at my face and threatened to 'smack me one' when I dropped some trays. Two days later he called me a "clumsy oaf". On many occasions he has made offensive remarks to me in front of the other team members.

4. I have complained to the Production Team Manager, Mr Brown, on a number of occasions about things that Mr Smith has said to me but nothing has happened and Mr White has continued his bullying behaviour towards me.

5. On 27th October 2019 there had been difficulties at home - my wife was ill and I had to make arrangements for the children to be looked after. As a result of this I was late in for work and as soon as I arrived John White started criticising me, accusing me of having a lie in. I told him to stop but he still persisted. I accept that I lost my temper and pushed him but he over-reacted and started hitting me.

6. On 30th October 2019 I attended a disciplinary hearing conducted by Mr Jones. I told him about Mr White's bullying behaviour towards me in the past and that on this occasion he provoked me. I had complained about Mr White's behaviour towards me in the past but nothing had been done to stop this. On 2nd October I had problems at home, which I was worrying about. Mr Jones said that this was no excuse and that he had no alternative but to dismiss me.

7. I accept that I was wrong to push Mr White and have apologised for doing this but I consider that to dismiss me for this incident was unfair. I have never been in trouble before and have had no warnings about my behaviour. I also consider that my dismissal was unfair when compared to the way Mr White was treated - he was only given a final warning. Mr White provoked the incident and he over-reacted. He has been in trouble in the past for disciplinary matters.

8. I do not consider that when deciding to dismiss me the Respondent took into account all the circumstances, including the fact that I had been provoked. I consider that the decision to dismiss me was unreasonable and unfair.

9. In addition to compensation for unfair dismissal I claim the notice pay to which I am entitled.

10. The Respondent failed to inform me of my right to appeal the dismissal and it is therefore in breach of the ACAS Code of Practice on Grievance and Disciplinary Procedures and any damages awarded should be increased by up to 25%.

ET1 Section 8.2: Details of claim - unfair dismissal (2)

1. I have been employed by the Respondent since 1st October 2010 as an Administration clerk in the Distribution section at the Respondent's factory in High Road, Bigtown. I am the only black female employee in the Distribution section.

2. On several occasions in 2012 and 2013 I have been asked to carry out various supervisory duties when one of the supervisors has been off sick. I was told that I had carried out these duties satisfactorily. When a full time supervisory post became vacant and advertised I was encouraged to apply for this. Because of my experience I considered that I would have a good prospect of obtaining this post.

3. In January 2019 I attended an interview conducted by Mr Smith, my Line Manager. I considered that the interview went well but I was disappointed to learn that I had not been successful. I found out the person who was appointed was a white male applicant who had not worked for the Respondent and did not have as much experience as I had with distribution procedures. In fact this employee left after six months and the post was advertised again.

4. In July 2019 I attended another interview - again this was conducted by Mr Smith. I considered that he made various negative comments in the interview about my ability to cope with the additional duties and extra responsibility. He suggested that I might have difficulty getting the respect of the other clerks in the department. It seemed as if he felt that because I was female and black I would not have the authority to carry out the work of a supervisor. I was very disappointed when I learnt that James Lewis, a white employee, who had only been working in the Distribution section for two years had been appointed to the post.

5. When I spoke to some of the other employees in the Distribution section they said that I was never going to be promoted because the company would not want a black female supervisor.

6. On 12th October 2019 I raised a grievance regarding the discrimination I had suffered. The grievance meeting took place on 23rd October 2019. It was conducted by Mr Jones, the Head of the Distribution section, who heard both from myself and Mr Smith. Mr Smith said that he was not influenced by the sex, race or colour of the applicants when he decided who to appoint for the post but this was not the impression I was given during the interview. I do not feel that my concerns were given any real consideration in the grievance hearing.

7. After my grievance hearing was rejected Mr Smith's attitude towards me changed. He made sarcastic comments about me complaining to the managers about him, he has referred to me as "getting too big for my boots" and "wanting to play with the big boys". He has also become more critical of my work. Other employees referred to me as a "snitch" and accused me of "telling tales". When I complained to Mr

Smith about this behaviour he said "you will just have to get used to it".

8. I consider that I have been discriminated against because I am black and a female, I do not consider that my complaints have been taken seriously and I have been subjected to harassment and victimisation because I have complained. I regard this behaviour as a breach of the implied term of trust and confidence and I am no longer prepared to put up with this treatment. On 30th October 2019 I sent the Respondent a letter informing them that I had resigned.

9. In the circumstances I consider that I have been constructively dismissed by the Respondent and I claim damages for unfair dismissal and my notice pay.

10. I consider that I have been subjected to direct discrimination on the grounds of my race and/or my sex in rejecting my application for the post of supervisor on two occasions, in respect of the remarks made to me by Mr Smith in the second interview, in rejecting my grievance and in the comments made by Mr Smith and other employees to me after my grievance had been rejected.

11. Further I consider that I have been subjected to harassment under section 26(1) of the Equality Act 2010 in that the comments made by Mr Smith both during the second interview, after my grievance had been rejected and the comments made by other employees had the purpose or effect of violating my dignity and creating a hostile, degrading, humiliating or offensive environment for me.

12. Further I consider that I have been victimised under section 27 of the Equality Act 2010 in that I had done a protected act, namely bringing a grievance alleging discrimination against me contrary to the provisions of the Equality Act 2010 and as a result of doing this protected act I have been subjected to a detriment as set out in paragraph 7 above.

13. I claim damages for injury to feelings in respect of the discrimination I have been subjected to. I am entitled to interest on any sums awarded to me for injury to feelings.

ET1 Section 8.2: Details of claim - constructive unfair dismissal

1. I have been employed by the Respondent since 1st October 2011 as a Production Line Worker at the Respondent's factory in High Road, Bigtown.

2. I work on the evening shift, working from 2.00pm to 10.00pm. I have been working this shift for the last three years.

3. In May 2019 Mr Brown became the Production Line Manager. Since then he has been trying to get me to change my shift so that I work alternate morning and evening shifts on different weeks. He told me that other team members have agreed to this and that I am the only one who has refused. I have explained to Mr Brown that because I take my children to school in the morning it is not possible for me to work the morning shift.

4. Since I refused to agree to change my shift Mr Brown has made life difficult for me at work in different ways. Before this I would do regular overtime at the weekends, both on Saturdays and Sundays but since then I have not been asked to do any overtime. When I spoke to Mr Brown about this in July he said that overtime was only available to those people who were prepared to work flexible shifts.

5. In addition, his attitude towards me has been increasingly unfriendly. He continually criticises my work in front of other members of the production team. For example on 4th July 2019 he criticised me for coming back late from my lunch break, when I was the first team member to return. On 3rd August he called me "a lazy slacker" in front of the other team members and said that if it was down to him I would be "out on my ear".

6. I raised a grievance about Mr Brown's behaviour. At the grievance meeting on 25th October 2019 I explained to Mr Ford what the problem was and that I was unable to do the morning shift because I had to take my children to school. I also told him about Mr Brown's behaviour towards me.

7. Mr Ford said that he had looked into the position about overtime and because there had been a decline in production none of the members of my team had been given overtime recently. He appeared sympathetic when I explained how Mr Brown treated me and said Mr Brown would be spoken to about this.

8. I had hoped that after the grievance hearing the position would improve but in fact matters have got worse. Mr Brown has continued to criticise me in front of the other team members and he continually makes sarcastic comments about me not wanting to work on the morning shift. He has made it clear that he does not want me as part of his team.

9. The continued criticism has affected my health and I have been depressed and unable to sleep. I have had to see my GP on several occasions for anti-depressants. I cannot put up with Mr Brown's behaviour any further. The Respondent has made no effort to help me or improve the situation. I consider that this failure constitutes a breach of the implied term of trust and confidence by the Respondent. On 30th October 2019 I sent the Respondent a letter informing them that I had resigned.

10. In the circumstances I consider that I have been constructively dismissed by the Respondent and I claim damages for unfair dismissal and my notice pay.

ET1 Section 8.2: Details of claim - protected disclosure detriment and dismissal

1. I have been employed by the Respondent since 15th November 2011 on the Production Line at the Respondent's factory in High Road, Bigtown. In December 2012 I was promoted to team leader.

2. On 15th October 2019 I was working on the production line when the conveyor belt got stuck because some of the larger items got jammed in it. Mr Brown, the Production Line Manager, told me to clear the jam without switching the conveyor belt off. I told him this would be dangerous and I might get my hand caught. He told me it would waste far too much time to shut the machine off and then have to start it up again. I refused to clear the jam unless the conveyor belt was turned off. Mr Brown got another member of the team to clear the jam and in order to do this he had to put his has hand into the machinery and he almost got his hand trapped when the conveyor belt started up again.

3. Later the same day Mr Brown told me that he did not want me as team leader if I was not prepared to do what he told me. I was demoted from the position of team leader. As a result of this demotion I suffered a reduction in pay.

4. On 18th October 2019 I raised a grievance about my demotion and explained how it had occurred. I sent a copy of this grievance to Mr Jones, the Managing Director. My grievance was not upheld.

5. On 30th October 2019 I was informed that the Respondent was making a number of employees on the production line redundant because of down turn in orders. I had a meeting with Mr Brown at which I was informed that I was being made redundant. I pointed out that there were two other members of the production line team who were junior to me. Mr Brown said that the decision had been made on the basis of work performance and it was considered that my performance was not as good as that of the other team members.

6. I consider that my complaint about the events of 18th October 2019 constituted a qualifying disclosure under section 43B(d) of the Employment Rights Act 1996 that the health and safety of an individual had been endangered. The fact that an employee was told to put his hand into the machinery of the conveyor belt, while it was still on, meant that the health and safety of that individual was endangered.

7. I made this disclosure in good faith to Mr Brown, my Line Manager, to Mr Ford, the Production Manager and to Mr Jones, the Managing Director. As result of making this protected disclosure I was subjected to a detriment, that is my demotion as team leader and the reduction in pay.

8. I do not believe that the true reason for my dismissal was because of redundancy.

I believe that I was dismissed because I made this protected disclosure. No proper redundancy selection procedure was carried out and also there were other team members who had not been employed for as long as me. At no stage had I been told that my performance was below standard and at my last appraisal my level of commitment and performance were both marked as "excellent".

9. In any event my dismissal was unfair. The Respondent did not carry a proper redundancy selection procedure - it was based solely on Mr Brown's judgement as to my performance. I believe my performance had been better than other team members who were not selected for redundancy and I had been employed by the Respondent for longer than these team members. I was given no examples of ways in which my performance was below standard and the fact that I had received good appraisals was ignored. I was not offered any alternative positions, although I later found out that there were suitable vacancies in other departments. There was a job in the post room I could have done and there was a vacancy in the Quality Control section.

10. I claim damages in respect of the detriment I suffered as a result of making a protected disclosure under section 49 of the Employment Rights Act 1996. I also claim damages for injury to feelings.

11. I claim that I was automatically unfairly dismissed for making a protected disclosure under section 103A of the Employment Rights Act 1996.

12. Further and alternatively I claim I was unfairly dismissed under section 98(2) of the Employment Rights Act 1996.

ET1 Section 8.2: Details of claim - disability discrimination

1. I have been employed by the Respondent since 15th November 2006 on the Production Line at the Respondent's factory in High Road, Bigtown. This job involves standing at the assembly line conveyor belt for long periods.

2. In January 2019 I was involved in a car accident which resulted in a severe injury to my back. As a result of this accident my back is now permanently weakened. My mobility is limited so that I can only walk a few hundred yards before I need to have a rest. I am unable to stand for more than 20 minutes and then I will need to sit down for at least 10 minutes.

3. When I returned to work in May 2019 I explained the problem to my Line Manager, Mr Brown. He told me that there were no other positions available and I would have to go back working on the assembly line. He told me just to take it easy and have a rest when I needed one.

4. At first I was able to manage although during the day I would have to take increasingly longer rest breaks. I asked if it was possible for me to be provided with a stool to sit on while I worked as this would ease the pressure on my back. Mr Brown told me that this was not possible and that I would just have to do as best as I could.

5. I did not want to make too much fuss about my back because I was concerned that the Respondent might find some excuse to sack me if they did not think that I was up to the job.

6. Since September 2019 my back condition has become increasingly worse. I have now been signed off work for four weeks by my GP. He says that if I continue putting my back under strain by working standing up I will do further damage to my spine.

7. My back condition is a permanent physical impairment. It has a substantial and long term adverse effect on my ability to carry out normal day-to-day activities. In particular it has a significant adverse effect on my ability to walk for a distance and to stand for any length of time. As such my back constitutes a disability.

8. The requirement that I have to work whilst standing up puts me at a substantial disadvantage in comparison to the other members of the production line team who are not disabled.

9. The Respondent has a duty to take such steps as are reasonable in order to prevent this requirement from putting me at a disadvantage. In particular, the Respondent failed to provide me with a stool and to allow me to do my work sitting down. This would have been a reasonable step for the Respondent to take.

The Respondent is accordingly in breach of the Equality Act 2010 and guilty of disability discrimination towards me.

10. I claim damages for disability discrimination including damages for earnings lost since I have been off sick and damages for injury to feelings.

11. I also ask the tribunal to make a recommendation that I be provided with a stool and be allowed to work on the assembly line sitting down.

ET3 Section 6: Details of response to unfair dismissal claim

1. The Respondent is a company specialising in the manufacture of metal brackets. The Claimant has been employed by the Respondent since 1ˢᵗ October 2011 as a Production Line Worker at the Respondent's main factory premises in High Road, Bigtown.

2. The Claimant works as part of a team of four. Mr White is one of the other members of the Claimant's team. Mr White has worked for the Respondent for 15 years and is one of the most experienced production line workers.

3. The Claimant alleges in his claim form that Mr White had been in trouble in the past for disciplinary matters. In 2008 Mr White had been given a written warning for persistent lateness. This is the only disciplinary matter against Mr White. He has never been disciplined with regard to any incidents involving either physical or verbal aggression. There have been no complaints about his behaviour.

4. The Claimant refers to an incident that is alleged to have taken place on 5ᵗʰ June 2019. He alleges that he was threatened by Mr White. Mr White denies that any such incident occurred. No complaint was made about any such incident by the Claimant either at this time or at any time about Mr White's behaviour towards him.

5. The Respondent does not tolerate any bullying by members of staff and this policy is set out in the company handbook, which the Claimant was given when he started working for the Respondent. Any complaints about bullying are taken seriously and if the Claimant had made any allegations that he was being bullied these would have been investigated and, if proved, would have been dealt with. There is also a formal grievance procedure which the Claimant could have used but he did not do so.

6. On 27ᵗʰ October 2019 Mr Brown, the Production Line Manager, saw an incident involving the Claimant and Mr White. He did not see how this started but he saw that they were fighting. It appeared to him that the Claimant had lost his temper and he was the aggressor and that Mr White was trying to defend himself and telling the Claimant to calm down.

7. Mr Brown sent them both home. He asked the other team members whether they had seen what had started the fight but none of them had seen this.

8. On 30ᵗʰ October 2019 disciplinary hearings were held with both the Claimant and Mr White. The Claimant admitted that he had started the fight but said that he had been provoked by Mr White. The Claimant was asked why he had not used the company procedure on bullying and he said he did know about this.

9. Mr White also said that the fight had been started by the Claimant. Mr White

denied that he had provoked him - he accepted that he had made a comment about the Claimant having a lie-in but this was just a joking comment. The Claimant then lost his temper and he started pushing Mr White aggressively. Mr White did not retaliate but was trying to defend himself and to calm the Claimant down.

10. Both disciplinary hearings were conducted by Mr Jones and he decided on the appropriate penalties for both the Claimant and Mr White. He took into account the fact that the Claimant appeared to be the aggressor and started the fight, he did not accept that there had been any real provocation by Mr White, although it would have better if he had not made the comment to the Claimant, even as a joke.

11. The Company handbook on disciplinary procedures at section 10 lists examples of gross misconduct and this includes fighting in the workplace.

12. In the circumstances it was considered that the Claimant was guilty of gross misconduct, the Respondent could not tolerate such behaviour and they had no alternative but to dismiss him. Whilst it was accepted that Mr White was involved in the fight he was not the aggressor and was trying to defend himself. In these circumstances it was felt that a final warning was the appropriate penalty.

13. The Respondent accepts that the Claimant and Mr White received different penalties but there were good reasons for this and the Respondent was entitled to take the view that the Claimant's misconduct was more serious and merited dismissal. The Respondent denies that the dismissal was unfair.

14. If it is found that the Claimant's dismissal was unfair the Respondent will contend that the Claimant was guilty of contributory fault and it was his behaviour that resulted in his dismissal. In these circumstances any award should be reduced by up to 100%.

15. The Claimant was verbally informed of his right to appeal against his dismissal by Mr Jones and therefore there should be no percentage uplift on any damages awarded for failure to comply with the ACAS Code of Practice on Grievance and Disciplinary Procedures.

ET3 Section 6: Details of response to constructive unfair dismissal claim

1. The Respondent is a company specialising in the manufacture of metal brackets. The Claimant has been employed by the Respondent since 1st October 2011 as a Production Line Worker at the Respondent's main factory premises in High Road, Bigtown.

2. The Claimant has worked on the evening shift since he started work. In 2012 it was decided that a new flexible shift pattern should be introduced and this would result in increased production and more efficient use of the production line system. It was made clear to all employees that this new shift system was optional and that no employee would be forced to change his shift pattern if he did not want to.

3. The three other members of the Claimant's team agreed to the change in shift patterns. The Claimant explained that because he took his children to school in the mornings he was unable to do an early shift.

4. On 15th October 2019 the Claimant raised a grievance outlining three complaints; i) that Mr Brown was trying to get the Claimant to change his shift pattern; ii) that the Claimant's overtime had been stopped; and iii) that Mr Brown criticised the Claimant in front of his work colleagues.

5. The grievance meeting took place on 25th October 2019 and was conducted by Mr Ford. Having investigated the matter he found that overtime generally had been reduced because of a downturn in production and this applied to all the members of the production line team not just to the Claimant. The Claimant's grievance regarding overtime was not upheld.

6. Mr Ford also found that there had been several occasions when Mr Brown had to point out to the Claimant that his work was below standard. The Claimant accepted that Mr Brown was justified in speaking to him about his performance but said it was humiliating to be told this in front of his work colleagues.

7. Mr Brown was spoken to about this and told if he had occasion to speak to the Claimant in future about his performance he would do so in private. The Claimant's grievance on this point was upheld.

8. It was explained that the Respondent was trying to introduce a more flexible working pattern and if he was able to make other arrangements for his children getting to school it would be helpful if he could change his shift but that this was not something the Respondent was going to insist on.

9. On 26th October 2019 the Claimant was informed of the outcome of the grievance meeting.

10. It is denied that following the grievance meeting Mr Brown criticised the Claimant's performance in front of other team members. On several occasions Mr Brown had speak to the Claimant about his performance. The first occasion occurred on 30th October 2019 when the Claimant went outside the factory premises to smoke a cigarette. Mr Brown spoke to the Claimant and told him that this was unacceptable. This was not said in front of any other employees.

11. Two days later on 2nd November 2019 Mr Brown again found the Claimant smoking outside the factory. He was told that as this was the second time this had occurred it would be treated as a disciplinary matter. This conversation did not take place in front of the Claimant's work colleagues. The Claimant said "I'm not going to put up with this harassment any more." That was the last day the Claimant came in to work.

12. It is denied that Mr Brown made sarcastic comments to the Claimant and it is denied that Mr Brown did not want the Claimant as part of his team or that Mr Brown gave this impression.

13. It is denied that the Respondent was in breach of the implied term of trust and confidence or in breach of any term of the contract of employment. It is contended that the reason the Claimant resigned was because he was facing a disciplinary allegation in relation to taking unauthorised smoking breaks

14. If it is found that the Claimant was constructively dismissed and that the dismissal was unfair, the Respondent will contend that the Claimant was guilty of contributory fault in taking unauthorised smoking breaks and it was this behaviour that resulted in his dismissal. In these circumstances any award should be reduced by up to 100%.

15. Further the Respondent will contend that, had the Claimant not resigned, he would have faced a disciplinary hearing in relation to taking unauthorised smoking breaks and the Claimant would probably have been dismissed for gross misconduct. The Respondent contends that the Claimant would have been dismissed in any event and the Respondent relies on the principle in *Polkey v AE Dayton* to limit any compensatory damages awarded to the period in which a disciplinary hearing would have taken place.

16. Although the Claimant had raised a grievance on 21st October 2019, which was dealt with by the Respondent the Claimant did not raise a further grievance in relation to Mr Brown's behaviour after 25th October 2019. It was this behaviour that the Claimant relied on when he resigned and in the circumstances the Claimant has failed to follow the ACAS Code of Grievances and any damages awarded should accordingly be reduced by up to 25%.

ET3 Section 6: Details of response to protected disclosure detriment and dismissal claim

1. The Respondent is a firm specialising in the manufacture of metal brackets. The Claimant has been employed by the Respondent since 1st October 2011 as a Production Line Worker at the Respondent's main factory premises in High Road, Bigtown. In December 2012 the Claimant was promoted to team leader.

2. On 18th October 2019 the Claimant was working on the production line when the conveyor belt got stuck. This is not an unusual situation and can occur two or three times a week. It happens when several of the larger brackets get jammed against each other. The usual procedure is to use a stick to clear the items. There is no danger of an employee's hands getting caught in the machinery. Over the last year the procedure has been used on at least 100 occasions without anyone being injured.

3. The Claimant was asked by Mr Brown the Production Line Manager to clear the blockage. The Claimant refused saying that his hand might get caught. It was pointed out to him that he would be using the stick to clear the jammed and his hand would be nowhere near the machinery. The Claimant still refused and in the end Mr Brown had to ask another member of the team to clear the blockage.

4. Mr Brown considered that the Claimant had refused to obey a direct order without any reasonable excuse. This had occurred in front of the other members of the team and had undermined Mr Brown's authority. Mr Brown considered that the Claimant's behaviour did not show the proper qualities for a team leader and felt it was not appropriate for the Claimant to continue as a team leader. The Claimant did not suffer any reduction in pay.

5. The Claimant raised a grievance about his demotion. This grievance was heard by Mr Ford on 25th October 2019 and the grievance was not upheld.

6. As a result of the recession a number of the Respondent's customers have gone out of business over the past two years. This has led to a considerable drop in orders. Because of this the Respondent has had to take the decision to reduce the number of employees working one the production line.

7. All the employees working on the production line were put into the selection pool. Out of the 30 employees, the Respondent was going to have to make 10 employees redundant. A selection matrix was drawn up with five different criteria which included punctuality, disciplinary record, length of service, commitment and work performance with marks out of 5.

8. The selection matrix was initially scored by the employee's Line Manager and this was checked by the Production Manager. The total number of marks available was 25. The Claimant only scored 12 marks overall and was one of the lowest three

scores. All those employees with less than a total of 15 were made redundant. The Claimant had low scores in a number of areas including his performance.

9. On 30th October 2019 the Claimant had a meeting with Mr Brown. The Claimant was given the opportunity at this meeting to discuss his scores. He said that he did not agree with the low scores he had been given but this was not accepted by Mr Brown.

10. Following the meeting on 30th October 2019 the Claimant was sent a letter informing him that he had been made redundant. He was informed of his right to appeal against the decision to dismiss him but did not do so. The letter gave him details of the company website where all vacancies were advertised. The Claimant did not apply for any of the jobs advertised.

11. The Respondent denies that the Claimant made a protected disclosure. If it is found that the Claimant did make a protected disclosure the Respondent denies that this was the reason for the Claimant's dismissal. The Claimant was dismissed for redundancy and the Respondent will contend that a fair selection procedure was followed.

12. If it is found that the selection procedure was flawed in any way the Respondent will contend that the Claimant's position was redundant and the Claimant would have been dismissed for redundancy in any event and the Respondent relies on the principle in *Polkey v AE Dayton* to limit any compensatory damages awarded to the Claimant.

ET3 Section 6: Details of response to claim for disability discrimination

1. The Respondent is a firm specialising in the manufacture of metal brackets. The Claimant has been employed by the Respondent since 15th November 2006 as a Production Line Worker at the Respondent's main factory premises in High Road, Bigtown.

2. The Claimant's work hours are from 9.30am to 5.00pm. There is a 15 minute break at 11.00am and 3.30pm and a one hour lunch break from 1.00pm to 2.00pm The Claimant's job involves some standing at the assembly line conveyor belt but there is a regular rotation of tasks.

3. The Respondent was aware that the Claimant was involved in an accident in 2019 and had several weeks off work. On his return to work on 24th May 2019 the Claimant asked his Line Manager, Mr Brown, whether there were any alternative positions available but he did not explain why he wanted an alternative position.

4. In September 2019 the Claimant did inform Mr Brown that his back was causing him problems. Mr Brown told the Claimant that he should take extra long breaks if he needed to and that there were chairs available in the canteen which he could use if he needed to ease his back pain.

5. The Respondent denies that the Claimant asked if he could be provided with a stool to sit on while he worked. In any event given the nature of the job carried out by the Claimant it would not have been possible for him to carry out this job whilst sitting on a stool as his job involved him moving up and down the conveyor belt.

6. The Respondent does not accept that the Claimant's back condition constitutes a disability for the purposes of the Equality Act 2010. The Respondent does not accept that the Claimant has a physical impairment which has a significant adverse effect on his ability to carry out day-to-day activities.

7. If it is found that the Claimant is disabled it is denied that the Respondent discriminated against the Claimant on account of his disability, or at all. It is contended that, by allowing the Claimant to take extra long rest breaks, the Respondent had carried out a reasonable adjustment which prevented the Claimant's disability putting him at a disadvantage.

8. It is contended that there were no other possible adjustments that could have been made that would have prevented the Claimant's disability putting him at a disadvantage when compared to other non-disabled employees. In particular it is contended that the provision of a stool would not have constituted a reasonable adjustment because it was not possible for the Claimant to do his job when sitting on a stool. Further it is contended that the requirement of assembly line workers

to stand was a proportionate means of achieving a legitimate end.

9. The Claimant's claim for disability discrimination is denied.

Request by the Respondent for additional information of the ET1 in a claim for constructive unfair dismissal

Mr Jones
Bigtown Manufacturing
Limited
100 High Road
Bigtown

Mr A N Smith
123 Hillside Road
Bigtown

21ˢᵗ October 2019

Dear Mr Smith,

This is a Request for Additional Information of the ET1 in the case of:

Andrew Smith v Bigtown Manufacturing Limited Claim No. 1234987/2019

Under paragraph 2 referring to Mr Brown:

> *"Since then he has been trying to get to me to change my shift"*

Please state each and every occasion that you allege Mr Brown tried to get you to change your shift, giving details of the date, time and place where the conversation took place and the words that were used by Mr Brown.

Under paragraph 8:

> *"Mr Brown has continued to criticise me in front of the other team members"*

Please state each and every occasion that you allege Mr Brown criticised you in front of other team members, giving details of the date, time and place where the conversation took place, the words that were used by Mr Brown and the names of the other team members who were present when the conversation took place.

Under paragraph 8:

> *"Mr Brown has continued to criticise me in front of the other team members"*

Is it the Claimant's case that the Claimant informed the Respondent of this criticism and, if so, give details of the date on which it is alleged that the Claimant informed the Respondent of this criticism and to whom the Claimant give this information.

Yours sincerely
Mr Jones

Request by the Claimant for additional information of the ET3 response

A.N. Smith
123 Hillside Road
Bigtown

Mr Jones
Bigtown Manufacturing Limited
100 High Road
Bigtown

12th October 2019

Dear Mr Jones,

This is a Request for Additional Information of the ET3 in the case of

Andrew Smith v Bigtown Manufacturing Limited Claim No. 1234987/2019

Under paragraph 4:

> *"Mr Brown…felt it was not appropriate for the Claimant to continue as team leader. The Claimant did not suffer any reduction in pay"*

Does the Respondent accept that the Claimant was demoted?

Does the Respondent accept that as a result of this demotion the Claimant suffered the loss of various benefits including team leader bonus?

Under paragraph 5:

> *"the grievance was not upheld".*

Did Mr Brown consult with any other members of the Management before coming to the decision not to uphold the grievance?

If so, please give the names of all those persons Mr Brown consulted with before coming to his decision and state what advice, if any, they gave Mr Brown.

Please state all facts and matters relied on by Mr Brown in his decision not to uphold the grievance.

Under paragraph 6:

> *"a number of the Respondent's customers have gone out of business over the past two years. This has led to a considerable drop in orders."*

Please give details of all the customers that have gone out of business in the past two years and state what percentage of the total business these customers would have provided.

Please give details of the extent to which there has been a drop in orders.

Yours sincerely

Mr Smith

Request by the Claimant for additional documentation

A.N. Smith
123 Hillside Road
Bigtown

Mr Jones
Bigtown Manufacturing Limited
100 High Road
Bigtown

12th October 2019

Dear Mr Jones,

This is a Request for Additional documentation in the case of

Andrew Smith v Bigtown Manufacturing Limited Claim No. 1234987/2019

1. In paragraph 2 of the ET3 you refer to the usual procedure when items get jammed in the conveyor belt.

2. Can you provide any documentation that you have from the manufacturer and/ or supplier of the conveyor belt, which sets out the recommended procedure for dealing with situations when the conveyor belt has become jammed.

3. Can you provide any risk assessments or training documents which relate to situations when the conveyor belt has become jammed.

4. In paragraph 8 of the ET3 you refer to the marking of the selection matrix and that the Claimant was one of the lowest three scores. Can you provide copies of any documentation that the Managers were provided with explaining how the matrix selection marking should be carried out. Can you provide a list of the marks of all the employees who took part in the selection process.

5. In paragraph 9 of the ET3 you refer to the Claimant's meeting with Mr Brown on 30th October 2019. Can you provide a copy of the transcript of this meeting.

Yours sincerely

A Smith

Questionnaire relating to a claim for disability discrimination

A.N. Smith
123 Hillside Road
Bigtown

Mr Jones
Bigtown Manufacturing Limited
100 High Road
Bigtown

12th October 2019

Dear Mr Jones,

This is a Request for Further Information in the case of

Andrew Smith v Bigtown Manufacturing Limited Claim No. 1234987/2019

1. Please state whether the Respondent was aware that the Claimant had sustained a severe injury to his back in an accident in 2019 and if so, which of the Respondent's employees were aware of this and when they knew of this.

2. Please state whether the Respondent was aware of the Claimant's ongoing back symptoms in 2019 and, if so, which of the Respondent's employees were aware of this and when they knew of this.

3. Please state who made the decision that the Claimant was not allowed a stool to sit on whilst doing his job.

4. If the decision was made by Mr Brown state whether he made the decision alone or whether he consulted anyone else before making the decision and, if so, state with whom he consulted and what advice he was given.

5. Please state whether any consideration was given to any other adjustment or steps that could be taken to prevent the Claimant's disability putting him at a substantial disadvantage when compared to non-disabled employees and if so, what consideration was given and by whom.

6. Were any other adjustments identified and, if so, why were these adjustments not implemented?

7. Do the Respondents have an Equal Opportunities policy? If so provide details or a copy of the policy.

8. Have the Respondent's managers undergone any Equal Opportunity training and, in particular any training with regard to disability discrimination? If so, give

details of the training and specify which managers have undergone such training.

Yours sincerely

AN Smith

Request by the Claimant to the Tribunal for specific disclosure of documents

A.N. Smith
123 Hillside Road
Bigtown

The Regional Secretary
Cardiff and the Vale Magistrates Court
Fitzalan Place
Cardiff
CF24 0RZ

24th November 2019

Dear Sir

This is a Request for specific disclosure of document in the case of

Andrew Smith v Bigtown Manufacturing Limited Claim No. 1234987/2019

On 12th October 2019 I sent a letter to the Respondent, a copy of which I have enclosed with this letter, requesting that they provide me with certain documents.

The Respondent has not replied to my letter.

The documents I requested were:

- any documentation that they have from the manufacturers and/or suppliers of the conveyor belt which set out the recommended procedure for dealing with situations when the conveyor belt has become jammed.

- any risk assessments or training documents that relate to situations when the conveyor belt has become jammed.

The reason that these documents are relevant to the issues in the case is that in paragraph 2 of the ET3 the Respondent refers to the usual procedure when items get jammed in the conveyor belt, which is to remove the jammed item without turning off the conveyor belt. I consider that this procedure is dangerous and likely to be contradicted by the documents I have requested.

I also requested copies of any documentation that the Managers were provided with explaining how the matrix selection marking should be carried out and a list of the marks of all the employees who took part in the selection process. This documentation is relevant to my allegation that the redundancy procedure was carried out unfairly.

I also requested a copy of the transcript of my meeting with Mr Brown on 30th

October 2019. Again this is relevant to the issue of whether the redundancy procedure was carried out fairly.

I would ask the tribunal to make an order that the Respondent do state which of these documents they have and do provide disclosure of these documents within 14 days of making the order.

I would also ask that in the event of the Respondent's failure to comply with this order within the specified time that the Response be struck out and the Respondent be barred from defending the claim.

Yours sincerely

A N Smith

List of documents

IN THE CARDIFF EMPLOYMENT TRIBUNAL   Claim No.
                                                1234987/2019

BETWEEN

ANDREW SMITH

Claimant

and

BIGTOWN MANUFACTURING LIMITED

Respondent

CLAIMANT'S LIST OF DOCUMENTS

15/11/2011	Terms and Conditions of Employment
12/10/2019	Grievance letter from Claimant
21/10/2019	Invitation to grievance meeting from Respondent
26/10/2019	Letter setting out the outcome of grievance meeting from Respondent
28/10/2019	Letter inviting Claimant to redundancy meeting
30/10/2019	Claimant's notes of redundancy meeting
30/10/2019	Dismissal letter

Witness statement by the Claimant

IN THE CARDIFF EMPLOYMENT TRIBUNAL   Claim No.
1234987/2019

BETWEEN:

ANDREW SMITH

Claimant

and

BIGTOWN MANUFACTURING LIMITED

Respondent

WITNESS STATEMENT

OF THE CLAIMANT

I, Andrew Smith, of 123 Hillside Road, Bigtown, make this statement in support of my claim for damages for making a protected disclosure and for unfair dismissal.

1. I have been employed by the Respondent since 15th November 2011 on the Production Line at the Respondent's factory in High Road, Bigtown. In December 2012 I was promoted to team leader.

2. On 15th October 2019 I was working on the production line when the conveyor belt got stuck because some of the larger items got jammed in it. Mr Brown, the Production Line Manager, told me to clear the jam without switching the conveyor belt off. I told him this would be dangerous and I might get my hand caught. He told me it would waste far too much time to shut the machine off and then have

to start it up again.

3. I refused to clear the jam unless the conveyor belt was turned off and said that it was in breach of the health and safety policy to put my hand into the machinery whilst it was still turned on. Mr Brown then got another member of the team, John White, to clear the jam. In order to do this John White had to put his has hand into machinery and he almost got his hand trapped when the conveyor belt started moving.

4. I have seen a copy of the manufacturer's instructions for this type of conveyor belt and at page 20 of this document it recommends that the conveyor belt should be turned off if it becomes jammed.

5. In the afternoon of 15th October 2019 Mr Brown came up to after the lunch break. He said that I had refused to obey an order that he had given and that he no longer wanted me as team leader if I was not prepared to do what he told me. Although this demotion has not affected the amount of pay I get each week it has meant that I no longer get the team leader bonus.

6. On 18th October 2019 I raised a grievance about my demotion and explained how it had occurred. I sent a copy of this grievance to Mr Jones, the Managing Director. There was a grievance meeting held on 25th October 2019 with Mr Ford, Head of Production, when I explained that it was unfair that I should have been demoted from team leader just because I was not prepared to risk an injury. I do not consider that Mr Ford was really interested in my complaints and my grievance was not upheld.

7. In October 2019 there was an announcement by Mr Jones that because of a drop in orders the company would be making a number of employees on the production line redundant. He said that this would be done fairly by using a selection procedure that had been agreed with the employee's representatives.

8. On 30th October 2019 I had a meeting with Mr Brown at which I was informed that I was being made redundant. I was given a copy of my scores. I had been marked down on all areas, which I considered very unfair because all my appraisals had been excellent. I pointed out that two other members of the production line team, John White and Alan Gray, were both junior to me. Mr Brown said that the decision had been made on the basis of work performance and it was considered that my performance was not as good as that of the other team members. I consider that Mr Brown was biased against me because of the incident on 15th October 2019 and had given me low marks because I raised a grievance about the matter.

9. I consider that my complaint about the events of 15th October 2019 constituted a qualifying disclosure under section 43B(d) of the Employment Rights Act 1996 that the health and safety of an individual had been endangered. The fact that

another employee, John White, was told to put his hand into the machinery of the conveyor belt, whilst it was still on, meant that the health and safety of that individual was endangered.

10. I made this disclosure in good faith to Mr Brown, my Line Manager. As a result of making this protected disclosure I was subjected to a detriment, that is my demotion as team leader and the loss of my team leader bonus. I also made this disclosure in my grievance to Mr Jones, the Managing Director, and to Mr Ford in the grievance meeting and as a result of this I believe the decision was made to dismiss me and the redundancy procedure was used as a way of achieving this.

11. I do not believe that the true reason for my dismissal was because of redundancy. No proper redundancy selection procedure was carried out. There were other team members who had not been employed for as long as me and whose work performance was not as good as mine. I believe I was deliberately marked down on the selection matrix so that I could be dismissed.

12. In any event my dismissal was unfair. The Respondent did not carry a proper redundancy selection procedure, it was based on solely on Mr Brown's judgment as to my performance. I believe my performance had been better than other team members who were not selected for redundancy and I had been employed by the Respondent for longer than these team members. I was given no examples of ways in which my performance was below standard and the fact that I had received good appraisals was ignored.

13. At no time during the redundancy procedure was I told about or offered any alternative positions. About three weeks after my dismissal I later found out that there had been suitable vacancies in other departments. There was a job in the post room I could have done and there was a vacancy in the Quality Control section.

14. I claim damages in respect of the detriment I suffered as a result of making a protected disclosure under section 49 of the Employment Rights Act 1996. These damages include the loss of the team leader bonus which I would have received if I had not been demoted. I also claim damages for injury to feelings to include the humiliation of being demoted as team leader, a post which I had held for almost two years.

15. I claim that I was automatically unfairly dismissed for making a protected disclosure under section 103A of the Employment Rights Act 1996.

16. Further and alternatively I claim I was unfairly dismissed under section 98(2) of the Employment Rights Act 1996 because no proper redundancy selection procedure was carried out, not was I offered any alternative position.

17. I have been unable to find another job since being dismissed. I have signed on

at the Job Centre and with various on-line job agencies. I will provide the tribunal with copies of the all the job applications that I have made and the interviews I have attended.

Witness statement by a witness on behalf the Claimant

IN THE CARDIFF EMPLOYMENT TRIBUNAL   Claim No.
1234987/2019

BETWEEN :

ANDREW SMITH

Claimant

and

BIGTOWN MANUFACTURING LIMITED

Respondent

WITNESS STATEMENT OF

OF JOSEPH GREEN

I, Joseph Green, of 321 Highside Road, Bigtown, make this statement in support of the Claimant's claim in the employment tribunal.

1. I have been employed by the Respondent since September 2010. I work on production line at the Respondent's factory in High Road, Bigtown. I work as part of the team that includes the Claimant, Andrew Smith and John White.

2. I am aware that there has been ill feeling between Mr Smith and Mr White for some time. Mr White has worked for the Respondent since 2007 and often behaves as if he is a team leader and orders us around. Although he has never made any

threatening remarks to me I have heard him make such remarks to Mr Smith.

3. There was one occasion in June 2019 (I am not sure of the exact date) when Mr Smith was carrying a number of trays and as he walked past Mr White he dropped one of the trays. Mr Smith immediately turned round and appeared to threaten Mr Smith. He raised his fist and waved it in Mr Smith's face. Mr White said something to him but I could not hear what was said.

4. There was another occasion some days later when I heard Mr White call Mr Smith "a clumsy oaf". This was said in front of all the team members.

5. I was present on 27th October 2019 when there was a fight between Mr Smith and Mr White. Mr Smith had turned up about 15 minutes late for his shift. Mr White started speaking to him. I could not hear everything that was said but I definitely heard a reference to Mr Smith having "a lie in". I did not see how the fight started but from what I could see it was Mr White who was punching Mr Smith. The fight was then broken up by Mr Brown who sent them both home.

6. I have known Mr Smith for three years and he has never been involved in any incident like this before. I consider it to be totally out of character for him to be involved in a fight and it must have been caused by some provocation by Mr White who can behave in a bullying way.

Witness statement by a witness on behalf of the Respondent

IN THE CARDIFF EMPLOYMENT TRIBUNAL   Claim No.
                                                  1234987/2019

BETWEEN :

ANDREW SMITH

Claimant

and

BIGTOWN MANUFACTURING LIMITED

Respondent

WITNESS STATEMENT OF

OF SAMUEL BROWN

I, Samuel Brown of 100 High Road, Bigtown, make this statement on behalf of the Respondent.

1. I am the Production Line Manager for the Respondent company at their factory premises in High Road, Bigtown. I have held this position for 11 years. The Respondent is a firm specialising in the manufacture of metal brackets.

2. I have known Mr Smith, the Claimant, for nine years since 2011 when he started working as a Production Line Worker on the assembly line. In December 2012 the Claimant was promoted to team leader.

3. On 15th October 2019 I was in my office at the factory when I was informed that the conveyor belt had become jammed. This is a common occurrence and can happen two or three times a week. It happens when several of the larger brackets get jammed against each other. There is a stick provided which is used to push the brackets along and clear the jam. The problem is normally sorted out by whoever is working at the conveyor belt, and this will normally only take a few seconds. There is no danger of an employee's hands getting caught in the machinery because they are using the stick. Over the last year this procedure has been used on at least 100 occasions without anyone being injured. The conveyor belt does not need to be turned off.

4. When I was informed of the problem, I went over the conveyor belt. The Claimant was standing by the conveyor belt. I do not know why he had not done anything to sort the problem out - it is his responsibility as team leader and I would have expected him to have dealt with the situation without the need for me to be involved.

5. I asked the Claimant to sort the problem out and clear the blockage, he refused and said that he was not going to do so unless the conveyor belt was turned off. I was not impressed by his manner and his failure to take responsibility for the problem. I asked one of the other team members, Mr White, to sort the problem out. This was done quickly and easily by Mr White using the stick. The Claimant has suggested that Mr White almost had his hand trapped when the conveyor belt started moving - this is totally untrue as Mr White's hand was nowhere near the machinery.

6. I am very aware of the Respondent's responsibility for the health and safety of its employees and would never ask any employee to do anything that I regarded as dangerous.

7. I considered that the Claimant had refused to obey a direct order without any reasonable excuse. Because this had occurred in front of the other members of the team I felt it had undermined my authority and I considered that the Claimant's behaviour did not show the proper qualities for a team leader. In the circumstances I felt it was not appropriate for the Claimant to continue as a team leader.

8. The Claimant raised a grievance about the matter. This grievance was heard on 25th October 2019. I did not consider that the Claimant had any good grounds for refusing to do what I had asked and I did not uphold the grievance. The Claimant was informed of this decision by letter dated 25th October. He was told of his right to appeal but I understand he did not do so.

9. As a result of the recession a number of the Respondent's customers have gone out of business over the past two years. This has led to a considerable drop in orders, over the last year this has been about 50% of our orders and as a result the

company has had to cut back on its production. This has meant that we need less employees working on the production line.

10. All the employees working on the production line were put into the selection pool. Out of the 30 employees, the Respondent was going to have to make 10 employees redundant. It was agreed that the fairest way to select employees was to draw up a selection matrix with different criteria which included punctuality, disciplinary record, length of service, commitment and work performance with marks out of 5. This method was agreed with the employee's representative

11. I carried out the initial scoring of those employees on the production line and my scores were checked by the Production Manager. The total number of marks available was 25. The Claimant scored 12 marks overall because he scored lowly in several categories. This was because his punctuality had been poor and I considered that his work performance was poor. This meant that the Claimant scored one of the lowest three scores. All those employees with less than a total of 15 were made redundant.

12. On 30th October 2019 the Claimant had a meeting with myself. The Claimant was given the opportunity at this meeting to discuss his scores. He said that he did not agree with the low scores he had been given but was not able to give any good reasons for this.

13. Following the meeting on 30th October 2019 the Claimant was sent a letter informing him that he had been made redundant. He was informed of his right to appeal against the decision to dismiss him but did not do so. The letter gave him details of the company website where all vacancies were advertised. The Claimant did not apply for any of the jobs advertised.

14. The Claimant was demoted from his position as team leader because of his unreasonable refusal to do something he had been asked to do. The only reason that the Claimant was dismissed was redundancy.

Application to the Tribunal for a witness order

A.N. Smith
123 Hillside Road
Bigtown

The Regional Secretary
Cardiff and the Vale Magistrates Court
Fitzalan Place
Cardiff
CF24 0RZ

24th January 2020

Dear Sir,

This is an application for a witness order in the case of

Andrew Smith v Bigtown Manufacturing Limited Claim No. 1234987/2019

I am the Claimant in this case and I have brought a claim for unfair dismissal against the Respondent.

I was dismissed for fighting with another employer. I am contending that the dismissal was unfair because I had been subjected to bullying and threats by the other employee involved. On the day of the incident I had been provoked by the other employee. He had been aggressive and was punching me and yet this employee was not dismissed but only received a final written warning.

I wish to call as a witness in support of my case Mr Joseph Green, who lives at 321 Highside Road, Bigtown. He witnessed the bullying and threats I have been subjected to and he witnessed the incident on 27th October 2019 for which I was dismissed. He has made a witness statement which I attach to this application but says that he is not prepared to attend the tribunal hearing because he is still employed by the Respondent.

I am applying to the tribunal for a witness order to compel Mr Green to attend the tribunal hearing on 6th June 2020. His evidence is relevant to issues that the tribunal will have to decide and it is important to my case that the tribunal hears his evidence.

Yours sincerely

Andrew Smith

Offer letter from Claimant

A.N. Smith
123 Hillside Road
Bigtown

Mr Jones
Bigtown Manufacturing Limited
100 High Road
Bigtown

12ᵗʰ March 2020

Dear Mr Jones,

This is an offer of settlement in the case of

Andrew Smith v Bigtown Manufacturing Limited Claim No. 1234987/2019

I have brought a claim for unfair dismissal arising out of my dismissal for gross misconduct on 31ˢᵗ October 2019 for fighting with John White.

I consider that I have a good prospect of succeeding in my claim and I have supporting evidence from a witness, Joseph Green, who can confirm that Mr White had bullied me on a number of occasions. I had complained about this to Mr Brown but nothing had been done. The decision to dismiss me was clearly unfair as Mr White, who was more guilty than me, was not dismissed.

I have not been able to find another job and have now been out of work for five months. I will be claiming damages of more than £7,500 when the case comes to be heard by the tribunal.

In the circumstances I would be prepared to withdraw my claim if the Respondent agrees to pay £5,000 and to provide me with a reference.

I look forward to hearing from you

Yours sincerely

Andrew Smith

Offer letter from Respondent including a cost warning

Mr Jones
Bigtown Manufacturing Limited
100 High Road
Bigtown

Mr A N Smith
123 Hillside Road
Bigtown

21st March 2020

Dear Mr Smith,

This is an offer of settlement in the case of

Andrew Smith v Bigtown Manufacturing Limited Claim No. 1234987/2019

The Respondent is prepared to offer you the sum of £2,500 if you agree to withdraw your claim for unfair dismissal. The Respondent would also require you to agree to a confidentiality clause.

The Respondent does not accept that you are likely to succeed in your claim. You accepted that you were fighting with another employee. Fighting on the shop floor is an act of gross misconduct which merits summary dismissal. Your dismissal comes within the band of reasonable responses that was open to the Respondent.

If you do not accept this offer and continue with your claim, and your claim is either dismissed or you are awarded less than £2,500, the Respondent will bring a claim for their costs and will bring the attention of the tribunal to the contents of this letter. The Respondent's legal costs are likely to be more than £10,000. The Respondent will contend that your refusal to accept this offer and to continue with a case in which you have little prospect of succeeding constitutes unreasonable behaviour under rule 76 of the Employment Tribunal (Constitution and Rules of Procedure) Regulations 2103 Schedule 1.

Yours sincerely

Mr Jones

Settlement agreement reached before bringing a claim

This document records the agreement that has been reached between Andrew Smith ("the employee") and Bigtown Manufacturing Limited ("the employer"). This agreement is intended to be legally binding on both the employee and the employer and its terms are enforceable in a court of law.

The employer will pay to the employee by 4.00pm on 30th March 2020 the sum of £5,000 in full and final settlement of all claims that the employee may have arising under his contract of employment with the employer or arising out of the termination of this contract of employment other than any claim for damages for personal injury or any claim arising under the employer's pension scheme.

Signed by the employee

Signed on behalf of the employer

Settlement agreement incorporating a reference and confidentiality clause

IN THE CARDIFF EMPLOYMENT TRIBUNAL   Claim No.
1234987/2019

BETWEEN :

ANDREW SMITH

Claimant

and

BIGTOWN MANUFACTURING LIMITED

Respondent

SETTLEMENT AGREEMENT

Andrew Smith ("The Claimant") and Bigtown Manufacturing Limited ("The Respondent") have agreed as follows:-

1. The Respondent will by 4.00pm on 14th October 2020 pay to the Claimant the sum of £5,000. The Claimant will accept this sum in full and final settlement of his claim in the employment tribunal claim no. 1234987/2019 for unfair dismissal and notice pay and all other claims, other than any claim for personal injury or any claim arising under the Respondent's pension scheme, which the Claimant has or may have against the Respondent arising out of his employment with the Respondent or the termination of this employment whether at common law or under the statutory provisions set out in Schedule 1 these being provisions which an employment tribunal has jurisdiction to hear.

2. On payment of the said sum the Claimant will withdraw his claim against the Respondent which is currently before the employment tribunal (Claim no. 1234987/2019).

3. The terms of this agreement are confidential and shall not be disclosed by either party save to their legal advisors or as required by law and the Claimant may disclose the terms to his wife and other members of his family who living at his home address. This clause does not prevent the Claimant making a protected disclosure under section 43A of the Employment Rights Act 1996.

4. On any request by any person or company for a reference for the Claimant the Respondent will provide on headed note paper a reference in the form agreed by the parties and set out in the Schedule 2 to this agreement.

5. The Claimant confirms that, before signing this agreement, he has received independent legal advice from Jo Bloggs, solicitor of 246 Bigtown Road, as to the terms and effects of this agreement and in particular its effects on his ability to pursue his right in an employment tribunal. The said advisor is a qualified lawyer in respect of whom there is in force a contract of professional indemnity insurance covering the risk of a claim by the Claimant in respect of any loss arising in consequence of the advice.

6. The conditions regulating compromise agreements under the Employment Rights Act 1996 and/or Equality Act 2010 and/or Working Time Regulations 1998 are satisfied in relation to this agreement.

Signed for the Claimant

Signed for the Respondent

Schedule 1

Trade Union and Labour Relations (Consolidation) Act 1992 sections 68, 86, 137, 145A and 145B, 146, 152, 153, 168, 168A, 169, 170, 191, 192, 238 and 238A, and paragraphs 156, 161 and 162 of Schedule A!.

Employment Rights Act 1996 sections 8, 13, 15, 28, 63F, 80(1), 80F, 80G, 92, 135 and Parts V, VI, VII and X.

National Minimum Wage Act 1998 sections 10 and 23.

Employment Relations Act 1999 section 10.

Part 5 of the Equality Act 2010 in respect of direct discrimination, indirect discrimination, duty to make adjustments, harassment, victimisation.

Working Time Regulations 1998 regulations 10(1), 10(2), 11(1), 11(2), 11(3), 12(1), 12(4), 13, 13A, 14(2), 16(1), 24, 24A, 27(2), 27A(4)(b).

Maternity and Parental Leave Regulations 1999 regulation 19.

Part-Time Workers (Prevention of Less Favourable Treatment) Regulations 2000 regulations 5 and 7(2).

Fixed-Term Employees (prevention of Less Favourable Treatment Regulations 2002 regulations 3, 6(2), 8 and 9.

Schedule 2

Andrew Smith was employed by Bigtown Manufacturing Limited from 1st October 2011 until 30th October 2019. He was employed as a Production Line worker in the Bigtown factory at 100 High Street Bigtown. His job involved working on the production line conveyor belt and checking the quality of manufactured items. Mr Smith was always punctual and a hard worker and he was willing to do overtime when asked.

Application to the Tribunal to strike out claim or make a deposit order

Mr Jones
Bigtown Manufacturing Limited
100 High Road
Bigtown

The Regional Secretary
Cardiff and the Vale Magistrates Court
Fitzalan Place
Cardiff
CF24 0RZ

24th January 2020

Dear Sir,

This is an application that the tribunal either strike out the claim or make a deposit order in the case of

Andrew Smith v Bigtown Manufacturing Limited Claim No. 1234987/2019

The Claimant, Mr Smith, has brought a claim for unfair dismissal against the Respondent.

The Claimant was dismissed on 31st October 2019 for an act of gross misconduct in that he was fighting with another employee whilst on the shop floor.

There was a full disciplinary hearing on 30th October 2019 when the Claimant was given the opportunity to put his case.

The Claimant had admitted fighting but said that he had been provoked. The Respondent did not accept that the Claimant had been provoked or, if he had, that this would have been an excuse for starting a fight.

The Claimant contends that his dismissal was unfair because the other person involved in the fight was not dismissed but only received a final written warning.

The Respondent having heard from both the employees involved in the fight and from the Manager, Mr Brown, who witnessed the incident, took the view that the Claimant's behaviour was more blameworthy in that he had started the fight and there had been no real provocation.

In these circumstances we contend that the Claimant has no real prospects of succeeding in his claim and therefore we would ask that the Tribunal should strike out the claim.

Alternatively we would ask that this would be an appropriate case to make a deposit order on the basis that the Claimant has little reasonable prospects of success.

Yours sincerely

Mr Jones

Application to postpone the tribunal hearing

A.N. Smith
123 Hillside Road
Bigtown

The Regional Secretary
Cardiff and the Vale Magistrates Court
Fitzalan Place
Cardiff
CF24 0RZ

24th January 2020

Dear Sir,

This is an application to postpone the tribunal hearing in the case of:

Andrew Smith v Bigtown Manufacturing Limited Claim No. 1234987/2019

I am the Claimant in this case and I have brought a claim for unfair dismissal against the Respondent.

I was dismissed for fighting with another employer. I am contending that the dismissal was unfair because I had been subjected to bullying and threats by the other employee involved. On the day of the incident I had been provoked by the other employee, he had been aggressive and was punching me and yet this employee was not dismissed but only received a final written warning.

The case is listed for a full hearing on 6th March 2020. I wish to call as a witness in support of my case Joseph Green. He witnessed the bullying and threats I have been subjected to and he witnessed the incident for which I was dismissed. He has made a witness statement which I attach to this application.

When the tribunal wrote on 12th November 2019 informing me that the case had been listed for hearing on 6th March 2020 I spoke to Mr Green and he said that this was fine for him. Mr Green contacted me last week and said that he would now not be able to attend the tribunal hearing because he will be in hospital that day. He has been waiting for some time for an operation on his knee and last week the hospital informed that the operation would take place on 5th March 2020 and Mr Green would be in hospital for three days after the operation.

Mr Green did explain about the tribunal hearing but was informed that if he was not available for the operation on 5th March it might be another six months before they would be able to give him a new date. Mr Green says that he cannot wait this long.

Mr Green's evidence is vital to my case and I consider it most important that the tribunal hears his evidence. In these circumstances I would ask that the tribunal postpone the hearing listed for 6th March 2020 to another date. As far as I am aware the Respondent would not be prejudiced by this postponement.

Yours sincerely

Andrew Smith

Schedule of loss

IN THE CARDIFF EMPLOYMENT TRIBUNAL
 Claim No.
 1234987/2019

BETWEEN :

ANDREW SMITH

Claimant

and

BIGTOWN MANUFACTURING LIMITED

Respondent

SCHEDULE OF LOSS

The Claimant has brought a claim for unfair dismissal, automatic unfair dismissal and detriment for making a protected disclosure, failure to pay holiday pay and failure to provide a statement of terms and conditions of employment.

The Claimant reserves the right to update and/or amend this Schedule of Loss.

1. DETAILS

Claimant's date of birth
 8th July 1972

Employment commenced	23rd April 2005

Employment commenced   23rd April 2005

Effective date of termination   29th July 2019

Age at EDT   47

Gross Annual salary   £40,000

Net Annual salary   £30,000

Annual Employer's Pension Contribution £2,400

UNFAIR DISMISSAL

2. BASIC AWARD

8 years' service @ 1 week's pay of £525   £4,200

6 years' service @ 1 ½ week's pay of £525   £4,725

Total Basic Award   **£8,925**

3. COMPENSATORY AWARD

The Claimant is still looking for work. He did two weeks' temporary work in September 2019 but has been unable to find a permanent job.

a) PAST LOSSES

i) Past Loss of Earnings

Net Pay £2,500 a month

Loss of earnings from 29.07.19 to 29.04.20 (7 months)   £17,500

Loss of pension contribution 7 months   £1,400

Less income received from temporary work   £1,000

Total   £17,900

ii) Job seeking expenses

The Claimant attends the Job Centre once a week for which his travel costs are £5.00. He has attended ten job interviews for which his travel expenses are £50. The Claimant has not received any state benefits.

Expenses	£55

iii) Loss of Statutory rights

Loss	£500

b) FUTURE LOSSES

i) Future Loss of Earnings

12 x £2,500	£30,000

ii) Future Loss of Pension Contributions

12 x 200	£2,400

iii) Future Job Seeking Expenses

12 x £55	£660
Total Compensatory award	**£51,515**

4. ACAS UPLIFT

The Respondent failed to follow to ACAS Code of Practice on Disciplinary and Grievance Procedures in that the Respondent failed to provide the Claimant with the true reason for his dismissal, the Respondent failed to inform the Claimant that he had the right to appeal. The Claimant contends that in the circumstances the full uplift of 25% on the compensatory award would be appropriate.

Uplift of 25% on compensatory award	£12,878.75

5. INJURY TO FEELINGS

The Claimant contends that he suffered a detriment for making protected disclosures and that he was dismissed for making protected disclosures and/or because of his age. The Claimant contends that the award for injury to feelings should be in middle *Vento* band.

Injury to feelings	£15,000

ACAS uplift of 25%	£3,750
Total award	£18,750

6. FAILURE TO PAY HOLIDAY PAY

Claimant's leave year	1st April to 31st March
Amount of holiday accrued at EDT	5.02 weeks
Amount of holiday taken	4.2 weeks
Holiday owed	0.82 weeks
Weekly net pay	£576.92
Holiday pay owing	£473

Uplift for failure to follow ACAS Code

The Claimant lodged a grievance regarding the failure to pay his holiday pay. He received no response to his letter. The Claimant contends that in the circumstances the full uplift of 25% would be appropriate.

Uplift on holiday pay	£118.25
Total holiday pay	£591.25

7. AWARD FOR FAILURE TO PROVIDE A STATEMENT OF TERMS AND CONDITIONS

4 x £525	£2,100

8. TAX LIABILITY

To the extent that the award, not including the award for injury to feelings exceeds £30,000 it will be subject to taxation. Of the amount over £30,000 the first £12,500 is tax free, then the next £37,500 is subject to tax at a rate of 20% and the next £100,000 is taxed at 40%.

Accordingly the Claimant will seek to gross up his award to provide for such tax to be paid on sums awarded.

Application by Claimant for a reconsideration of the judgment

A.N. Smith
123 Hillside Road
Bigtown

The Regional Secretary
Cardiff and the Vale Magistrates Court
Fitzalan Place
Cardiff
CF24 0RZ

24th January 2020

Dear Sir,

This is an application for reconsideration of the judgment in the case of

Andrew Smith v Bigtown Manufacturing Limited Claim No. 1234987/2019

I am the Claimant in this case and I have brought a claim for unfair dismissal against the Respondent.

On 20th January 2020 I was informed by a friend of my mine who works for the Respondent company that there had been a hearing at the tribunal on 15th January 2020 and because I had not attended my claim was dismissed. I had no knowledge of this hearing date and have been waiting for some months to hear from the tribunal when the hearing took place. I do not know why I was not informed that the hearing was listed for 15th January. The only possibility I can think is that since sending my ET 1 to the tribunal I have moved to a new address. When I sent in my ET1 in September 2019 I was living at 123 Station Road, Bigtown and this was the address I put on my form.

On 5th November 2019 I moved to my current address at 123 Hillside Road. On 7th November 2019 I sent a letter to the tribunal office informing them of this move and telling them to send all correspondence to my address. But since this date I have received no correspondence from the tribunal.

I make my application for a reconsideration of the judgment under rule 70 of the Employment Tribunal (Constitution and Rules of Procedure) Regulations 2013 Schedule 1 on the basis that I did not receive notice of the proceedings and also on the basis that it is in the interests of justice that a reconsideration of the judgment should be undertaken.

Yours sincerely
A Smith

Application by Respondent for a reconsideration of the judgment

Mr Jones
Bigtown Manufacturing Limited
100 High Road
Bigtown

The Regional Secretary
Cardiff and the Vale Magistrates Court
Fitzalan Place
Cardiff
CF24 0RZ

24th January 2020

Dear Sir,

This is an application for reconsideration of the judgment in the case of

Andrew Smith v Bigtown Manufacturing Limited Claim No. 1234987/2019

At the hearing which took place on 15th January 2020 the Employment Judge found that the Claimant had been unfairly dismissed. The Judge then heard evidence regarding the level of damages. The Claimant gave evidence and said that he had been out of work since the date of dismissal. The Judge awarded the Claimant his past loss of earnings on this basis.

The Respondent has discovered since the date of this hearing that in fact the Claimant had worked for a number of months after his dismissal and had been paid for this work. I attach to this letter a copy of a statement from Mr Brown, the Production Line Manager, explaining how he received this information.

The Respondent makes this application for a reconsideration of the judgment under rule 70 of the Employment Tribunal (Constitution and Rules of Procedure) Regulations 2013 Schedule 1 on the basis that new evidence has become available which would effect the amount of damages that the Claimant was awarded. This was not evidence that was available to the Respondent at the time of the hearing nor was it evidence that the Respondent could reasonably have obtained.

The Respondent also makes this application on the basis that it is in the interests of justice that a reconsideration of the judgment should be undertaken.

Yours sincerely

Mr Jones

Appeal letter

A.N. Smith
123 Hillside Road
Bigtown

The Registrar
Employment Appeal Tribunal
5th Floor, 7 Rolls Building
Fetter Lane
London
EC4A 1NL

24th January 2020

Dear Sir,

In support of appeal against the judgment in the case of in the case of

Andrew Smith v Bigtown Manufacturing Limited Claim No. 1234987/2019

I enclose the following documents :-

- Notice of Appeal

- Judgment of the employment tribunal

- Written reasons for the decision of the employment tribunal

- Claim form ET1

- Response form ET3

Yours sincerely

A Smith

Grounds of appeal Section 7 Form 1: Notice of Appeal From Decision of Employment Tribunal

- The tribunal's decision (at paragraph 30 of the written reasons) that the Appellant's refusal to clear a jam in the conveyor belt because he thought it could be dangerous did not constitute a protected disclosure under section 43B(d) of the Employment Rights Act 1996 because it was not a "disclosure of information" was wrong in law.

- The tribunal's decision (at paragraph 30 of the written reasons) that the Appellant's refusal to clear a jam in the conveyor belt because he thought it could be dangerous did not constitute a protected disclosure under section 43B(d) of the Employment Rights Act 1996 because it did not "tend to show that the health and safety of any individual has been or is likely to be endangered." was perverse having regard to the finding of fact that the Respondent's risk assessment had identified there was a risk of injury in clearing a jam if the conveyor belt was not turned off.

- When the Appellant sought to make oral submissions on this point, the tribunal judge indicated that he did not need to address the tribunal on this point as it was accepted that it was "a matter of common sense".

- The tribunal's decision at paragraph 39 that there was no requirement on the Respondent to look for and/or offer the Appellant an alternative position was wrong in law and contrary to the decision in the case of *Williams v Compair Maxam Ltd* [1982] ICR 157 where Browne-Wilkinson J said at page 162 paragraph F: "The employer will seek to see whether instead of dismissing an employee he could offer him alternative employment."

Case   Website   Summary

Employment Status: Employee/self-employed

Autoclenz Ltd v Belcher & Ors [2011] UKSC 41	ECU (Employment Cases Update)	Vehicle cleaners were working under a contract which stated that they were self-employed. The Supreme Court held they were employees - the written terms of the contract did not reflect the reality of the situation or the true intention of the parties.
Hewlett Pack-ard v O'Murphy [2001] UKEAT 612/01/2609	EAT	The fact that the employer pays the worker's tax will be irrelevant if there is no contract between them.
Johnson Underwood Ltd v Montgomery & Anor [2000] UKEAT 509/98/1804	Bailii	The requirement of mutual obligation, that is the obligation on one side to offer work and on the other side to accept work, is normally an essential requirement of a contract of employment.
Ready Mixed Concrete v Ministry of Pensions [1968] 2 QB 497	Swarb	The earliest significant case considering the distinction between an employee and self-employed person, setting out three essential elements of a contract of employment.
Carmichael & Anor v National Power Plc [1999] UKHL 47	Bailii	In this case there was no obligation on workers to do the work offered to them - they were contracted on a casual and "as required" basis. It was held they were not employees.
O'Kelly v Trusthouse Forte [1983] ICR 728	Oxcheps	The tribunal decision as to whether the Claimant is a worker or self-employed is a question of fact based on the evidence and not law.

Employment Status: Agency workers

McMeechan v Secretary of State for Employment [1996] EWCA Civ 1166	Bailii	An agency worker can be an employee of the agency.

Case	Website	Summary
Brook Street Bureau (UK) Ltd v Dacas [2004] EWCA Civ 217	Bailii	An agency worker can be an employee of the client.
Hewlett Packard v O'Murphy [2001] UKEAT 612/01/2609	EAT	An agency worker might not be an employee at all.

Disciplinary procedures: General

Salford Royal Hospital NHS Trust v Roldan [2010] EWCA Civ 522	Employment Cases Update	It is particularly important to conduct a fair investigation and test allegations where a finding could have serious consequences for an employee with regard to obtaining future employment.
Bentley Engineering v Mistry [1979] ICR	N/A	No particular form of procedure is required for a disciplinary hearing so long as it is fair.
Harris and Shepherd v Courage [1982] IRLR	N/A	Where there are pending criminal proceedings against an employee, the employer will need to consider carefully whether there can be a fair disciplinary hearing.
Linfood Cash & Carry v Thomson [1989] IRLR 235	Swarb	This case sets out guidelines where an employer is relying on evidence from an informant who does not wish to be identified.
Moyes v Hylton Castle Working Men's Club [1986] IRLR 482	N/A	Where possible the person making the decision should not be a witness to the misconduct.
Clark v Civil Aviation Authority [1991] UKEAT 362/89/1806	EAT	A fair appeal can correct a procedurally defective disciplinary hearing and render the dismissal fair.

Case   Website   Summary

Case	Website	Summary
Securicor v Smith [1989] IRLR 356	Swarb	Where two employees involved in the same incident are given different punishments this can be fair if one of the employee's conduct was considered more blameworthy. See also *Kier Islington v Pelzman* UKEAT/0266/10/DM (Employment Cases Update).
London Borough of Harrow v Cunningham UKEAT 1098/94/0211	Bailii	Where two employees involved in the same incident are given different punishments this can be fair if one of the employees has a worse disciplinary record.

Disciplinary procedures: Suspension

Gogay v Hertford-shire County Council [2000] EWCA Civ 228	Bailii	Unwarranted suspension of an employee can be a breach of the implied term of trust and confidence.
McClory v Post Office [1993] IRLR 159	Mondaq	There is no duty on an employer to explain why he was suspending an employee or to allow the employee an opportunity to explain why he should not be suspended.

Disciplinary procedures: Previous warnings

Auguste Noel v Curtis [1990] IRLR 326	N/A	Previous unexpired warnings for different matters can be taken into account when dismissing an employee.
Airbus UK Ltd v Webb [2008] EWCA Civ 49	Bailii	Where an employer takes into account an expired final warning when considering dismissal this would not inevitably mean that the dismissal was unfair but it would usually do so.

Case Website Summary

Dismissal: Has there been a dismissal?

Kwik-Fit v Lineham [1992] IRLR 156	Swarb	When an employer or employee says something in the heat of the moment that can be interpreted as a resignation or dismissal the other party should confirm that what is said is really intended to be a dismissal or resignation.
Southern v Franks Charlesly [1981] IRLR (see also *Burton v Glycosynth* UKEAT/0811/ O4DZM (EAT website))	N/A	When considering the words used by an employer in dismissing or an employee in resigning the tribunal must consider the normal meaning of the words used.

Dismissal: Capability dismissal

Dunning & Sons v Jacomb	Oxcheps	In a capability dismissal the employee should have been given a warning regarding the possibility of dismissal.

Dismissal: Sickness absence dismissal

East Lindsey District Council v Daubney [1977] UKEAT 7/77/2004	Bailii	When considering dismissal for ill health absence an employer should try to obtain medical evidence about the prognosis of the employee's condition.
Links & Co v Rose [1991] IRLR 353	N/A	When considering a dismissal for ill health absence an employer should where possible carry out a consultation with the employee.
Lynock v Cereal Packaging [1988] IRLR 511	Oxcheps	Where the employee is off sick the employer should consider various factors before dismissing including likelihood of the illness recurring and the impact of the absence on the other employees.

Case   Website   Summary

Dismissal: Redundancy dismissals

Williams & Ors v Compair Maxam Ltd [1982] UKEAT 372/81/2201	Bailii	This case sets out the basic principles of a fair redundancy procedure.
Volkes v Bear [1974]	Oxcheps	The employer should be considering alternative positions for an employee facing redundancy.

Dismissal: Implied terms

Malik v BCCI [1997] UKHL 23	Bailii	House of Lords confirmed that there is an implied term of trust and confidence. Where the employer is conducting a dishonest business this will be a breach of the term.
Transco Plc v O'Brien [2002] EWCA Civ 379	Bailii	There is an implied obligation to treat all employees in an equally fair manner.

Dismissal: Cases where there has been a finding of constructive dismissal

Cantor Fitzgerald International v Callaghan & Ors [1999] EWCA Civ 622	Bailii	Employer reduced employee's pay.
Derby City Council v Marshall [1979] IRLR 261	N/A	The employer insisted on the employee working hours he was not contractually required to work.

Case	Website	Summary
O'Brien v Associated Fire Alarms [1969] 1 All ER 93; *Courtaulds Northern Spinning v Sibson* [1988] IRLR 305; *Aparau v Iceland Frozen Foods Plc* [1999] EWCA Civ 3047	Swarb; Bailii	All cases where the employer transferred the employee's place of work and the distance of the move was a relevant factor.
British Aircraft Corp v Austin [1978] IRLR 332; *Bracebridge Engineering v Darby* [1990] IRLR 3; *W A Goold (Pearmak) Ltd v McConnell & Anor* [1995] UKEAT 489/94/2804	Bailii	All cases where the employer refused to investigate complaints/grievances promptly and reasonably.
Palmanor v Cedron [1978] IRLR 303	N/A	Employer was abusive to employee, the type of business being a relevant factor.
Wigan Borough Council v Davies [1979] ICR 411	Oxcheps	Employer failing to protect an employee from harassment by other employees.
Hilton Hotels v Protopapa [1990] IRLR 316	Swarb	Employer criticising an employee in front of their subordinates in a humiliating and degrading manner.
Waltons & Morse v Dorrington [1997] UKEAT 69/97/1905	Bailii	The employer failed to provide a suitable/ safe working environment.
Marriott v Oxford & District Co-Op [1970] 1 QB 186	N/A	The demotion of an employee will normally be a breach of contract and entitle the employee to resign and claim constructive dismissal.

Case	Website	Summary
Rigby v Ferodo [1987] IRLR 516	Swarb	Where the employer reduced an employee's wages this will normally amount to a breach of contract. Rather than resign the employee can bring a claim for the difference in pay.
Alcan Extrusions v Yates [1996] IRLR 327	N/A	Where the employer introduces new working patterns which constituted a substantial departure from the old system this constituted a breach of contract.

Dismissal: Last straw doctrine

Case	Website	Summary
Garner v Grange Furnishing [1977] IRLR 206; *Woods v WM Car Services (Peterborough)* [1981] IRLR 34; *Lewis v Motorworld Garages* [1985] IRLR 46	Oxcheps	Three cases in which the employers' actions over a period of time amounted to conduct likely to destroy the relationship of trust between the parties but where the employee actually resigns over a relatively trivial incident.
Waltham Forest v Omilaju [2004] EWCA Civ 1493	Bailii	An innocuous or lawful act by the employer cannot constitute the last straw.

Dismissal: Unfair dismissals - general principles

Case	Website	Summary
Iceland Frozen Foods Ltd v Jones [1982] UKEAT 62/82/2907	Bailii	Whether an employer acted unreasonably under section 98 ERA 1996 in dismissing the employee is a question of fact for the tribunal based on the evidence. This finding can only be appealed if it was perverse or if it was based on an incorrect application of legal principles.
HSBC Bank Plc v Madden [2000] EWCA Civ 3030	Bailii	The test for unfair dismissal is whether it was within the band of reasonable responses that was open to the employer even though not all employers might have dismissed the employee.

Case	Website	Summary
British Home Stores Ltd v Burchell [1978] UKEAT 108/78/2007	Bailii	This is the main case setting out the test for fair dismissal in a misconduct case. The employer does not need to prove that the employee was in fact guilty of the misconduct but the employer must satisfy the tribunal that he genuinely believed that: the employee was guilty of the misconduct; he had reasonable grounds for that belief; and he had carried such investigation into the misconduct as was reasonable in the circumstances.
Pay v Lancashire Probation Service [2003] UKEAT 1224/02/2910	Bailii	Where an employee's activities outside the workplace are not compatible with his position within the company and might damage the reputation of the company his dismissal can be fair.

Dismissal: Some other substantial reason

Case	Website	Summary
Perkin v St Georges Healthcare NHS Trust [2005] EWCA Civ 1174	Bailii	A breakdown in the employment relationship caused by the employer's manner, in this case his managerial style, can constitute a fair reason for a dismissal for some other substantial reason.

Dismissal: Varying the terms of the employment contract

Case	Website	Summary
Chubb Fire v Harper [1983] IRLR 311	Swarb	Where the employer wishes to vary the terms of the contract and dismisses any employees who refuse to accept the new terms, the question the tribunal will have to consider on a claim for unfair dismissal is whether the employer acted reasonably.

Case	Website	Summary
Hollister v National Farmers' Union [1979] IRLR 23	Oxcheps	Where the employer dismisses an employer who refuses to accept changes to his contract, when considering whether the dismissal is unfair the tribunal will have to consider a variety of factors such as the significance of the changes to both employer and employee and whether the employee has been consulted.

Dismissal: Notice

Case	Website	Summary
Hills v Parsons [1971] 3 WLR	N/A	Where the contract does not provide for a notice period the tribunal will consider what a reasonable period of notice would be - the more senior the position the longer the notice period will be considered to be appropriate.
Delaney v Staples [1991] IRLR 112	Swarb	This case sets out the different circumstances when a payment in lieu of notice can be made and what the legal effect of this is.
Abrahams v Performing Rights Society [1995] IRLR 486	Swarb	Where the employee's contract specifies the right to pay in lieu of notice, the employee is under no obligation to mitigate his loss.
Cerberus Software Ltd v Rowley [2001] EWCA Civ 78	Bailii	Where the contract of employment gave the employer the option of making a payment in lieu of notice, this was not a right to which the employee was entitled and therefore he had to mitigate his loss.

Dismissal: Expiry of fixed term contract

Case	Website	Summary
Labour Party v Oakley [1988] ICR 403	N/A	Where a fixed term contract expires it may constitute unfair dismissal if the employer acts unreasonably in not considering the employee for another suitable post.

Case   Website   Summary

Discrimination: General principles

Case	Website	Summary
EBR Attridge Law LLP & Anor v Coleman [2009] UKEAT 0071/09/3010	Bailii	This is the main case on discrimination by association. The Claimant who had a disabled child was discriminated against.
James v Eastleigh Borough Council [1990] UKHL 6	Bailii	The reason or motive for the discrimination was irrelevant.
Smith v Safeway Plc [1994] UKEAT 185/93/0912	EAT	The test for discrimination is objective not subjective - it does not matter if the employer does not consider the treatment discriminatory if a reasonable person would consider it to be so.
Bahl v The Law Society & Anor [2004] EWCA Civ 1070	Bailii	Because an employer behaves unreasonably does not necessarily mean that the behaviour is discriminatory.
Nagarajan v LRT [1999] UKHL 36	Bailii	Discrimination does not have to be deliberately intended - it can be unconscious behaviour by the employer.
X v Mid Sussex Citizens Advice Bureau & Ors [2011] EWCA Civ 28	Employment Cases Update	Equality Act 2010 does not apply to volunteer workers.

Discrimination: Burden of proof

Case	Website	Summary
Igen Ltd & Ors v Wong [2005] EWCA Civ 142	Bailii	Two stage test for shifting burden of proof in discrimination claims. The Claimant must prove facts from which discrimination can be inferred - the burden of proof then shifts to the Respondent.

Case   Website   Summary

Case	Website	Summary
King v The Great Britain-China Centre [1991] EWCA Civ 16	Bailii	Court considered the difficulties a Claimant has in proving discrimination and when inferences can be drawn from certain treatment by an employer.

Discrimination: Vicarious liability

Case	Website	Summary
Tower Boot Company Ltd v Jones [1996] EWCA Civ 1185	Bailii	An employer will be liable for the discriminatory acts of an employee done in the course of his/her employment.
Marks & Spencer Plc v Martins [1997] EWCA Civ 3067	Bailii	The tribunal will consider whether the employer has done enough to show that it has taken all reasonable steps to prevent discrimination. Examples of what would constitute reasonable steps are given.
London Borough of Hackney v Sivanandan [2013] EWCA Civ 22	Employment Cases Update	A discrimination claim can be made against an individual and an employer and damages can be awarded both individually and severally.
Lister and Others v Hesley Hall Limited [2001] UKHL 22	Bailii	When considering whether an employer is vicariously liable for the wrongdoing of an employee the tribunal must consider how close the connection is between the wrongful act and the employee's job.

Discrimination: Post-termination discrimination

Case	Website	Summary
Relaxion Group Plc v Rhys-Harper [2003] UKHL 33	Bailii	There can be discrimination after the employment relationship has ended, where the employer refuses to provide a reference on discriminatory grounds.

Discrimination: Comparators

Case	Website	Summary
Bullock v Alice Ottley School [1992] IRLR 564	N/A	When selecting a comparator there should be no material difference with the employee who is bringing the discrimination claim.

Case	Website	Summary
Shamoon v Chief Constable of the Royal Ulster Constabulary [2003] UKHL 11	Bailii	If there is no actual comparator the tribunal can accept a hypothetical comparator.
Eweida v British Airways Plc [2010] EWCA Civ 80	Employment Cases Update	A Christian who was not allowed to wear a cross at work did not choose a valid comparator when comparing herself to a Sikh who was permitted to wear a metal bracelet as this was a religious requirement whilst wearing a cross was not.

Discrimination: Age

Case	Website	Summary
Incorporated Trustees of National Council of Ageing v Secretary of State for Business C-388/07	Curia Europa	An employer has a defence to a claim for age discrimination if he can show it was justified being a proportionate means of achieving a legitimate end. This will also apply to government bodies.
Homer v Chief Constable of West Yorkshire Police [2012] UKSC 15	Employment Cases Update	Where an employer imposes hidden age barriers such as a particular educational qualification that could only have been obtained after a certain date, this can amount to discrimination.
Seldon v Clarkson Wright and Jakes (A Partnership) [2012] UKSC 16	Employment Cases Update	A fixed retirement age will have to be justified. Examples are given of what might constitute justification.

Discrimination: Disability

Case	Website	Summary
Abedah v BT [2001] IRLR 23	Swarb	It is for the tribunal, not the medical expert, to make a specific finding that a Claimant is or is not disabled in a disability discrimination case.

Case	Website	Summary
Leonard v Southern Derbyshire Chamber of Commerce [2000] UKEAT 789/99/1010	Bailii	When considering disability and the issue of substantial adverse effect on day to day activities, the tribunal should concentrate on what the Claimant cannot do, not on what he can do.
Matthew Goodwin v Patent Office [1998] UKEAT 57/98/2110	Bailii	When considering whether an impairment has a substantial adverse affect on day to day activities the tribunal should not be considering whether the Claimant is able to do his job but must consider the sort of activities common to most people.
Coca-Coal Enterprises v Shergill EAT/0003/02	EAT	Sport is not an everyday activity.

Discrimination: Reasonable adjustments

Case	Website	Summary
Chief Constable of Lincolnshire v Weaver UKEAT/0622/07	EAT	An employer can take into account the impact of any proposed adjustments on the employer.
O'Hanlon v HM Revenue & Customs [2006] UKEAT 0109/06/0408	Bailii	Failure to pay full pay when employee is off sick does not constitute failure to make a reasonable adjustment.
Garrett v Lidl Ltd [2009] UKEAT 0541/08/1612	EAT	Moving an employee to a different workplace can be a reasonable adjustment.
Chief Constable of South Yorkshire Police v Jelic [2010] UKEAT 0491/09/2904	Employment Cases Update	Swapping roles with another employee can be a reasonable adjustment.

Case   Website   Summary

Discrimination: Pregnancy related

Brown v Rentokil C - 394/96	Curia Europa	A rule that an employee who was off sick for more than 26 weeks would be dismissed was discriminatory when applied to a woman who was off sick with a pregnancy related illness.
Ramdoolar v Bycity Ltd UKE-AT/0236/04/DM	EAT	In order to succeed in a claim for pregnancy related discrimination the Claimant must show that the employer knew or should have suspected the employee was pregnant.

Discrimination: Religous

Panesar v Nestle [1980] IRLR 60	N/A	When considering whether a PCP is proportionate the tribunal must consider whether the means are reasonable and justified. A ban on long hair was justified for reasons of hygiene and safety.
Ladele v London Borough of Islington [2009] EWCA Civ 1357	Bailii	Prohibition of sexual orientation discrimination took precedence over religious beliefs where a registrar refused to carry out same sex marriages as it was contrary to her religious beliefs.
McClintock v Department of Constitutional Affairs [2007] UKEAT 0223/07/3110	Bailii	Employer must know or should have been aware of religious beliefs to be liable for religious discrimination.

Discrimination: Sex

R v Secretary of State for Employment ex parte Equal Opportunities Commission [1994] UKHL 2	House of Lords	Most part-time workers are women therefore less favourable treatment of part-time workers can amount to sex discrimination.

Case   Website   Summary

Home Office v Holmes [1984] IRLR 299	N/A	Refusal to allow a woman to return to work on a part-time basis can be discrimination.
London Underground Ltd v Edwards [1998] EWCA Civ 876	Bailii	The tribunal was entitled to take into account knowledge that more women than men have child care responsibilities and were therefore less likely to be able to work full time.

Discrimination: Harassment

Conn v City of Sunderland [2007] EWCA Civ 1492	Bailii	Conduct that is oppressive and unacceptable will constitute harassment.
Bracebridge v Derby [1990] IRLR 3	N/A	A tribunal can find that there has been harassment of an employee on the basis of just one incident.

Wages: Definition of wages

Bruce & Ors v Wiggins Teape (Stationery) Ltd [1994] UKEAT 1050/93/1305	Bailii	Wages include overtime pay.
Yemm v British Steel [1993] IRLR 117	N/A	Wages include shift payments.
Thames Water Utilities v Reynolds [1995] UKEAT 1090/94/2211	Bailii	Wages include holiday pay.
Robertson v Blackstone [1998] IRLR 376	N/A	Wages include commission.
Delaney v Staples [1992] ICR 483	Swarb	Wages include payments made whilst on garden leave.

Case   Website   Summary

Bear Scotland Ltd & Bailii   Holiday pay should include commission and
Ors v Fulton & Ors   regular overtime payments.
(Working Time Regu-
lations: Holiday pay)
[2014] UKEAT
0047/13/0411

International Packag- Bailii   Reduced working hours resulting in reduced
ing Corporation (UK)   wages can constitute unlawful deduction of
Ltd v Balfour & 57   wages.
Ors [2002] UKEAT
31/02/2310

Horkulak v Cantor   Bailii   Abusive language can amount to a breach of
Fitzgerald Inter-   the implied term of trust and confidence.
national [2003]
EWHC 1918 (QB)

Protected discosure

Parkins v Sodexho   Bailii   Failing to comply with a legal obligation can
Ltd [2001] UKEAT   be the subject of a protected disclosure.
1239/00/2206

Bolton School v Evans Bailii   An employee can be fairly dismissed for an
[2006] EWCA Civ   unlawful act even where the purpose of the
1653   act was to highlight failings. Here the em-
                                  ployee had hacked into the employer's com-
                                  puter system to highlight lack of security.

Cavendish Munro   Bailii   It is not sufficient just to make an allegation,
Professional Risks   - factual information must be provided to
Management Ltd   constitute a protected disclosure.
v Geduld (Rev 1)
[2009] UKEAT
0195/09/0608

Case Website Summary

Time limits: General

Cambridge & *Peterborough* *Foundation NHS* *Trust v Crouchman* [2009] UKEAT 0108/09/0805	Bailii	The employee discovered new information, which was not reasonably available earlier, after the three month time limit for bringing a claim had expired. The new information provided grounds for bringing an unfair dismissal claim and he was allowed to bring his claim out of time.
James W Cook v Tip- *per* [1990] ICR 716	Oxcheps	An employee was allowed to bring his claim out of time where he had been misled by his employer.
Times Newspaper *v O'Regan* [1977] IRLR 101	N/A	Where the employee's advisor is at fault with regards to the time limits, the tribunal will not normally extend the time limit for an unfair dismissal claim where the test is whether it was reasonably practicable to bring the claim in time.

Time limits: Discrimination

Chohan v Derby Law *Centre* [2004] UKE-AT 0851/03/0704	Bailii	Where the employee's advisor is at fault with regards to the time limits, the tribunal will normally extend the time limit for a discrimination claim where the test is whether it is just and equitable.
Hendricks v Commis- *sioner of Police of the* *Metropolis* [2002] EWCA Civ 1686	Bailii	For limitation purposes a number of separate acts extending over a period can be treated as a continuing act if they are part of an ongoing state of affairs.

Damages

W Devis & Sons *Ltd v Atkins* [1977] UKHL 6	Bailii	Where, after the dismissal of an employee, the employer discovers that the employee was guilty of misconduct during the employment, this can be a reason for refusing or reducing the compensatory award.

Case	Website	Summary
Polkey v AE Dayton Services Ltd [1987] UKHL 8	Bailii	Where the tribunal finds that the dismissal was procedurally flawed and therefore unfair it should then go on to consider whether the employee would have been dismissed in any event if a fair procedure had been carried out. This can be expressed in percentage terms and any award reduced accordingly.
Gunton v Richmond [1980] ICR 755	Oxcheps	Where the employee has failed to carry out a proper disciplinary procedure but the dismissal would otherwise be fair, damages may be limited to the period it would have taken for a fair procedure to be carried out.
Wilding v British Telecommunications Plc [2002] EWCA Civ 349	Bailii	The Court of Appeal set out the basic principles relating to mitigation of loss in employment cases. The burden of proof is on the employer to show that the employee has failed unreasonably to mitigate his loss.
Nelson v BBC (No 2) [1980] ICR 110	Oxcheps	This case sets out the factors to be taken into account when considering contributory conduct. The conduct must have contributed to the dismissal.
Vento v Chief Constable of West Yorkshire Police [2002] EWCA Civ 1871	Bailii	This case sets out the three bands of awards for injury to feelings in employment cases.
Da'Bell v National Society for Prevention of Cruelty To Children [2009] UKEAT 0227/09/2809	Bailii	Updates the *Vento* bands.
HM Prison Service v Salmon [2001] UKEAT 21/00/2404	Bailii	Damages may be awarded for psychiatric injury resulting from discrimination.

Case	Website	Summary
Dunnachie v Kingston-upon-Hull [2004] UKHL 36	Bailii	No damages are recoverable for psychiatric injury caused by the manner of dismissal in unfair dismissal cases.

Costs

Case	Website	Summary
Vaughan v London Borough of Lewisham & Ors UKEAT /0534/12/SM	Employment Cases Update	The Employment Appeal Tribunal upheld an £87,000 costs award against an unrepresented Claimant of limited means.

Internet sites

Advisory Conciliation and Arbitration Service ("ACAS")	www.acas.org.uk
Government services and information	www.gov.uk
Acts of Parliament	www.legislation.gov.uk
Employment Rights Act 1996	www.legislation.gov.uk/ukp-ga/1996/18/contents
The Employment Law Bar Association	www.elba.org.uk
Employment Law Association	www.elaweb.org.uk
Personnel Today	www.personneltoday.com
Employment Tribunal Claims (a helpful blog site by Naomi Cunningham and Michael Reed)	www.etclaims.co.uk
Caselaw	www.bailii.org
Employment Appeals Tribunal	www.gov.uk/courts-tribunals/employ-ment-appeal-tribunal
Ministry of Justice	www.justice.gov.uk
Equality and Human Rights Commission	www.equalityhumanrights.com
European Court of Justice	www.europa.eu
UK Parliament	www.parliament.uk
Employment Claims Toolkit (schedule of loss calculator)	www.employmentclaimstoolkit.co.uk
Employment Cases Update (free case summaries and articles)	www.employmentcasesupdate.co.uk
Swarb	www.swarb.co.uk

Internet sites

Oxford Centre for Higher Education Policy Studies	www.oxcheps.new.ox.ac.uk
UK Business Briefing website	www.mondaq.co.uk
Curia Europa (judgments from the European courts)	https://europa.eu/european-union/index_en:
House of Lords	www.parliament.uk/business/lords
Litigants in person: new guidelines for lawyers (Guide published by the Law Society)	www.lawsociety.org.uk/support-services/advice/articles/litigants-in-person-new-guidelines-for-lawyers-june-2015
Presidential guidance - case management	https://www.judiciary.gov.uk/wp-content/uploads/2013/08/presidential-guidance-general-case-management-20180122.pdf
Help on making a claim to the employment tribunal	www.gov.uk/employment-tribunals

Books

Employment Tribunal Remedies Handbook (lists all the remedies and how to calculate them): https://bathpublishing.com/collections/employment-law/products/employment-tribunal-remedies-handbook-2020-21

Selwyn's Law of Employment (this is the main text book)

Harvey on Employment Law (this is the main practitioner's work)

Butterworth's Employment Law Handbook (this sets out the relevant Statutes and Statutory Instruments)

Main Acts and Regulations

Employment Rights Act 1996	www.legislation.gov.uk/ukpga/1996/18/contents
Employment Act 2002	www.legislation.gov.uk/ukpga/2002/22/contents

Main Acts and Regulations

Equality Act 2010	www.legislation.gov.uk/ukp-ga/2010/15/contents
Employment Relations Act 1999	www.legislation.gov.uk/ukp-ga/1999/26/section/10
Fixed Term Employees (Prevention of less favourable treatment) Regulations 2002	www.legislation.gov.uk/uksi/2002/2034/contents/made
Flexible Working (Eligibility, Complaints and Remedies) Regulations 2002	www.legislation.gov.uk/uksi/2009/595/made
Health Protection (Coronavirus, Restrictions) (England) Regulations 2020	www.legislation.gov.uk/uksi/2020/350/contents/made
National Minimum Wage Act 1998	www.legislation.gov.uk/ukp-ga/1998/39/contents
Part Time Workers (Prevention of less favourable treatment) Regulations 2000	www.legislation.gov.uk/uksi/2000/1551/contents/made
Trade Union and Labour Relations (Consolidation) Act 1992	www.legislation.gov.uk/ukp-ga/1992/52/contents
Transfer of Undertakings (Protection of Employment) Regulations 2006	www.legislation.gov.uk/uksi/2006/246/contents/made
Working Time Regulations 1998	www.legislation.gov.uk/uksi/1998/1833/contents/made

ACAS Codes of Practice and Tribunal Guidance documents

All the following Codes of Practice and Guidance documents can be found on the ACAS website (www.acas.org.uk):

ACAS Code of Practice 1 - Disciplinary and Grievance Procedures

ACAS Code of Practice 2 - Disclosure of information to trade unions

ACAS Code of Practice 3 - Time off for trade union duties and activities

ACAS Code of Practice 4 - Settlement Agreements

ACAS Code of Practice 5 - Handling in a reasonable manner requests to work flexibly

Useful templates for letters, forms and checklists (free to download)

Advisory booklet - Managing conflict at work

Disciplining staff - letters for all the stages of a formal disciplinary procedure under the ACAS Code of Practice on Discipline and Grievance

Hiring staff - free documents to help you hire staff

Managing staff - free documents to help you manage staff

ACAS Guide to Discipline and grievances at work (this guide complements the ACAS Code of Practice 1 - Disciplinary and Grievance Procedures)

ACAS Guide to Asking and Responding to Questions of Discrimination in the Work Place

ACAS Guide to Bullying and Harassment at Work

ACAS Guide to Redundancy Handling

ACAS Guide to Settlement Agreements (this guide complements the ACAS Code of Practice 4 - Settlement Agreements)

Coronavirus (Covid-19): advice for employers and employees

Tribunal offices

A full list of tribunal offices with postal and email addresses, telephone numbers, maps and directions can be found at www.gov.uk/employment-tribunal-offices-and-venues

Index

Printed in Great Britain
by Amazon